This is the most helpful discussion I have read on the two-fold nature of prophecy in the Corinthian Church. It spells out the very important implications for strengthening each church today. I therefore highly recommend this book for all ministers and also members of their churches.

Dr. Bruce W. Winter
Director of the Institute for Early Christianity
in the Graeco-Roman World
Principal Emeritus Queensland Theological Seminary,
Brisbane, Australia

I endorse the book written by Rev. Vijai Singh Tagore for several reasons. The first is for the author's outstanding scholarship that is evident as one reads the book carefully. He has made a sincere and genuine attempt to mine the best of evangelical scholarship with which to grapple the study of prophecy. The second reason is because he has taken a subject that has current relevance in the context we live in. There is growing confusion as to what constitutes the work of the Holy Spirit, particularly with reference to the gifts, and especially prophecy. A work of this type will help towards bringing sound biblical discussion to the table. The third reason is that Rev. Tagore represents a young generation of academics who seek to engage with issues creatively and sincerely. Whether you agree, or disagree, with his conclusions there is no escaping the fact that he can support his arguments forcefully. I wish him the very best and look forward to more writing by the author.

Rev. Dr. Matthew Ebenezer
Principal and Professor of Church History
and Pastoral Care Counselling
Presbyterian Theological Seminary, Dehradun, India

The vexed problem of prophecy in 1 Corinthians receives an insightful solution in this book by Vijai Singh Tagore. He refuses the easy exegetical options often chosen by others and insists on taking seriously what the Apostle wrote. He does not simply equate prophecy with preaching. He affirms its revelatory character, but does not allow it to rival the authority of Scripture. Here is an honest and fresh approach that sees congregational prophecy as one of the appointed means through which God still speaks to his church.

Dr. Gregory Goswell
Academic Dean
Christ College, Sydney, Australia

Vijai Singh Tagore's Corinthian Prophecy is an honest attempt to define the nature and function of prophecy in 1 Corinthians 12-14. In it he draws a clear distinction between 'canonical' and 'congregational' prophecies and attributes the prophecy mentioned in Paul's first letter to Corinth as congregational in nature. He argues that the prophets in the Corinthian congregation prophesied not for inscripturation purpose, but for exhortation and edification of the church under divine revelation. This kind of prophecy is one of the gifts of the Holy Spirit given to the church for building up the Body of Christ. As a gift it is available to all the believers at all times. By making a careful distinction between canonical and congregational prophecies, Tagore moves the debate beyond the cessationist and the continuationist camps for which he deserves our appreciation.

Dr. Simon Samuel
Principal and Professor of
New Testament Studies and Christian Origins
New Theological College, Dehradun, India

Prophecy is a minefield for any student of Scripture, particularly with regard to the Corinthian correspondence. That God continues to give to some Christians a clearly supernatural insight into His Word and ways is incontestable. How that connects with biblical prophecy is contestable. Vijai Tagore has given us a detailed examination of the evidence from First Corinthians to help us think more clearly on this issue. This may not be the last word on the subject, but it is a carefully-considered, challenging and helpful word.

Rev. Dr. Peter Barnes
Minister at Revesby Presbyterian Church, Sydney, Australia
Part-time Church History Lecturer at Christ College,
Sydney, Australia

How do we hear from God? Corinthian Prophecy tackles this vital question by examining the nature of prophecy in the Bible, and especially the place of congregational prophecy present in the Corinthian church. Its shows us the foundational importance of the Old Testament prophets for the canon, and the ongoing value of a different form of prophecy by which God recalls his people to the truths of Scripture and applies these to their circumstances. This book provides a basis for making an essential distinction, so that the church is clear about where its primary authority lies, but also enjoys the benefits of the continuing work of the Spirit. It will leave you better informed about the nature of revelation and stimulated to think about ministries in the church today.

Rev. Dr. John McClean
Vice-Principal and Lecturer in Systematic Theology
Christ College, Sydney, Australia

This book is an enquiry into the nature of Corinthian prophecy, a controversial topic. The author addresses the issues with aplomb through a detailed textual investigation, and brings clarity to the discussion on prophecy in the early church

Dr. Mohan Chacko
Principal Emeritus and Professor of Theology and Mission
Presbyterian Theological Seminary, Dehradun, India

Biblical Hermeneutics Rediscovered

The Series as the name suggests will focus on Biblical Hermeneutics, i.e., literary works concerned with methods of interpreting the Old and New Testaments of Bible via different stream of topics like Literature & Poetry, Indigenous Philosophizing, Ethical response towards Ecology, Health & Healing, Science & Technology, Feminist Theology, Sociological approach towards Human Rights, Law & Politics, Arts, History of Ideas, Ancient Civilizations, Cultural Contiguity, Religious Cosmologies & Mysticism, Appraisal of various Theologians, World Peace & Harmony, Global Capitalism, Network Marketing, Cybertheology, Population & Demographics, Epigraphic Studies, Contextualized Education, and many others. We welcome a Mss. on any topic/s mentioned, whether they are original works, scholarly monographs, collections of conference papers, revised dissertations, or translations of historical documents. Through the Series we, the Publishers, are striving to put forward published works that may help Institutions, Academic Bodies, Researchers, Scholars and the World at large in furthering their respective knowledge and understanding on the concerned subject. We welcome your comments on our efforts and further suggestions on how we can enshrine new ray of analysing & explaining the written texts through our upcoming books.

Biblical Hermeneutics Rediscovered - 10

Corinthian Prophecy

Exegetical and Theological Analysis

Vijai Singh Tagore

CWI

Christian World Imprints™

First Published in 2018 by

Christian World Imprints™
Christian Publishing & Books from India
H-12 Bali Nagar, **New Delhi-110015**
info@christianworldimprints.com
www.ChristianWorldImprints.com
Phone: +91 11 25465925

ISBN: 978-93-5148-239-0 (HB) ISBN: 978-93-5148-240-6 (PB)

Cataloging in Publication Data--DK
Courtesy: D.K. Agencies (P) Ltd. <docinfo@dkagencies.com>

Tagore, Vijai Singh, 1982- **author**.
Corinthian prophecy : exegetical and theological analysis / Vijai Singh Tagore.
pages cm. -- (Biblical hermeneutics rediscovered ; 10)
Includes bibliographical references.
ISBN 9789351482390 (HB)
ISBN 9789351482406 (PB)

1. Prophecy--Christianity. 2. Bible. Corinthians, 1st, 12-14--Hermeneutics. I. Title. II. Series: Biblical hermeneutics rediscovered ; 10.

LCC BS2675.52.T34 2017 | DDC 227.206 23

Printed in India.

To

Suchitra

My best friend and companion for life

Contents

Foreword xi
Abstract xv
Acknowledgements xvii

Chapter 1: Introduction 1
1.1 The Issue and Theses 1
1.2 Methodology 9
1.2.1 Primacy of the Text of 1 Corinthians 12-14 10
1.2.2 Limitations of Methodology 12
1.2.3 Approach 13

Chapter 2: Debates on the Nature of NT Prophecy 15
2.1 The Cessationist View 15
2.2 The Continuationist View 20
2.3 Prophecy as Contemporary Preaching (or Teaching) 27
2.4 Conclusion 33

Chapter 3: An Overview of Prophecy in the Bible 37
3.1 Prophecy in the Old Testament 38
3.1.1 The Pentateuch 38
3.1.2 The Historical Books (Former Prophets) 40
3.1.3 The Prophetic Books (Latter Prophets) 43
3.1.4 Conclusion 45
3.2 Prophecy in the Intertestamental Period 46
3.3 Prophecy in the New Testament 50
3.3.1 The Gospels and Acts 52

3.3.2 Pauline Material 58
3.3.3 Non-Pauline Epistles and Revelation 62
3.3.4 Conclusion 64

Chapter 4: The Nature of Corinthian Prophecy 65
4.1 Distribution: A Widely Distributed Gift of the Spirit (1 Cor 12:10 [cf. v. 7], 29; 14:1 [cf. v. 39], 3, 24, 29-31 [cf. 11:4-5]) 66
4.2 Origin: Rooted in Revelation (14:30 [cf. vv. 6, 26]) 74
4.2.1 A Spontaneous Phenomenon 82
4.2.2 Distinct from Preaching and Teaching 88
4.3 Content: A Diverse and Responsive Phenomenon (1 Cor 14:3 [cf. 4b], 19 [v. 31], 24-25; 13:2) 91
4.3.1 Its General Function: οἰκοδομὴν (*oikodomen*, "edification") καὶ (*kai*, "and") παράκλησιν (*paraklesin*, "exhortation") καὶ παραμυθίαν (*kaiparamuthian*, "encouragement") (1 Cor 14:3 [cf. vv. 4, 31]) 93
4.3.2 Its Teaching Aspect (1 Cor 14:31 [cf. v. 19]) 98
4.3.3 As Gospel Proclamation (1 Cor 14:24-25) 102
4.3.4 Its Relation to μυστήρια (*musteria,* "mysteries") and γνῶσιν ([*gnosin*, "knowledge"] 13:2) 108
4.4 Authority: Subject to διακρίσις (*diakrisis,* "judgment or discernment" in 1 Cor 14:29, 37-38 [cf. 12:10; 1 Thess 5:21; 1 John 4:1]) 113
4.5 Distinction from Tongues: Interpreted Tongues not Equivalent to Corinthian Prophecy 123
4.6 The Cessation or Continuation of Congregational Prophecy (1 Cor 13:8-10) 131
4.7 Conclusion 139

Conclusion 141
Bibliography 147
Index of Authors 159
Index of Subjects 162

Foreword

I have a very distinct memory from when I was a teenager. We were in church. It was the evening service, and during the singing of a hymn, a cataclysmic sound was heard from outside. We all turned our heads as the organist stopped playing. A car had swerved out of control off the road and smashed through the front fence of the church yard and knocked down the church's sign. Fortunately no-one was hurt, but the front fence and the church's sign were both demolished.

Several months after this event I was at a congregational meeting. The car in the accident was insured, and because its driver was at fault, the church received a payment to cover the cost of the repairs. But the church also had insurance. Although we had already received money from the owner of the car, some argued that we should also claim through the church's insurance policy. The argument raged. Is this a double payout? Is this ethical? It was at this point that someone from the congregation spoke. This person spoke with conviction, and at length, and it was this speech that stopped the conversation. We were reminded from God's Word that a double claim is not only against Scriptural teaching, but that obedience to God and to his Word is of greater value than any financial gain.

That speech was over forty years ago, and although I cannot remember many sermons or Bible studies from that time, I still remember that moment. It was a time when God's people were reminded of God's standards in a specific situation. But what word should we use to define what was happening? It was not preaching. It was not a new revelation. It was the application of God's Word to a real situation. Was it prophecy?

What is New Testament prophecy? Paul mentions it as a gift of the Spirit that should be exercised in proportion to our faith (Rom 12:6). It is a gift that should not be despised (1 Thess 5:20) and it was exercised at the time the council of elders laid their hands on Timothy (1 Tim 4:14). Even the apocalyptic revelation given to the apostle John by the Lord Jesus is described as prophecy (Rev 1:3; 22:7) and as such it should be treated as the Word of God (Rev 1:2). This revelation to John has such authority that it should neither be added to nor subtracted from (Rev 22:18,19). From this data, questions abound. Is all prophecy the same? Why are some prophecies added to the canon (e.g. Revelation) and others not?

The nature of New Testament prophecy receives its most extended discussion in chapters 12-14 of Paul's first letter to the Corinthians and it is to these chapters that Vijai Singh Tagore turns to define the practice. What was happening in Corinth and what relevance does this have to today's church?

This book charts a course through some important questions. How does prophecy relate to the sufficiency of Scripture and a closed canon? How does prophecy related to debates between "Cessationists" and "Continuationists"? Can we neatly fit all the biblical data into one of these two categories? Do we expect miraculous or spirited gifts today?

This book is an excellent treatment of 1 Corinthians 12-14 and how it sheds light on the nature of New Testament prophecy. Not all New Testament prophecy is the same. Whereas some prophecy will find its way into the canon, that is not the case in all instances. If some prophecy is an application of God's revelation, and not an instance of fresh revelation, it means that there may be no conflict between belief in prophecy and an adherence to the completion of the canon and an assertion of *Sola Scriptura.* It's not always "either/or".

God continues to speak to his church; he has not taken a vacation. God continues to apply his Word to his people in specific situations. The prophet Joel prophesied that "your sons and your daughters shall prophesy" (Joel 2:28). This Scripture is fulfilled in the "last days" on the Day of Pentecost (Acts 1:17). We continue to live in these last days. I am sure you will glean much from reading this important work.

Dr. Ian Smith
Principal
Christ College
Sydney, Australia

Abstract

This book is an effort to define the nature and function of Corinthian prophecy as described in 1 Corinthians 12-14. It proposes that the gift of prophecy exercised in the Corinthian church can be labeled as a "non-canonical" or "congregational" form of prophecy. It was distinct from the canonical (inscripturated) form of prophecy recorded in Scripture that often brought new doctrinal revelation and was mostly limited to a few particular individuals. Distinctively, in the post-Pentecost New Testament (NT) church, congregational prophecy became a widely exercised gift of the Spirit among believers and provided guidance and edification to the NT churches. Its content was diverse, based on previous revelation but not recorded in Scripture. Therefore, it is this book's assertion that there are two levels of prophecy in the NT, canonical and congregational, and Paul is describing the nature and function of congregational prophecy in 1 Corinthians. Moreover, while canonical prophecy ceased with the NT having being completed, congregational prophecy continues in various forms in the post-apostolic church.

Support for these assertions will be sought in three areas. Firstly, a survey of the three popular views on NT prophecy, namely the cessationist, the continuationist, and the view that identifies prophecy as contemporary preaching/teaching, will provide the background of debates on Corinthian prophecy, which lays the theological foundations for the proposed view. Secondly, a detailed survey of the phenomenon of prophecy through the various stages in biblical history will clarify the proposed distinction between canonical and congregational prophecy present in biblical data. Thirdly, but most importantly, an exegesis of the relevant passages on prophecy in 1 Corinthians 12-14 will define the nature and function of Corinthian prophecy that falls under the category of congregational prophecy. In the end, a conclusion will be drawn proposing a definition of congregational prophecy and a few pastoral reflections.

Acknowledgements

No research is a product of one person but involves many beside the primary researcher. This work has been greatly assisted by others whom I wish to acknowledge.

I owe a debt of gratitude to many godly individuals and institutions who have been instrumental in various ways in training and guiding me in my Christian journey. This book is the evidence of that. These include: the Australian Presbyterian World Mission, in particular the Rev. Kevin and Mrs. Julie Murray, the Presbyterian Women Association and PCANSW congregations in Australia, the Revesby Presbyterian Church and the Presbyterian Theological Centre (now called *Christ College*) in Sydney, and the Presbyterian Theological Seminary in India.

The individuals include: Dr. Ian Keith Smith (the main force behind this research), Dr. Peter Barnes, Dr. John Davies, Dr. John McClean, Dr. Gregory Goswell, Mr. David Evans, Mr. Franco and the late Heather Salaun, Rachel Salaun, and the numerous friends both at Christ College and Revesby Presbyterian Church in Sydney who listened to my arguments and sharpened my thinking with their comments and questions.

My loving gratitude: to my wife Suchitra, for her patience and constant encouragement with this project to finish; to our children Adiel and Isabelle who refresh me each day with their smiling faces when I am mentally and physically exhausted; to our extended families in Bhutan and India for their prayer support.

I am also grateful to Mr. Sudhanshu Kanda at Christian World Imprints, New Delhi, India, for his assistance with the editorial and publishing outputs.

I thank my heavenly Father, who has been my unfailing help and strength when I felt overwhelmed dealing with such a controversial topic and with an enormous amount of material accompanying it. May He receive all the glory and praise, and use this small work to bless His Church universal. Amen!

"To each is given the manifestation of the Spirit for the common good" (1 Cor 12:7)

Chapter 1

Introduction

1.1 The Issue and Theses

This book is an effort to define the nature and function of Corinthian prophecy as described in 1 Corinthians 12-14. It proposes that the gift of prophecy exercised in the Corinthian church can be labeled as a "non-canonical" or "congregational" form of prophecy. The subject of New Testament (NT) prophecy as one of the spiritual gifts has remained a controversial issue, especially since the rise of Pentecostalism and the Charismatic movements in the early and the mid-twentieth centuries. This has resulted in divergent views regarding spiritual gifts, particularly prophecy (and tongues) in 1 Corinthians 12-14.[1] Since then, much has been written on the subject of NT prophecy, particularly on Corinthian prophecy

[1] Gaffin suggests that the divergent views "stem from the difficulty of having to reconstruct a coherent overall picture from somewhat disparate materials, found almost entirely in Acts, Paul, and Revelation" (Richard B. Gaffin, *Perspectives on Pentecost: New Testament Teaching on the Gift of the Holy Spirit* [Philadelphia: P&R, 1979], 58). See Chapter 2 for a discussion on popular views regarding NT prophecy.

as the main focus.[1] However, to this author's knowledge, not

[1] Cf. E. Fascher, *Prophetes: Eine sprach- und religionsgeschichtliche Untersuchung* (Geissen: Topelmann, 1927); H. A. Guy, *New Testament Prophecy: Its Origin and Significance* (London: Epworth Press, 1947); E. Best, "Prophets and Preachers," *SJT* 12 (1959): 129-50; Donald Gee, *Spiritual Gifts in the Work of Ministry Today* (Springfield, Mo.: Gospel Publishing House, 1963, 1979); T. M. Crone, *Early Christian Prophecy: A Study of its Origin and Function* (St. Mary's University Press: Baltimore, 1973); M. E. Boring, "What Are We Looking For? Toward a Definition of the Term 'Christian Prophet,'" *SBL Seminar Papers* (Missoula, MT: SBL, 1973), 142-54; idem, "Prophecy (Early Christian)," *ABD* 5: 495-502; D. L. Baker, "The Interpretation of 1 Corinthians 12-14" *EvQ* 46 (1974): 224-34; G. Dautzenberg, *Urchristliche Prophetie* (Stuttgart: W. Kolhlhammer, 1975); U. B. Muller, *Prophetie und Predigt im Neuen Testament* (SNT 10; Gutersloh: Gerd Mohn, 1975); B. Yocum, *Prophecy: Exercising the Prophetic Gifts of the Spirit in the Church Today* (Ann Arbor: Word of Life, 1976); J. Panagopoulos, ed., *Prophetic Vocation in the NT and Today*, NovTSup 45 (Leiden: E. J. Brill, 1977); T.W. Gillespie, "A Pattern of Prophetic Speech in 1 Corinthians," *JBL* 97 (1978): 74-95; E. Earle Ellis, *Prophecy and Hermeneutic in Early Christianity* (Grand Rapids: Eerdmans, 1978); T. L. Wilkinson, "Tongues and Prophecy in Acts and 1st Corinthians," *VoxR* 31 (1978): 1-20; David Hill, *New Testament Prophecy* (London: Marshall Morgan & Scott, 1979); Rendtorff, "προφήτης," (prophetes, *prophet*) *TDNT* 6:796-812; R. Meyer, "προφήτης," *TDNT* 6:812-28; G. Friedrich, "προφήτης," *TDNT* 6:828-61; R. R. Wilson, "Prophecy and Ecstasy: A Reexamination," *JBL* 98 (1978): 321-37; D. E. Aune, *Prophecy in Early Christianity and the Ancient Mediterranean World* (Grand Rapids: Eerdmans), 1983; R. P. Martin, *The Spirit and the Congregation: Studies in 1 Corinthians 12-15* (Grand Rapids: Eerdmans, 1984); T. Callan, "Prophecy and Ecstasy in Greco-Roman Religion and 1 Corinthians," *NovT* 27 (1985): 125-40; R. Clements, *Word and Spirit: The Bible and the Gift of Prophecy Today* (Leicester: UCCF, 1986); D. A. Carson, *Showing the Spirit: A Theological Exposition of 1 Corinthians 12-14* (Colorado Spring: Authentic Media, 2010); G. Houston, *Prophecy: A Gift for Today?* (Downers Grove: IVP, 1989); A. C. Wire, *The Corinthian Women Prophets: A Reconstruction through Paul's Rhetoric* (Minneapolis: Augsburg Fortress, 1990); Mark J. Cartledge, "Charismatic Prophecy: A Definition and Description," *JPT* 5 (1994): 79-120; F. D. Farnell, "The Current Debate about New Testament Prophecy," *BSac* 149 (1992): 277-303; idem, "The Gift of Prophecy in the Old and New Testaments," *BSac* 149 (1992): 387-410; idem, "Does the New Testament Teach Two Prophetic Gifts?" *BSac* 150 (1993): 62-88; idem, "When Will the Gift of Prophecy Cease?" *BSac* 150 (1993): 171-202; Gordon D. Fee, *God's Empowering Presence: The Holy Spirit in the Letters of Paul* (Peabody: Hendrickson, 1994); Thomas W. Gillespie, *The First Theologians: A Study in Early Christian Prophecy* (Grand Rapids: Eerdmans, 1994); D. B. Martin, *The Corinthian Body* (London: Yale

much has been written on the subject of Corinthian prophecy in the last one and a half decades. At the same time, no unanimous conclusions have been reached among scholars regarding the nature and function of prophecy in Corinth. The cessationist camp largely identifies Corinthian prophecy with Old Testament (OT) prophecy and sees it having ceased with the completed Scripture. The continuationist camp generally (if not always) sees the Corinthian phenomenon distinct from OT prophecy and as still continuing in the post-apostolic church. Yet, another famous view identifies Corinthian prophecy with contemporary preaching and teaching, and so continuing today as well. Efforts have been made to reconcile the three camps through various arrangements and proposals regarding Corinthian prophecy but none of these efforts has gone un-critiqued or unquestioned. The best known of all among such efforts to reconcile the three camps is Grudem's view of NT prophecy. Grudem suggests two distinct types of prophecy in the NT, namely 1) apostolic prophecy that was fully infallible and authoritative like the OT canonical prophecy; 2) the weaker type prophecy amongst the congregation more generally, similar to the prophetic phenomenon in the intertestamental period.[1] According to Grudem, the apostolic prophecy gave the foundational revelation which became inscripturated as the New Testament and ceased with the apostles. The weaker type of prophecy had little to do with providing doctrine but served for the edification and direction of the church or individuals about matters on which the Scripture is

---

University Press, 1995); Christopher Forbes, *Prophecy and Inspired Speech in Early Christianity and its Hellenistic Environment* (Peabody: Hendrickson, 1997); Max Turner, *The Holy Spirit and Spiritual Gifts: Then and Now* (UK: Paternostser Press, 1996); Wayne Grudem, ed., *Are Miraculous Gifts for Today? Four Views* (Grand Rapids: Zondervan, 1996); idem, *The Gift of Prophecy in the New Testament and Today* (Wheaton: Crossway books, 2000); Rowland S. Ward, *Blessed by the Presence of the Spirit: The Authentic Charismatic Church* (Melbourne: New Melbourne Press, 1997). For an extended bibliography see Anthony C. Thiselton, *The First Epistle to the Corinthians,* NIGTC (Grand Rapids: Eerdmans, 2000), 903-907.

[1] See Grudem, *Prophecy,* chs. 3-4. For other similar efforts see Clements, *Word and Spirit;* Houston, *Prophecy*; Gee, *Spiritual Gifts.*

generally silent. Grudem concludes that this non-apostolic weaker type prophecy did not cease with apostolic prophecy and is still alive today. He therefore puts all non-apostolic NT prophecy, including the Corinthian prophecy, under this category. For Grudem, it was fallible and less authoritative since it consisted of "merely speaking human words to report something God brings to mind."[1] It was a mixture of divine insight (revelation) and human fallible interpretation of divine revelation. Grudem's view has received both commendations (see Chapter 2) and critique.[2]

This book can be seen as a reconciliatory effort to build bridges amongst the three camps by reclassifying Corinthian prophecy in the light of Paul's discussion in 1 Corinthians 12-14. Clarifications regarding the terminology used in this book will be undertaken first. Despite some conceptual similarities and common terminology, this work differs from Grudem's view in the following respects. This book proposes two distinct types of prophecy in the NT, being canonical and congregational prophecy in preference to Grudem's primary distinction of apostolic and non-apostolic prophecy. Grudem's distinction between apostolic and non-apostolic prophecy is not the key distinction, since there is non-apostolic prophecy which was included in the canon. Here, canonical prophecy refers to all inscripturated prophecy and congregational prophecy to non-inscripturated prophecy. This book's distinction within NT prophecy is more appropriate since NT canonical prophecy was available to both the apostles and some

---

[1] Grudem, *Prophecy*, 51.

[2] For critiques of Grudem's view see Kenneth L. Gentry, Jr., *The Charismatic Gift of Prophecy: A Reformed Response to Wayne Grudem* (Memphis, TN: Footstool, 1989); Gaffin, "A Cessationist View," *Are Miraculous Gifts for Today?*; Edmund P. Clowney, *The Church* (Illinois: IVP, 1995), 257-68; Sinclair B. Ferguson, *The Holy Spirit* (Illinois: IVP, 1996), 210-11; Turner, *Holy Spirit,* 208-212; Farnell, "Does the New Testament," 62-88; idem, "Fallible New Testament Prophecy/Prophets? A Critique of Wayne Grudem's Hypothesis," *The Master's Perspective on Contemporary Issues* (ed. R. Thomas; Grand Rapids: Kregel, 1998), 40-47; O. Palmer Robertson, *The Final Word* (Edinburgh: Banner of Truth, 1993).

of the NT prophets who were not apostles (Eph 2:20; 3:5).[1] The distinction between canonical and non-canonical (congregational) prophecy is also more accurate since not all NT prophecy was meant for inscripturation.[2] Gaffin also recognises this distinction and affirms that there were different kinds of revelation in NT prophecy, one from the apostles and the prophets for canonisation (i.e. canonical prophecy), and another through the Spirit to be used in the church for edification, not for canonisation. He also argues that not all prophets in the Bible were involved in receiving and writing down canonical revelation but served local churches by providing guidance and edification.[3] It necessarily follows that not only Corinthian prophecy but most Pauline references to NT prophecy fall under the category of congregational prophecy (1 Cor 12-14; Rom 12:6; 1 Thess 5:20-21; 1 Tim 1:18 [cf. 4:14]) since none of these prophecies was ever recorded in the NT Scriptures.[4] A further implication is that this non-inscripturated form of prophecy (i.e. congregational prophecy) was widely exercised amongst the congregation members for edification and guidance, whereas canonical prophecy was confined to the apostles and some NT prophets for inscripturation. Forbes explains "congregational prophecy" as referring to prophecy exercised by NT Christians who, though "not considered 'prophets' in any regular or official sense, none the less occasionally prophesied."[5] Forbes affirms that "there is important evidence that *for Paul*, all Christians were capable of prophesying occasionally. At any point the Spirit might speak through any believer with all the authority of the Lord … anyone might occasionally prophesy; those who

[1] Paul sees two distinct groups in Eph 2:20 and 3:5 as apostles and prophets entrusted with foundational, doctrinal type new revelation. See Gaffin, *Perspectives*, 61-62 (contra Grudem, *Prophecy*, 54-83).

[2] The contents of prophesying mentioned in Acts 21:9, 1 Corinthians 12-14, Rom 12:6, 1 Thess 5:20-21, 1 Tim 1:18 (cf. 4:14) are not actually recorded in the NT but only mention the act of prophesying.

[3] Gaffin, *Perspectives*, 99-100.

[4] Ephesian 2:20 and 3:5 refer to prophetic revelation that was new doctrinal revelation for inscripturation. Therefore, they belong to canonical prophecy.

[5] See Forbes, *Prophecy*, 242, 243-46.

did so regularly or in a notable fashion became known as prophets in the stronger sense."[1] Hence, such occasional prophesying is rightly to be categorised as congregational prophecy since it was not only widespread, but its content also never became part of the NT Scriptures. This proposed distinction is also consistent with the fact that prophecy was not a necessary condition for inscripturation of NT Scripture[2] (e.g. Hebrews, James, Jude). Turner points out that "the gift of prophecy was in any case not needed in order to write what came to be acknowledged as NT Scriptures (cf. the Gospels, Acts, etc.) … Pauline letters are not 'prophecies,' but apostolic teaching."[3]

A further distinction from Grudem's view is that congregational prophecy in the NT is not to be regarded as "merely speaking human words to report something God brings to mind"[4] but as a revelation from the Spirit, since it originates from the Spirit. This holds even though there is a qualitative difference, in regard to the content and authority, between canonical and congregational prophecy and the revelation that comes through each. Therefore, Farnell's distinction between the two is preferable to Grudem's because Farnell sees congregational prophecy as being of a less enduring nature than canonical prophecy since the former consisted of "temporal and local prophetic advice to Christian communities" of the NT.[5]

And lastly, this author is fully aware that the proposed distinction between canonical and congregational prophecy is not a biblical one but an analytical one. These are helpful and even

---

[1] Forbes, *Prophecy,* 246.

[2] There is a good number of NT books that are non-apostolic and not "prophecy" in a strict sense (e.g. Hebrews, James, Jude).

[3] Turner, *Holy Spirit*, 211 (cf. D.A. Carson and John. D. Woodbridge, eds., *Hermeneutics, Authority and Canon* [Leicester: IVP, 1986]; David G. Dunbar et al., "The Canon: How God Gave His Word to the Church: Viewpoints," *Christianity Today*, vol. 32, no.2 [1988]: 23-38). The same applies to the writing of OT Scripture (see, Craig S. Keener, *Gifts and Giver: The Holy Spirit for Today* [Grand Rapids: Baker, 2001], 122).

[4] Grudem, *Prophecy*, 51.

5 Farnell, "Gift of Prophecy," 388 n. 3.

unavoidable categories which are needed in order to understand and distinguish the Corinthian prophetic phenomenon from the inscripturated form of prophecy.

Therefore, this book proposes that the form of prophecy exercised in the Corinthian church was congregational prophecy, distinct from the canonical (inscripturated) form of prophecy. This is evident from Paul's description of Corinthian prophecy. An exegetical examination of 1 Corinthians 12-14 suggests that Paul saw the gift of congregational prophecy potentially available and widely exercised beyond those designated as prophets (1 Cor 12:10 [cf. v. 7], 29; 14:1 (cf. v. 39], 3, 24, 29-31 [cf. 11:4-5]). There is also evidence in the text that for Paul congregational prophecy consisted of spontaneous revelation from God to individual believers (1 Cor 14:30 [cf. vv. 6, 26]) for the "edification and encouragement and consolation" (1 Cor 14:3 [cf. v. 4]) of the church. Paul also distinguished congregational prophecy from other forms of speech (e.g. preaching and teaching) due to its revelatory nature while affirming its ability to instruct and teach the church (1 Cor 14:31 [v. 19]). There is also evidence that congregational prophecy was a diverse and responsive phenomenon, addressing current issues and situations by providing specific applications of previously revealed biblical truths (OT Scripture and apostolic teachings).[1] Ciampa and Rosner also describe Corinthian prophecy as "more highly occasion-or situation-focused" activity of the Spirit that acted as a "responsive phenomenon"[2] (i.e. addressing specific local issues and situations) unlike canonical prophecy that often (though not always) brought forth fresh or new redemptive revelations from God to be inscripturated (cf. Eph 2:20; 3:5; Rev 1:3; 22:7, 10, 18, 19). It necessarily follows that Corinthian prophecy did not bring new redemptive, doctrinal revelation (whether oral or written) but

---

[1] This explains why the content of Corinthian prophecy is not recorded in the NT Scripture since it was often of temporary nature. Paul regards this as an essential difference between prophecy and tongues (see Chapter 4).

[2] Roy E. Ciampa and Brian S. Rosner, *The First Letter to the Corinthians* (PNTC; Grand Rapids: Eerdmans, 2010), 581.

could include reiteration of previous doctrinal revelation (1 Cor 14:19, 31) for the edification of believers, including Spirit-inspired gospel proclamation for the conversion of unbelievers visiting Christian gatherings (1 Cor 14:24-25). Paul also distinguished congregational prophecy from speaking in tongues, being more productive and preferable in the assembly (1 Cor 14:1-5, 13-17, 22, 28) due to its intelligible nature and humanward direction (14:3) unlike tongues that was both unintelligible and Godward (1 Cor 14:2).[1] At the same time, Paul subjects congregational prophecy to the rule of evaluation/weighing (1 Cor 14:29 [cf. 12:10; 1 Thess 5:21; 1 John 4:1]) and to his own apostolic authority/teachings (1 Cor 14:37). This implies a qualitative difference in authority between canonical and congregational prophecy. Lastly, Paul nowhere indicates the cessation of congregational prophecy at any time before the coming the of the τελειον (*teleion* [perfect, mature, complete]), which refers to "the state of affairs brought by the arrival of the *parousia*" (1 Cor 13:8-10).[2] In other words, there is no exegetical evidence in 1 Corinthians 12-14 of congregational prophecy having ceased with canonical prophecy. In fact, it is the congregational prophecy that seems to be the dominant form of prophecy not only in Corinth but also in other NT congregations (cf. Acts 21:4, 9; 1 Thess 5:19-21; 1 Tim 1:18; 4:14), particularly after Pentecost when the Holy Spirit was poured upon the church indiscriminately, unlike in the OT where the Spirit of prophecy was limited to certain individuals.[3]

The approach proposed by this book to prophecy in 1 Corinthians 12-14 can be regarded as modified cessationism or continuationism. It affirms the sufficiency and finality of written Scripture by maintaining the cessation of canonical prophecy. However, it is open to the continuation of congregational prophecy

---

[1] In prophecy God addressed humans (1 Cor 14:3) and so it was didactic, whereas in tongues it was humans who addressed God (14:2) since tongues consisted of prayers and doxological praise to God.

[2] Carson, *Showing the Spirit,* 69.

[3] See Forbes, *Prophecy,* 244-45; Gaffin, *Perspectives,* 60; Gordon Fee, *The First Epistle to the Corinthians* (NICNT; Grand Rapids: Eerdmans, 1987), 595.

in the post-apostolic church.[1] In doing so, it partially agrees with both traditional cessationist and popular continuationist views (see Chapter two for more on this) since it upholds the view that in terms of new redemptive/doctrinal revelation, prophecy ceased, but in terms of providing occasional specific guidance and edification to the church, congregational prophecy still continues in the post-apostolic period.

1.2 Methodology

It is generally held that 1 Corinthians 12-14 provides the most detailed information and substantial discussion on the nature and function of prophecy in the NT.[2] However, this portion of Scripture contains many interpretive problems with numerous proposals being made in regard to the nature of Corinthian prophecy. Though, the divergent views fall under one of the three

---

[1] While there is evidence that Corinthian type congregational prophecy continued in the post-apostolic church, it had also started to decline. Reasons for its decline have been attributed to the rise of false prophets and prophetic claims along with the rise of Montanism that resulted in the church's rejection and suppression of such prophetic claims to protect herself from false teaching (See Carson, *Showing the Spirit*, 184-86; Forbes, *Prophecy*, 248-50; Aune, *Prophecy*, 189). Carson reminds us that "it must be remembered that this theological stance was an ecclesiastical reaction. The fact that the church made room for prophecy until the Montanist abuse strongly suggests that what the church understood by 'prophecy' up to that time *did not in any way jeopardize the apostolic deposit*" (italics his, Carson, *Showing the Spirit*, 186). On the other hand, Forbes, while accepting such a possibility, affirms that there is yet no "convincing explanation of the decline of Christian prophecy. In some places it does seem to have been subsumed into new structures, and in others to have become well integrated with them" (Forbes, *Prophecy*, 250). Theologically, it can be argued that the decline (not complete cessation) of congregational prophecy was a natural result in view of a completed and sufficient revelation recorded in the Scripture that was available in the post-apostolic church unlike in the Corinthian church. However, this still does not necessarily imply a complete cessation of congregational prophecy today.

[2] Fee affirms there is enough material in 1 Corinthains 12-14 to get a fair picture of how Paul understood prophecy and tongues (Fee, *First Epistle to the Corinthians*, 597-98 [also Gaffin, *Perspectives*, 59]).

broader categories,[1] variations exist among scholars within each of these broader categories in regard to what exactly Christian prophecy looked like in the first century Corinthian world. Often the different conclusions are heavily consequent on the methods of approach used by different scholars. It is therefore important that the method of approach adopted by this research be stated.

1.2.1 Primacy of the Text of 1 Corinthians 12-14

This research work holds that the text must be the primary source in determining the nature, function, and content of Corinthian prophecy. A careful reading of many scholarly studies shows that Corinthian prophecy has often been described in the light of background materials about the religious environment of the first century Greco-Roman world. Parallels in regard to terminology or to conceptual similarities in various non-biblical sources have been sought to define Corinthian prophecy.[2] These non-biblical sources include Hellenistic mystery religions,[3] Gnosticism,[4] Hellenistic Judaism,[5] and the revelation traditions of Jewish

---

[1] Namely, the cessationist, the continuationist, and the view that identifies NT prophecy with contemporary preaching or teaching.

[2] Forbes provides a good discussion and critique of such approaches (See Forbes, *Prophecy* [also Aune, *Prophecy*; Hill, *Prophecy*]).

[3] Cf. Crone, *Early Christian Prophecy*; Fascher, *Prophetes*; also R. Reitzenstein, *Hellenistic Mystery Religions*, trans. J. Steely (Pittsburgh: Pickwick Press, 1978), who associates Christian prophets with ecstasy and miracle in the later Hellenistic cults of the papyri.

[4] Cf. W. Schmithals, *Gnosticism in Corinth* (Nashville: Abingdon Press, 1971); R. Jewett, *Paul's Anthropological Terms: A Study of their Use in Conflict Setting,* AGJU 10 (Leiden: Brill, 1971); Robert M. Grant, *Paul in the Roman World: The Conflict at Corinth* (Louisville: Westminster John Knox Press, 2001).

[5] Cf. B. A. Pearson, *The Pneumatikos-Psychikos Terminology in 1 Corinthians: A Study in the Theology of the Corinthian Opponents of Paul and its Relation to Gnosticism,* SBLDS 12 (Missoula, MT, 1974); similarly R. A. Horsley has argued for the personified wisdom found in Philo as providing background to understanding prophecy in 1 Corinthains 12-14 (Horsley, "Wisdom of Word and Words of Wisdom in Corinth," *CBQ* 39 [1977]: 224-39; idem, "Pneumatikos

apocalyptic discourse[1] among others.[2] There is value in such historical (even theological) reconstructions based on parallels in secondary sources since they can shed some light on the text and aid in understanding Corinthian prophecy. However, they must neither determine nor control the interpretation of the primary text.[3] Garland warns that by injudiciously allowing a mirror-reading or historical reconstruction to control the text, "the text can become the servant of preconceived impressions. The interpreter can read too much into what Paul says, read in his or her own biases, and misread Paul's argumentation in a particular passage."[4] It is, therefore, important not to lose focus on the primary text since it is the text that must control the outcomes. Background information informs in order to allow an appropriate understanding of the text. Paul Barnett advises that "the search for exegetical understanding may profitably begin *within* the text, rather than in sources external to it in Corinth's cultural and historical background ... background information illuminates the exegesis of the text but

---

vs. Psychikos: Distinctions of Spiritual Status among the Corinthians," *HTR* 69 [1976]: 269-88).

[1] Cf. G. Dautzenberg, *Urchristliche Prophetie* (Stuttgart: Kohlhammer, 1975); idem, "Zum religionsgeschichtlichen Hintergrund der διακρίσεις πνευμά των (1Kor 12:10)," *BZ* 15 (1971): 93-104; also with some modifications and differences, Aune, *Prophecy.*

[2] For parallels in the Torah Wisdom at Qumran and in Sirach, see J. A. Davis, *Wisdom and Spirit* (Lanham: UPA, 1984); Martin bases his reading of 1 Corinthains on the ancient (Greco-Roman) construction of human body (see Martin, *Corinthian Body*).

[3] Cf. J. L. Sumney, *Identifying Paul's Opponents: The Question of Method in 2 Corinthians* (Sheffield: JSOT Press, 1990), 70-94, chs. 7-9; also David G. Horrell and Edward Adams, eds., *Christianity at Corinth: The Quest for the Pauline Church* (Louisville: Westminster John Knox Press, 2004), 16-23; Thiselton, *First Epistle to the Corinthians,* 957-64.

[4] David E. Garland, *1 Corinthians*, BECNT (Grand Rapids: Baker, 2003), 13 (also see Robert H. Stein, *A Basic Guide to Interpreting the Bible: Playing by the Rules* [2nd ed., Grand Rapids: Baker, 2011], 205-206; Douglas J. Moo, *2 Peter, Jude*, NIV Application Commentary [Grand Rapids: Zondervan, 1999], 129-30; M. G. Barclay, "Mirror-Reading a Polemical Letter: Galatians as a Test Case," *The Galatians Debate*, ed. Mark Nanos [Peabody: Hendrickson, 2002], 372-76).

does not control it."[1] Therefore, this interplay between text and background information will be evident throughout the discussion in this book. This balance is needed since it is undeniable that an ancient document like 1 Corinthians needs to be read and understood against the background of its historical context.[2]

1.2.2 Limitations of Methodology

The limitations of this methodology are threefold. It is recognised that since the original questions of the Corinthian church cannot be accessed, but only Paul's answers,[3] postulation evaluation of the text will need to be made at times. Secondly, the occasional nature of the Corinthian letter is to be recognised in exegesis since it arose out of a specific occasion and is not a compendium of Paul's theology intended to describe the phenomenon of prophecy.[4] Paul's primary concern in writing 1 Corinthians 12-14 was not to define the nature of Corinthian prophecy but to correct the misconceptions about spiritual gifts and the improper exercise of the gifts of prophecy and tongues. A theology of prophecy can certainly be drawn from 1 Corinthians 12-14 but it is not an exhaustive theology, rather it is controlled by the Corinthian context. The use of secondary material relating to prophecy in other parts of the Bible (e.g. the OT, other Pauline, and non-Pauline sources) will be made to support, further explain,

---

[1] Paul Barnett, *The Corinthian Question: Why did the Church Oppose Paul?* (Nottingham: Apollos, 2011), 8-9.

[2] Cf. Ciampa and Rosner, *First Epistle to the Corinthian,* 35, 38; James Dunn, "Reconstructions of Corinthian Christianity and the Interpretation of 1Corinthians," in *Christianity at Corinth*, 308-309; Fee, *First Epistle to the Corinthians*, 1.

[3] Cf. Gordon Fee and Douglas Stuart, *How to Read the Bible for all Its Worth* (Grand Rapids: Zondervan, 1982), 46; Ciampa and Rosner, *First Epistle to the Corinthians*, 46.

[4] See Fee and Stuart, *How to Read the Bible,* 43-45; D. A. Carson and Douglas J. Moo, *An Introduction to the New Testament* (Nottingham: Apollos, 2005), 415; Ben Witherington III, *Conflict and Community in Corinth: A Socio-Rhetorical Commentary on 1 and 2 Corinthians* (Grand Rapids: Eerdmans, 1995), 39.

confirm, and test the exegetical findings of 1 Corinthians 12-14 on Corinthian prophecy.[1] This will determine the Pauline view of Corinthian prophecy. Hence, the methodology will primarily (but not exclusively) be exegetical.

Thirdly, only the passages/verses directly dealing with prophecy and related themes will be exegeted and discussed from 1 Corinthians 12-14.[2] This is because of the limitation of space and the focus of this book being exclusively on prophecy and not on other spiritual gifts. The relevant texts identified as the primary or high-priority passages that help define the nature of Corinthian prophecy are: 1 Cor 12:7, 10b, 28-29; 13:1-2, 8-10; 14:1-6, 13-17, 19, 22, 24-26, 29-32, 39. These passages are approached thematically rather than sequentially or chronologically, defining the main features, function, and content of Corinthian prophecy under appropriate titles.

1.2.3 Approach

The following chapter provides a brief overview and a critical evaluation of the three popular views of Corinthian prophecy. Similarities and differences between the views, along with their strengths and weaknesses are pointed out. Each of these views has certain points that this book builds upon to define Corinthian prophecy.

The third chapter provides an overview of prophecy in the Bible. It investigates the main form(s) of prophetic revelations along with some exceptions in the various parts of the Bible. It deals with the questions of the direction of prophecy (whether humanward or Godward or both), its general content and function, and groups and individuals who exercised it. In particular, it will be shown that canonical prophecy in the OT and parts of the NT was distinct from Corinthian congregational prophecy. The

---

[1] Cf. Gaffin, *Perspectives*, 59.

[2] Ciampa and Rosner also identify 1 Cor 13:2; 14:3; 24-25, 30-32, and 37 as providing "Paul's best clues as to his own understanding of prophecy" (Ciampa and Rosner, *First Epistle to the Corinthians*, 581).

information gathered here will be used to compare and explain Corinthian congregational prophecy.

The fourth chapter seeks to define Corinthian prophecy under six categories from the relevant passages in 1 Corinthians 12-14. Exegesis of relevant verses is done identifying Paul's understanding of Corinthian prophecy to be labelled as congregational prophecy. Information on prophecy from the OT and other parts of the NT will also be used and referred to so as to define, support, further explain, and confirm the congregational nature of Corinthian prophecy. Hence, differences and similarities between congregational and canonical prophecy will become clearer. If this hypothesis of congregational prophecy can be validated from the text, it may also build bridges among the three popular views on NT prophecy, offering a possible solution to the debate between the cessationist and continuationist camps. The final chapter summarises the conclusions of this book and offers some pastoral and theological reflections with the proposed definition of congregational prophecy.

Chapter 2

Debates on the Nature of NT Prophecy

It was pointed out earlier that research on Corinthian prophecy has been extensive and "answers to that question are *legion*."[1] The numerous proposed views can broadly be categorised as follows: the cessationist, the continuationist, and the view that identifies contemporary preaching as prophecy. The main concern of each regards the cessation or continuation of prophecy in the post-apostolic church; conclusions are largely dependent on an understanding of prophecy and of the role of a prophet. It is necessary to survey previous scholarship survey previous scholarship to build upon the works of those who have preceded us. Moreover, a critical evaluation of each of the major categories is also made. Nevertheless, there are elements in all three views that support this book's proposed view of Corinthian congregational prophecy.

2.1 The Cessationist View

The cessationist view finds its roots in the "Princeton view" with its first explicit expression found in the work of Benjamin

[1] Carson, *Showing the Spirit*, 92 (italics his).

Warfield.[1] Since then, it has been maintained (though with some variations) in the works of both dispensationalist and Reformed theologians such as John R. W. Stott,[2] Charles C. Ryrie,[3] Anthony A. Hoekema,[4] Robert G. Gromacki,[5] John F. Walvoord,[6] Merril F. Unger,[7] Edwin H. Palmer,[8] Walter J. Chantry,[9] Robert L. Reymond,[10] Robert L. Thomas,[11] Richard Gaffin,[12] Kenneth L. Gentry,[13] Norman Geisler,[14] F. D. Farnell,[15] John MacArthur,[16] O. Palmer

[1] Cf. B. B. Warfield, *Counterfeit Miracles* (Carlisle, PA: Banner of Truth, 1918) who proposed the cessation of all revelatory and miraculous gifts as a reaction to the charismatic movement.

[2] John R. W. Stott, *Baptism and Fullness: The Work of the Holy Spirit Today* (Leicester: IVP, 1964).

[3] C. C. Ryrie, *The Holy Spirit* (Chicago: Moody, 1965).

[4] Anthony A. Hoekema, *What about Tongue-Speaking*? (Grand Rapids: Eerdmans, 1966).

[5] Robert G. Gromacki, *The Modern Tongues Movement* (Philadelphia: P&R, 1967).

[6] John F. Walvoord, *The Holy Spirit at Work Today* (Wheaton: Van Kampen Press, 1954).

[7] Merril F. Unger, *The Baptism and Gifts of the Holy Spirit* (Chicago: Moody, 1974).

[8] Edwin H. Palmer, *The Holy Spirit* (Philadelphia: P&R, 1974).

[9] Walter J. Chantry, *Signs of the Apostles: Observations on Pentecostalism Old and New* (Carlisle, PA: Banner of Truth, 1976).

[10] Robert L. Raymond, *What about Continuing Revelations and Miracles in the Presbyterian Church Today: A Study of the Doctrine of the Sufficiency of Scripture* (St. Louis: P&R, 1977).

[11] Robert L. Thomas, *Understanding Spiritual Gifts* (Chicago: Moody, 1978).

[12] Gaffin, *Perspectives.*

[13] Gentry, *Gift of Prophecy.*

[14] Norman Geisler, *Signs and Wonders* (Wheaton: Tyndale, 1988).

[15] Farnell, "Current Debate"; idem, "Gift of Prophecy," 277-303; idem, "Does the New Testament Teach?" 62-88; idem, "When Will the Gift," 171-202.

[16] MacArthur seems to fit in all three camps since he distinguishes between the canonical revelatory prophecy (having ceased at the end of apostolic era) and the non-revelatory prophecy (continuing today as "the ability to proclaim

Robertson,[1] Edmund Clowney,[2] and Sinclair Ferguson.[3] Diversity exists among cessationist scholars, not only in regard to the degree and the basis of the cessation of certain gifts but also in regard to the nature and continuation of prophecy. All, however, agree that prophecy ceased with the apostolic period since it consisted of foundational redemptive revelations for inscripturation. The cessationist view generally regards NT prophecy as the same as OT prophecy in nature and function because NT prophets had the same foundational ministry as the apostles: speaking the divine word of revelation (cf. Eph 2:20; 3:5).[4] Once the church's foundation had been laid by the first century apostles and prophets, there was no further need for these offices.[5] Therefore, it is argued that with the completion of the all-sufficient biblical revelation in the Scriptures, prophecy also ceased with the NT completed because prophecy is revelatory in nature.[6] In the words of Hodge: "the gift of prophecy was the gift of revelation by which mysteries were communicated,"[7] and since revelation has ceased, all revelatory gifts have ceased too.[8] Hodge defines these *mysteries* (cf. 1 Cor 13:2) as "all the secret purposes of

---

truth powerfully") which he identifies with preaching (John F. MacArthur, Jr., *Charismatic Chaos* [Grand Rapids: Zondervan, 1992], 231 n. 20).

[1] Robertson, *Final Word.*

[2] Clowney, *Church.*

[3] Ferguson, *Holy Spirit.*

[4] Ferguson, *Holy Spirit*, 210, 214; Gaffin, *Perspectives*, 58; Clowney, *Church*, ch.16; Robertson, *Final Word*, ch.1.

[5] See Farnell, "When Will the Gift," 190; Stott, *Baptism and Fullness,* 100-101.

[6] Cf. Ryrie, *Holy Spirit*, 86; Stott, *Baptism and Fullness*, 101-02; Gentry, *Gift of Prophecy,* chs. 5-6; Palmer, *Holy Spirit*, 102; Ferguson, *Holy Spirit*, 221.

[7] Charles Hodge, *I & II Corinthians* (Edinburgh: The Banner of Truth, 1857), 267. However, Hodge sees NT prophets under the apostles since the apostles were permanently inspired and possessed infallible teaching at all times, unlike NT prophets who were only occasionally inspired and infallible (Hodge, *I&II Corinthians*, 262).

[8] Ferguson, *Holy Spirit*, 262-63.

God relating to redemption."[1] This view generally regards all NT prophecy (including Corinthian prophecy) as a means of bringing redemptive revelation for inscripturation by NT prophets and apostles who were the main "vehicles of divine revelation" under the New Covenant.[2] Hence, for most scholars in this camp, there is only one form of prophecy in the Bible, i.e., canonical or inscripturated prophecy.

According to the cessationist view, the primary content of NT prophecy was "forth-telling" rather than "fore-telling."[3] Prediction was only one of the elements of NT prophecy, not the main.[4] The content of NT prophecy mostly consisted of "occasional inspiration and revelations ... either in some new communications relating to faith or duty, or simply an immediate impulse and aid from the Holy Spirit, in presenting truth already known."[5] It was both new as well as a reiteration of previous redemptive revelation. The cessationist view also makes a strict distinction between prophecy and preaching/teaching due to the revelatory character of prophecy. Gaffin affirms that prophecy is not primarily an "interpretation of an already existing inspired text or oral tradition, but is itself the inspired, non-derivative word of God ... the element of revelation is plainly at its core."[6] Farnell similarly argues that "in the NT the presence or absence of revelation distinguishes prophecy from teaching"[7] (or preaching or evangelism or knowledge) since prophecy involves a "miraculous impartation of immediate revelation, which could not be known" otherwise.[8] The elements of prediction and revelation also confirm the spontaneous nature

---

[1] Hodge, *I&II Corinthians*, 267 (italics his); also Robertson, *Final Word*, 15-16, ch. 2.

[2] Robertson, *Final Word*, 16; Stott, *Baptism and Fullness*, 99-102; Gentry, *Gift of Prophecy*, ch.3.

[3] Robertson, *Final Word*, 3-4; also Hodge, *I & II Corinthians*, 247.

[4] Farnell, "When Will the Gift," 172.

[5] Hodge, *I & II Corinthians*, 247.

[6] Gaffin, *Perspectives*, 59-60.

[7] Farnell, "When Will the Gift,"182; cf. 182-85.

[8] Farnell, "When Will the Gift," 184.

of prophecy.[1] This view also regards tongues with interpretation as closely related and functionally equivalent or identical to prophecy (cf. Acts 2:14-18). As a result, it argues that tongues, being of a foundational and revelatory nature (i.e. consisting of Scripture-quality revelation), also ceased with prophecy.[2]

In summary, then, the cessationist view of NT prophecy is based on the revelatory nature of prophecy (and interpreted tongues) as a means of bringing forth the foundational redemptive revelation that became inscripturated in the Bible. Here, the argument for the cessation of prophecy is primarily grounded in the theological assertions regarding the completion, sufficiency, and authority of written Scripture. This view holds that since prophecy brings foundational, new, and doctrinal revelation, it cannot continue once Scripture is complete. This is also indicated from Gaffin's assertion that even if there was other prophecy (beside the canonical one) it was only to guide the NT church in matters that arose because the canon was, as yet, incomplete. In other words, according to Gaffin, when the NT was complete, any other (non-canonical) type of prophecy also ceased. It is interesting to note that, unlike many other cessationists, Gaffin, above, seems to accept that there was a non-canonical type prophecy in the NT church operating through the Spirit for the church's edification, beside the one from the apostles and the prophets for canonisation (i.e. canonical prophecy). Gaffin also argues that not all prophets in the Bible were involved in receiving and writing down canonical revelation but served local churches by providing guidance and edification.[3] According to Gaffin, this implies that prophetic revelation for canonisation was mainly given to the apostles and some of the NT prophets, while the other prophets (and individuals) were given prophetic revelations for the church's edification. Gaffin considers that both forms of prophecy ceased with the completion of the NT. Gaffin's distinction supports this

[1] Cf. Farnell, "When Will the Gift," 182-84.

[2] See Ferguson, *Holy Spirit*, 212-13, Clowney, *Church*, 255-68; Robertson, *Final Word*, 27-28; MacArthur, *Charismatic Chaos*, ch. 2.

[3] Gaffin, *Perspectives*, 99-100.

book's assertions of congregational prophecy as the other (non-canonical) type of prophecy. However, the proposed view in this book, unlike Gaffin, holds that non-canonical prophecy did not cease with the completion of the NT.

The cessationist view appears to be theologically rather than exegetically driven. This is recognised by the cessationist scholars themselves. Farnell agrees that the cessationist view is "based on theological deduction made from certain NT passages,"[1] and just as OT prophecy ceased when "the canon of the OT was closed, NT prophecy reasonably may be considered to have ceased following the same analogy."[2] In summary, this view generally (Gaffin being a rare exception) sees only one form of prophecy in the Bible that brought redemptive revelations for inscripturation and ceased with the completion of the NT.

2.2 The Continuationist View

The opposite of the cessationist view of Corinthian prophecy is the continuationist view. This includes both the Pentecostals/ charismatics and many evangelical and even Reformed scholars including Wayne Grudem,[3] Michael Green,[4] John Piper,[5] C. Samuel

---

[1] Cf. Rom 15:18-19; 2 Cor 12:12; Rev 22:18; Eph 2:20; 1 Cor 13:10. Thus Farnell also bases the cessationist argument on the foundational (Eph 2:20) and temporal (1 Cor 13:10) nature of NT prophecy.

[2] Farnell, "When Will the Gift," 185-86.

[3] Grudem, *Prophecy.*

[4] Micheal Green, *I Believe in the Holy Spirit* (London: Hodder and Stoughton, 1975).

[5] David Mathis, *Piper on Prophecy and Tongues* (Unpublished), [assessed 10 Sep, 2013]. Online: http://www.desiringgod.org/blog/posts/piper-on-prophecy-and-tongues.

Storm,[1] Gordon Fee,[2] D. A. Carson,[3] Robert L. Saucy,[4] Max Turner,[5] Christopher Forbes,[6] Craig S. Keener,[7] Jack Deere,[8] Douglas A. Oss,[9] Donald Gee,[10] and Graham Houston.[11] At the same time, significant variations exist even among continuationist scholars, not only in regard to the degree of the continuation of prophecy and other gifts, but also in regard to its nature (discussed later in this chapter).[12] All, however, agree that the NT does not indicate the cessation of all prophecy (along with other spiritual gifts) in the post-apostolic period, and that prophecy still continues in one or another form. This view generally regards prophecy by NT prophets (and other believers) as inferior or of a lower type (less authoritative and not infallible) to that of OT and apostolic prophecy. Grudem's view of two levels of NT prophecy, namely apostolic and ordinary congregational prophecy, has received commendation and sympathy from many leading evangelical and Reformed scholars.[13] His view is considered to provide a strong

---

[1] Samuel Storm, "A Third Wave View," in *Are Miraculous Gifts for Today*.

[2] Gordon Fee, *Paul, the Spirit, and the People of God* (Grand Rapids: Baker Press, 1996); idem, *God's Empowering Presence.*

[3] Represents a cautious moderate continuationist view (Carson, *Showing the Spirit*).

[4] Saucy, "An Open But Cautious View," in *Are Miraculous Gifts for Today?*

[5] Turner, *Holy Spirit.*

[6] Forbes, *Prophecy.*

[7] Keener, *Gifts and Giver*.

[8] A former cessationist affirming that the doctrine of cessationism originated in "experience," and not from Scripture. Jack Deere, *Surprised by the Power of the Spirit* (Grand Rapids: Zondervan, 1993), 99.

[9] Oss, "A Pentecostal View," in *Are Miraculous Gifts for Today?*

[10] Gee, *Spiritual Gifts.*

[11] Houston, *Prophecy.*

[12] For a survey of variations among continuationists, see also Mark J. Cartledge, "Charismatic Prophecy," 79-120.

[13] Grudem's work, *The Gift of Prophecy,* has commendations on its back cover page from J. I. Packer, Vern S. Poythress, L. Russ Bush, and Stanley Horton. Both Carson and Piper essentially agree with Grudem's thesis. See Carson, *Showing*

doctrinal and theological justification for continuing prophecy.[1] Here, apostolic prophecy is seen as an OT-type foundational prophecy, fully inspired and absolutely authoritative, bringing fresh redemptive revelation that became inscripturated in the NT. Accordingly, it is limited to and ceased with the apostles.[2] It is to be noted that the apostolic prophecy here is equivalent to the cessationist view of canonical prophecy. The difference between the two views is that the continuationist view limits NT canonical (apostolic) prophecy to the apostles only, whereas the cessationist view includes some of the NT prophets along with the apostles (cf. Eph 2:20; 3:5) as the recipients of canonical prophetic revelations.

According to the continuationist view, ordinary congregational prophecy is a weaker type, non-foundational prophecy, similar to prophecy in the intertestamental period, and exercised by ordinary Christian prophets in the NT. Grudem defines it as "speaking merely human words to report some things God brings to mind" suddenly.[3] This view argues that though ordinary congregational type prophecy is a spontaneous activity of the Spirit (including divine insights and revelation), it is potentially fallible since it is received and interpreted by humans in fallible words.[4] Samuel Storms also affirms that "although rooted in revelation, prophecy is occasionally fallible," because it "is the *human* report of a divine revelation" and involves *perception* (or reception), *interpretation*, and *application* by believers. Only the revelation itself is infallible

the Spirit, 95 and *Piper on Prophecy and Tongues* (Unpublished), [assessed 10 Sep, 2013]. Online: http://www.desiringgod.org/blog/posts/piper-on-prophecy-and-tongues. Grudem has actually expanded on some points advanced by other scholars before him (E.g. Guy, *Prophecy*).

[1] Cf. Michael G. Maudlin, "Seers in the Heartland," *Christianity Today* (January, 1991): 20.

[2] Grudem, *Prophecy*, 27-70. In the latest edition of his book, Grudem clarifies that the distinction between apostolic and ordinary Christian prophecy is not about different "kinds" but different levels of authority attached to each (see Grudem, *Gift of Prophecy*, 47-48).

[3] Grudem, *Prophecy*, 51.

[4] Grudem, *Prophecy,* chs. 3-4.

because God is responsible for it. Storms concludes that "in terms of the *revelation* alone, the New testament prophetic gift" is like the Old Testament prophetic gift.[1] However, Grudem differs from Storms here, arguing that though revelation is essential for prophecy, it does not necessarily mean absolute authority, even if it is correct. He supports this by suggesting that often the terms ἀποκαλύπτω (*apokalupto*, "I reveal") and ἀποκάλυψις (*apokalupsis*, "revelation") in the Bible can mean "authority of merely human words" like in "a sermon or the advice of a mature Christian" (cf. Phil 3:15; Eph 1:17) which is not equal to Scripture's authority.[2]

Grudem finds the pattern of two types of prophets (apostolic and non-apostolic) in the NT, also present among OT prophets as the "established, primary prophets" (including writing prophets) and the "bands of secondary prophets."[3] He argues that the latter's prophecies were not "equal in value or in authority" to the former since their prophecies were not preserved in the canonical Scriptures. Therefore, he regards the "bands of secondary prophets" as identical to NT ordinary Christian prophets and the "established, primary prophets" as the apostles. Prophecies by the apostles, like OT established prophets, were absolutely authoritative, were canonised and eventually ceased, whereas prophecies by ordinary prophets in the NT are like the prophesying of OT "bands of secondary prophets" that had lesser authority and were not canonised.[4] Grudem identifies the Corinthian prophecy with the latter type of prophesying. It must be noted though, that there is no indication in the latter 8th and 6th century prophets that groups like the "bands of secondary prophets" continued to

---

[1] Storm, "Third Wave View," 207.

[2] Grudem, *Prophecy*, 64-68, cf. 113-17. Notice that what Grudem refers to as "speaking merely human words to report some things God brings to mind" (51) in Phil 3:15 and Eph 1:17 is the Spirit's work of illumination. He seems to identify illumination very closely with ordinary congregational prophecy.

[3] Grudem, *Prophecy*, appendix one, 274-75.

[4] Grudem, *Prophecy*, appendix one, 274-76; also idem, "Prophecy/ Prophets," *NDBT*, 702-703.

exist.[1] Moreover, prophesying by such groups in the OT was an exception since it consisted of some kind of spontaneous inspired worship directed to God rather than oracular speech directed to humans (e.g. 1 Samuel 10; 1 Kings 18).[2] It is extremely unlikely that Corinthian prophecy was similar to the prophesying of such groups since Paul nowhere indicates that Corinthian prophecy was Godward (discussed further in Chapters 3 and 4). It is also important to note that though Gurdem's view of two levels of NT prophecy is well accepted in Pentecostal and charismatic circles, not all continuationist scholars agree with it.[3]

The continuationist view generally regards the purpose of NT prophecy as being to edify and direct the church by providing specific instructions on matters and situations on which the Scripture is generally silent or unclear. Green suggests that NT prophecy is "a direct word from God for the situation on hand," contributing to the edification of the Church and is still continuing today though diminished due to various factors in history.[4] This view also makes a strict distinction between prophecy and preaching/teaching due to the spontaneous revelatory character of prophecy. Green argues that though NT prophecy could have had various forms, it was distinct from preaching/teaching since

> the men of the first century knew preaching and teaching when they heard it, and they knew prophecy as well. The two were quite different ... it is one thing to prepare one's address in dependence on the HS, and to preach it in the power of same Spirit; it is quite another thing to find the Spirit taking over and speaking directly from Christ through you, in words that you never intended to use at all.[5]

---

[1] See Rendtorff, *TDNT* 6:800.

[2] See Turner, *Holy Spirit*, 189.

[3] Cf. Green, *I Believe*, 169; Turner, *Holy Spirit,* 210-12.

[4] Green, *I Believe,* 170, 172-74.

[5] Green, *I Believe*, 171 (also Grudem, *Prophecy*, 117-23 [cf. ch. 6]; James Dunn, *Jesus and the Spirit* [London: SCM Press, 1975], 228).

Fee regards the NT gift of prophecy as "new prophecy" of a "different kind" since it was not just limited to NT "prophets" but was "widely expressed and widely experienced" by NT believers (1 Cor 14:24-25, 30-31) with the goal of building up the church (Eph 4:11-16). Therefore, Fee regards Corinthian prophecy as "potentially available to all" believers.[1] Like Grudem, he also describes Corinthian prophecy as consisting of "spontaneous, understandable messages, orally delivered in the gathered assembly, intended for edification or encouragement of the people."[2] While Fee sees continuity between OT and NT prophecy, he also considers NT (Corinthian) prophecy as distinct because of the eschatological situation of the church. He explains that OT prophecy mostly consisted of judgment messages but NT prophecy brought encouragement and comfort.[3] Fee also maintains that prophecy is distinct from teaching/preaching due to its revelatory and spontaneous nature (1 Cor 14:29-32). He argues that in Paul's view, prophecy "does not mean a prepared sermon, but the spontaneous word given to God's people for the edification of the (church)."[4] Prediction in prophecy is seen as only one element in NT prophecy, and not necessarily the crucial one.[5]

The most particularised yet comprehensive view, within the continuationist classification, is that of Turner and Forbes. They do not fully agree with Grudem but affirm the revelatory nature of prophecy and argue for its distinction from preaching/teaching. Turner affirms that prophecy did not simply involve "general principles that could be deduced ... by illuminated reading of the Torah, or from the gospel tradition, or from apostolic *didache*," but specific directions or unsolicited guidance, solution for disputes, assurance, warning, at times prediction of the future, and even "the impartation of theological 'mysteries.'"[6] The main

---

[1] Fee, *Paul, the Spirit,* 171-72 (cf. idem, *First Epistle to the Corinthians*, 595).

[2] Fee, *God's Empowering Presence*, 891 (also *Paul, The Spirit,* 171).

[3] Fee, *God's Empowering Presence*, 892 (also *Paul, The Spirit,* 171-72).

[4] Fee, *First Epistle to the Corinthians*, 660 (cf. 595).

[5] Fee, *First Epistle to the Corinthians*, 595.

[6] Turner, *Holy Spirit,* 200, 202, 206, cf. ch.12.

characteristic of NT prophecy, for Turner, is the "necessity of God's revealing particularistic knowledge."[1] He further explains that though teaching might have "included exposition that related Scripture and tradition to the immediate needs of a congregation ... prophecy primarily denoted the declaration by a person of material revealed to him or her *directly* by supernatural source, rather than mediated through consideration of Scripture."[2] Forbes agrees with Turner here, distinguishing prophecy from preaching by suggesting that NT prophecy "was not normally the basic gospel proclamation or κήρυγμα (*kerugma*) itself, but might commonly be some application of its principles to a particular situation."[3] He claims that Paul nowhere calls preaching (or gospel proclamation) "a charisma" like he does for prophecy. Forbes supports this by arguing that on the examination of "the use of the various verbs (ἀγγέλλω [*angello*], κηρύσσω [*kerusso*], etc.) usually translated by English 'to preach,'" are found to be "overwhelmingly used of the proclamation of *past* revelation. Prophecy, on the other hand, is a proclamation of revelation only just received." In other words, "today's prophecy is tomorrow's preaching or teaching."[4]

Turner also explains that since NT prophecy was exceedingly varied, it could also be doctrinal in nature, not as offering "new theological revelation" but "pastoral 'words,'" based on "already known theology," to specific circumstances, with the exception of the eschatological prophecies.[5] Turner and Forbes also recognise the "didactic and prescriptive elements" in NT prophecy since the NT prophets were able to preach and teach (Acts 15:32), however, they object to identifying inspired preaching, homily, exegesis, and teaching with application or other forms of speech (e.g. words of wisdom and knowledge) with prophecy, despite their producing the same results as prophecy (1 Cor 14:3).[6] The objection is based

[1] Turner, *Holy Spirit*, 200.

[2] Turner, *Holy Spirit*, 203.

[3] Forbes, *Prophecy*, 236 (cf. 229).

[4] Forbes, *Prophecy*, 228 (italics his).

[5] Turner, *Holy Spirit*, 214.

[6] Turner, *Holy Spirit*, 201-202.

on the rationale that Pauline prophecy is by nature spontaneous and revelatory. Turner, therefore, concludes that "for Paul prophecy is the reception and subsequent communication of spontaneous, divinely given ἀποκάλυψις" (*apokalupsis*, "revelation").[1]

It can be summarised that diversity of opinions exists within the continuationist view. Some scholars either fully accept or have sympathy for Grudem's view, others do not. All, however, see Corinthian prophecy as distinct from OT canonised prophecy and apostolic writings for one reason or another. This indicates that a general distinction between inscripturated (canonical) and non-inscripturated (congregational) prophecy is maintained by all continuationists, as also proposed in this the proposed view in this book. All scholars also agree that NT prophecy was a widespread phenomenon, rooted in spontaneous revelations, and providing guidance and edification to the church, rather than bringing forth new redemptive revelation for inscripturation. At the same time, scholars agree that NT prophecy can include reiteration and application of previous revelation to immediate situations. Prediction is seen as an occasional element, and distinction between NT prophecy and preaching/teaching is also maintained.

2.3 Prophecy as Contemporary Preaching (or Teaching)

This view can be regarded as a more controversial and yet increasingly popular position that includes scholars such as David Hill,[2] E. Earle Ellis,[3] Ralph P. Martin,[4] E. Cothenet,[5] T. W.

---

[1] Turner, "Spiritual Gifts: Then and Now," *VoxEv* 15 (1985): 10; cf. 7-64 (Forbes, *Prophecy*, 229; Dunn, *Jesus and the Spirit*, 228).

[2] Hill, *Prophecy*; also "Christian Prophets as Teachers and Instructors in the Church," in *Prophetic Vocation*.

[3] Ellis, *Prophecy and Hermeneutic*.

[4] Martin, *Spirit and the Congregation*.

[5] Cothenet, "Les prophètes chrêtiens comme exegetes charismatiques de l'écriture," in *Prophetic Vocation*.

Gillespie,[1] J. I. Packer,[2] U. Muller,[3] J. Hering,[4] Robertson and Plummer,[5] Anthony C. Thiselton,[6] David Garland,[7] and Michael Horton.[8] Though, this view can be considered as a sub-category of the continuationist view since it also sees prophecy continuing today in some form, it differs from it due to its particular view of NT prophecy. Here too, significant variations exist among scholars within this sub-category but all agree that contemporary preaching (and exegesis or teaching with application) can be seen as a form of prophecy, even if not exactly the same. In other words, this view holds that the gift of prophecy continues today but in a limited and different sense to that in the NT. One of the main proponents of this view, J. I. Packer, defines prophecy, in general, as "the receiving and relaying of what purports to be a divine message," which includes "forth-telling God's present word to His people."[9] He argues that "any verbal enforcement of biblical teaching as it applies to one's present hearers may probably be called prophecy today" since it involves "application of revealed truth rather than augmentation of it."[10] For Packer, prophecy is "exhibited in every sermon or informal message," and has always been present "ever

---

[1] Gillespie, *First Theologians;* also "A Pattern of Prophetic Speech in 1 Corinthians," *JBL* 97 (1978): 74-95.

[2] J. I. Packer, *Keep in Step with the Spirit* (Leicester: IVP, 1984).

[3] Muller, *Prophetie und Predigt im Neuen Testament.*

[4] J. Hering, *The First Epistle of St. Paul to the Corinthians,* (trans, A. W. Heathcote and P. J. Allcock; London: Epworth, 1962).

[5] Archibald Robertson and Alfred Plummer, *A Critical and Exegetical Commentary on the First Epistle of St Paul to the Corinthians*, ICC (Edinburgh: T & T Clark, 1911).

[6] Although, Thiselton broadly sees NT prophecy as prophetic preaching, he sees a distinction between NT prophetic preaching and the modern/contemporary styles of pastoral preaching. He also distinguishes prophetic preaching from teaching (Thiselton, *First Epistle to the Corinthians*, 960-61, 1087-1094).

[7] Garland, *1 Corinthians.*

[8] Michael Horton, *The Christian Faith: A Systematic Theology for Pilgrims on the Way* (Grand Rapids: 2011), 884.

[9] Packer, *Keep in Step*, 214-15.

[10] Packer, *Keep in Step*, 214-15.

since the church began."[1] He also does not see any clear distinction between preaching and teaching since, he argues, "preaching is teaching God's revealed truth with application; such teaching with application is prophecy, always was, and always will be."[2] This view also sees continuity between OT and NT prophets in regard to their function in forth-telling God's word to his people. Packer explains that the main function of OT prophets was to preach the law and to call Israel to covenantal obedience which is similar to the function of NT prophets who preach the gospel for conversion, edification, and encouragement (1 Cor 14:3, 24, 25 [cf. Acts 15:32]).[3]

Packer also suggests that in view of Joel's prediction fulfilled in Acts 2:17-21, prophesying in the NT became "an activity in which all believers were able and perhaps expected to share (cf. Acts 19:6; 1 Cor 14:1, 23-25)," though not all were called prophets (1 Cor 12:29) "presumably because their sharing in prophetic ministry was too intermittent."[4] Therefore, he concludes that since prophecy "is in principle a universal Christian activity," it should not be expected to be absent in any age.[5] Here, Packer appears to apply a distinction between canonical (inscripturated) and non-canonical (congregational) prophecy in the Bible. He calls the latter "the potentially universal prophecy" (e.g. Acts 19:6; 1 Cor 14:1, 23-25), which was practised by many believers (not called "prophets") intermittently in NT churches.[6] He adds that this non-canonical or universal type of prophecy needs to be tested and weighed (1 Cor 14:29) since it is "less than infallible and irreformable," and is not in the "direct-speech-of-God verbal

---

[1] Packer, *Keep in Step,* 217.

[2] Packer, *Keep in Step,* 217. This is quite similar to Ellis' view of prophecy as exegesis and application of biblical texts (See Ellis, *Prophecy and Hermeneutics*, 186).

[3] Packer, *Keep in Step*, 215.

[4] Packer, *Keep in Step,* 214-15.

[5] Packer, *Keep in Step*, 215.

[6] Packer, *Keep in Step,* 214-15.

form" like canonical prophecy.[1] In fact, he regards prophecy as revelatory, only and particularly in connection with this type of universal/non-canonical prophecy.[2] Hence, Packer proposes two levels of prophecy in the NT, namely canonical and non-canonical ("the potentially universal" type) prophecy and sees the later type not only practised in Acts and Corinth but also continuing today.[3]

In this view, the revelatory nature of prophecy is either underemphasised or limited. For example, Packer considers NT prophecy to be revelatory only "sometimes" (1 Cor 14:26, 30) and "not every time." He suggests that such revelation would generally be about "a God-prompted application of truth that ... had been revealed already, rather than a disclosure of divine thoughts and intentions not previously known or not otherwise knowable."[4] Therefore, according to this view, prophecy is revelatory only occasionally and in a limited way with no new revelations to be added to Scripture. As such, prediction is not the main element in prophecy. In brief, Packer's view implies that any paraenetic ministry under the new covenant is a form of prophecy.[5]

Another prominent scholar in this camp is David Hill who sees prophecy as Spirit-inspired "pastoral preaching or proclamation."[6] His view is based on the various forms of the term παράκλησις (*paraklesis* "exhortation, consolation, comfort"), which are often used of early Christian prophetic speech, consisting of *kerygmatic* proclamation, correction, rebuking, warning, and guiding.[7] At the

---

[1] Packer, *Keep in Step*, 216.

[2] Packer, *Keep in Step,* 215.

[3] However, he also maintains that the present charismatic phenomenon of prophecy is not to be seen as the NT sign gift now restored. Unfortunately, he does not expand on this point further, see Packer, *Keep in Steps*, 217-19.

[4] Packer, *Keep in Step*, 215.

[5] Turner argues against this and affirms that such a view of prophecy "overlooks the fact that paraenesis is not a distinctive feature of Old or New Testament prophecy as such, but common to a variety of genres" (e.g. Sermon on the Mount). Thus 1 Corinthians 14:3 does not define "the distinctive character of 'prophecy'" (Turner, *Holy Spirit*, 204).

[6] Hill, *Prophecy*, 97, 213.

[7] Hill, *Prophecy*, 128-29, 103, 108, 195, 212.

same time, he recognises a functional difference between prophets and teachers and suggests that though "charismatic exegesis" of the OT might have been part of the prophet's ministry, it was "more characteristic of a Christian teacher."[1] A distinguishing feature of Hill's view is that he even sees prophecy as a "response of men to God and his word" by considering prayer and praise as a form of prophecy. Consequently, for Hill, prophecy is not just humanward but also Godward.[2] He also affirms the revelatory character of prophecy since he sees a Christian prophet as "a divinely inspired speaker who receives intelligible and authoritative revelations or messages" from God "to deliver publicly, in oral or written form, to Christian individuals and/or the Christian community."[3] Nonetheless, for Hill, such prophetic revelations from God, consisting of mysteries or the hidden purposes of God, are made known in the gospel with moral implications.[4] Hill also proposes two levels of prophecy functioning in the NT with two levels of authority attached to them. He distinguishes between occasional (i.e. congregational) prophecy and the regular prophecy by those designated as prophets and who also wrote the Scripture (e.g. Paul, Peter, John). He sees the former (as community-prophets) who were more like "guardians (and exponents) of the prophet-author's words" and played a secondary role. In other words, the community prophets prophesied occasionally using the content from the speeches of regular prophets (and apostles). This means that the prophetic speeches of the community prophets were to be tested, unlike Paul's prophetic speeches and writings. As such, he also argues that NT community prophets did not always enjoy "unchallengeable authority" like OT prophets and the apostles.[5] Here, Hill comes very close to sharing Grudem's view of two

---

[1] Hill, *Prophecy*, 211; also "Christian Prophets as Teachers," in *Prophetic Vocation*, 114, 123.

[2] Hill, *Prophecy*, 210.

[3] Hill, *Prophecy,* 8-9.

[4] Hill, *Prophecy*, 136.

[5] Hill, *Prophecy,* 135, 137-38, 195.

levels of prophecy except that Hill includes in prophecy pastoral preaching.

Another prominent view, belonging in this camp, is that of Thomas Gillespie who sees prophecy as "interpretation of the theological and ethical implications of the apostolic *kerygma*," and argues that a prophetic speech was more like "extended discourse of a sermonic kind rather than brief ejaculatory oracles."[1] Gillespie argues that Paul's restriction on the number of prophets in 1 Cor 14:29-30 and his instruction that a prophet should withdraw if another receives a revelation, shows that prophecy consisted of lengthy discourses.[2] However, Turner refutes it by pointing out that the same restriction also applies to tongues (1 Cor 14:27) which are understood to be "relatively short utterances." Moreover, the time required for judgment and reflection also supports that prophecy consisted of shorter discourses rather than long sermons.[3]

It is interesting to note that contrary to popular belief,[4] both Calvin and Luther also fit more accurately in this camp rather than solely in the cessationist camp. They both agree that the NT prophets ceased with the apostles, but they see the function of prophecy still continuing in "the interpretation of Scripture" (i.e. preaching).[5] In his commentary on Romans 12:6, Calvin affirms that "prophesying at this day amongst Christians is almost nothing else than a right understanding of the Scripture, and singular gift of expounding the same, since all the old prophecies and oracles of God have been finished in Christ and his gospel."[6] Similarly, Luther in his sermons on Romans 12, affirms that "'the interpreting of Scripture … is the noblest, highest, and greatest

[1] Gillespie, *First Theologians,* 63, 237, 262-63.

[2] Gillespie, *First Theologians*, 24-25.

[3] Turner, *Holy Spirit*, 205 (also Forbes, *Prophecy*, 227-29).

[4] Cf. Gentry, *Gift of Prophecy*, 108-16.

[5] Cf. David Starling, "The Analogy of Faith in the Theology of Luther and Calvin," *RTR* 72 (2013): 6-7.

[6] Jean Calvin, *Commentary upon the Epistle of Saint Paul to the Romans* (Edinburgh: Calvin Translation Society, 1844), 460 (as quoted by David Starling, "The Analogy of Faith," 7).

gift of prophecy."[1] He further affirms that "'prophesying does not mean to speak as the prophets once did of future things but to interpret the Prophets, the Psalms … we are prophets."[2] David Starling suggests that Calvin's "'almost nothing'" could point to the possibility that NT prophecy has not completely ceased, though Calvin himself does not elaborate on this.[3] At the same time, Calvin also recognises the necessity of *revelation* needed in prophecy that brings the *knowledge* to apply Scripture to present situations.[4] It appears that neither of the reformers saw the gift of prophecy as having completely ceased in his time.

It can be summarised here briefly that though diversity of opinions exists among scholars within this camp too, they all agree that NT prophecy still continues today in pastoral preaching, teaching, and in exegesis of Scripture with application. Some scholars also propose two levels of prophecy operating within NT prophecy as canonical and non-canonical (i.e. congregational or occasional) prophecy. They see that canonical (inscripturated) prophecy ceased with the first century apostles and prophets but congregational prophecy continues today in preaching (and teaching). Spontaneous revelation in prophecy is not completely denied or overlooked but is not regarded as the defining feature of NT prophecy. Revelation in prophecy is confined to God-prompted application of previous revealed truths. The term παρά κλησις (*paraklesis*) plays the key role in some scholars' view (e.g. Hill, Gillespie, Thiselton), constituting the main feature of NT prophecy.

2.4 Conclusion

The discussion above shows that there are certain features of NT prophecy with which all three groups agree. All views generally

[1] Sermon 17, (*WA* II, 39, 26), as quoted by Starling, "The Analogy of Faith," 7.

[2] Sermon 34, (*WA* I, 104, 16), as quoted by Starling, "The Analogy of Faith," 7.

[3] Starling, "The Analogy of Faith," 7.

[4] Calvin, *Paul to the Romans,* 438.

agree, to some extent, that NT prophecy was revelatory in some way. Here, "revelation" is generally understood as referring to immediately revealed biblical truths and their applications whether previously known or unknown. The cessationist and continuationist views see prophecy always rooted and originating in revelation, while the third view sees only occasional occurrences of revelation in NT prophecy. All views also agree that prediction was only one element of NT prophecy and not the main. All views agree that NT prophecy was an intelligible phenomenon and not ecstatic in the sense of a frenzied or uncontrolled phenomenon. They also agree that NT prophecy was to be weighed and tested on the basis of previous revelation (the OT and known apostolic traditions/teachings). Lastly, all three affirm the sufficiency of Scripture and regard canonical prophecy having ceased with the completion of NT Scripture. The proposed view in this book agrees with the three views on the features of NT prophecy pointed out above since these features are also present in Paul's discussion of Corinthian congregational prophecy in 1 Corinthians 12-14 (discussed in Chapter 4 later).

There are also certain points where this book does not agree with the three views. It disagrees with the cessationist view for seeing only canonical prophecy operating in the NT. This cessationist assertion is based on the assumption that prophecy was always needed and meant for writing Scripture. It was pointed out earlier that prophecy was not a necessary condition for the writing of NT Scripture.[1] The cessationist view seems to lack clear exegetical evidence to support the assumption that prophecy was a necessary condition for inscripturation.[2] Though, prophecy was one of the means of canonical revelation to be inscripturated, the NT shows that not all prophecy was inscripturated (e.g. Acts 19:6; 21:9; Rom 12:6; 1 Thess 5:20-21; 1 Tim 1:18; 4:14). In fact, none of the Corinthian prophecies were inscripturated (1 Corinthians

[1] Cf. Turner, *Holy Spirit*, 211 (cf. Keener, *Gifts and Giver*, 122; also see Carson & Woodbridge, eds., *Hermeneutics, Authority and Canon*; Dunbar et al., "The Canon: How God Gave His Word to the Churches," 23-38.

[2] Cf. Farnell, "When Will the Gift," 185-86.

11-14).[1] Here, the continuationist view is more accurate in seeing a congregational form of prophecy operating in the NT (alongside canonical prophecy), not for inscripturation, but for the guidance and direction of NT churches. This is also accepted by some scholars from the third camp who maintain the same distinction between canonical and non-canonical prophecy, and see the latter widely practised among the NT Christians as potentially available to all believers.[2] This book argues for the same in Chapter 4.

Furthermore, this study will argue against the view that identifies Corinthian prophecy with preaching/teaching[3] because it overlooks the essential nature of Corinthian prophecy as rooted in revelation and reduces it to a human activity controlled by human desire and effort. Here, the cessationist and continuationist views are more accurate in distinguishing NT prophecy from preaching/ teaching, maintaining its revelatory and spontaneous character.

The discussion on the three view has helped to identify the particular features of NT prophecy with which this book interacts. Chapter 4 will deal in detail with these features that are present in the congregation prophecy in the text of 1 Corinthians 12-14. Before turning to that, it is necessary to undertake an overview of prophecy in the Bible to further clarify and support the assertions above from the data on prophecy in the Bible. This will also contribute to defining Corinthian prophecy in Chapter 4.

---

[1] Gaffin, *Perspectives*, 99-100.

[2] Cf. Packer, *Keep in Step,* 214-16; Hill, *Prophecy,* 135, 137-38, 195.

[3] Cf. Packer, *Keep in Step,* 217; Ellis, *Prophecy and Hermeneutics*, 186; Hill, *Prophecy*, 97, 213; Gillespie, *First Theologians,* 63, 237, 262-63.

Chapter 3

An Overview of Prophecy in the Bible

Having looked at the traditional and contemporary views on NT prophecy as set out in 1 Corinthians, it is now necessary to consider the biblical data on prophecy in general regarding its main features, forms, and the individuals and groups that exercised it. This chapter investigates the phenomenon of prophecy through the various stages in biblical history from Genesis to Revelation. It particularly argues that prophecy in the Bible was diverse in content and was primarily humanward but could occasionally be Godward in some exceptional cases. Moreover, though humanward prophecy in the OT was mostly limited to those recognised as "prophets," congregational prophecy in the Corinthian church was widely exercised beyond the circle of prophets. This also serves as the main distinction between OT prophecy (and NT canonical prophecy) and congregational prophecy in Corinth and other NT churches. It will be shown that there is both continuity and discontinuity between the phenomenon of prophecy in the OT and the NT in regard to some features. The Corinthian congregational prophecy also demonstrates both continuity and discontinuity with prophecy in the OT and canonical prophecy in the rest of the NT.

Therefore, the discussion on the phenomenon of prophecy in the Bible, in this chapter, is both historical and biblical-theological.

3.1 Prophecy in the Old Testament

Prophecy in the OT largely consists of prophetic utterances providing exhortation and correction, occasional predictions, and infrequent spontaneous doxological praise to God.[1] A survey of the data on OT prophecy below will confirm that OT prophecy was distinct from Corinthian congregational prophecy in various ways despite some similar features shared by both. Due to limits of space and because the primary focus here is on the comparison between OT and Corinthian congregational prophecy, discussions on terminology and other issues are not covered here.

3.1.1 The Pentateuch

The Pentateuch offers foundational information in regard to OT prophecy despite having only a few individuals described as prophets, and among whom Moses serves as the leading one.[2] Moses' self-recognition and description as a prophet (cf. Deut 18:15; 34:10-11; cf. Num 12:6-8) has the idea of God's spokesperson or messenger to deliver his word to his people. Aaron is called Moses' prophet in being his spokesperson (Exod 7:1-2) but is better known not as a prophet but as a priest (Exodus 29). Both Aaron and Moses bring God's messages of judgment and warning to Pharaoh, and messages of hope and comfort to Israel, with the prophetic formula "Thus says the LORD" (Exod 4:22; 5:1; 8:1, 20; 9:1; 10:3; 11:4; 32:27). This shows two

---

[1] Cf. Rendtorff, *TDNT* 6: 796; John W. Hilber, "Diversity of Old Testament Prophetic Phenomena and New Testament Prophecy," *WTJ* 56 (1994): 243; J. A. Motyer, "Prophecy, Prophets," *NBD*, 964-72.

[2] Though, Abraham is the first one called a נביא by God (Gen 20:7), nothing particular about his prophetic activity is known except for his ability to offer an intercessory prayer (cf. Exod 32:11-14; 33:12-17; 1 Kgs 13:6), which was not characteristic of a prophet alone. At best, his prophetic function can be seen in his often receiving revelations from God (Gen 12:1-3, 7; 15:1, 4-5). See Grudem, *Prophecy*, 272; Motyer, "Prophecy," 965.

important things: 1) a prophet is always sent by God to deliver his word to others; 2) the prophetic message must always come from God and not from the prophets themselves. This is further confirmed by Deut 18:20-22 where a prophet must speak only what God commands or gives.[1] God also gives warnings about false prophets with particular rules for testing them. The main tests are the fulfilment of a prophecy (Deut 18:22) and a prophet's loyalty to God alone (Deut 13:1-5; cf. 18:20). In brief, from the example of Abraham, Moses, and Aaron, prophecy can be seen as a vehicle for God communicating with people through a prophet.

The prophesying of Miriam (Exod 15:20-21) and the seventy elders (Num 11:25-29) appear as exceptions. Miriam the prophetess, bursts into spontaneous doxological praise with singing and dancing with musical instruments, repeating what Moses and the Israelites were singing (cf. Exod 15:1 [cf. 21]). Whether her singing with music and dancing should be seen as prophesying is not clear but her being described as a prophetess may suggest that (15:20). The content of her song of praise is directed toward God rather than to people. The 70 elders, though never described as prophets, are said to have prophesied (Num 11:25) under the Spirit's inspiration at least once and not thereafter (cf. Num 11:25b). Their prophesying serves as initial confirmatory evidence of God's public demonstration of validating the 70 elders before Israel for their new office.[2] Horton notes that while Moses' prophetic ministry was continual, the elders' prophesying was a unique instance and an exception.[3] The content of their prophesying is not recorded but from the context, it appears to be similar to that of Miriam's doxological praise.[4] In both of these incidents, prophesying seems to consist of spontaneous doxological praise to God rather than a message from God to humankind. In other

---

[1] Cf. Grudem, *Prophecy*, 272 (cf. ch.1). Even Balaam recognises this (Num 22:38)

[2] See Horton, *Christian Faith*, 883; J. P. Baker, "Prophecy," *NBD,* 973.

[3] Horton, *Christian Faith*, 883.

[4] Cf. Turner, *Holy Spirit*, 189.

words, it was Godward rather than humanward, unlike in the prophetic activity of Moses.

In summary, prophecy in the Pentateuch was mostly humanward (i.e. messages from God to his people by a prophet) with the exception of occasional Godward prophesying consisting of spontaneous doxological praise to God. There was some predictive element in the prophetic utterances of Moses and Aaron. There is a woman prophet and an exception of occasional prophesying by those not designated as prophets. Warning against false prophets is also given with standards for testing them.

3.1.2 The Historical Books (Former Prophets)

There are hints of prophetic activity in Joshua and Judges. Joshua is not called a prophet but he continually receives direct messages from God (Josh 1:2-9; 3:9; 4:10; 5:2, 9; 6:2; 7:10) and speaks on his behalf to Israel using the prophetic formula "Thus says the LORD" (Josh 7:13; 24:2). In this manner, he serves like Moses as God's spokesperson to Israel. The book of Judges mentions Deborah the prophetess (Judg 4:4) and an anonymous prophet (Judg 6:8-10). The latter's message is much in line with the latter 8th century prophets, delivering God's word to Israel using the prophetic formula, "Thus says the LORD," and, using the Exodus history as the base, rebuking Israel for her backsliding. Deborah's main ministry is described as leading Israel as a judge (cf. 1 Sam 7:15) but her prophetic activity is seen in the reception and proclamation of a message from God to Barak (Judg 4:6-9) in the first person ("I"), exhorting and correcting Barak (v. 9, 14). In both cases prophesying is humanward and consists of exhortation and correction to individuals and to Israel based on previous revelations (Judg 6:8-10), with some predictive element (Judg 4:7-9). Here too, prophets are sent by God to deliver only what God reveals to them.

Between 1 Samuel and 2 Kings, a large number of individual prophets and considerable prophetic activity emerges. Some prophets are mentioned by name and seem to be more established and better known than other anonymous prophets (e.g. 1 Kgs

13:1-9, cf.11, 18, 21; 1 Kgs 20:13-14, 22, 28; 2 Kgs 21:10).[1] The prominent ones include Samuel (1 Sam 3:19-20), Gad (1 Sam 22:5), Nathan (2 Sam 7:2-17), Ahijah (1 Kgs 11:29; 14:2, 7), Jehu (1 Kgs 16:1-4, 7, 12), Elijah (1 Kgs 18:22), Shemaiah the man of God (1 Kgs 12:22; 2 Chr 12:5), Micaiah (1 Kgs 22:13-28), Elisha (2 Kgs 2:15), and Huldah the prophetess (2 Kgs 22:14-22). Their prophesying was humanward and consisted of God-given messages of exhortations, guidance, and corrections (with predictions of coming judgment), mostly delivered to kings (e.g. 2 Sam 7:4-17; 12:1-15; 24:11-14; 1 Kgs 21:17-24), other individuals (e.g. 1 Kgs 11:29-39; 13:11-22), and occasionally to Israel as a nation (e.g. 1 Kgs 18:21, 30-40).[2] There was often a predictive element in their prophecies regarding God's immediate will for individuals and for Israel (e.g. 1 Sam 10:2-7; 2 Sam 7:4-17; 24:11-13; 1 Kgs 11:31-32; 13:2; 16:1-4; 17:1; 2 Kgs 2:21). Although, consulting Yahweh through prophets appears to be commonplace (1 Sam 9:19-20 [cf. vv. 15-16]; 10:2-7; 1 Sam 28:6; 1 Kgs 14:2, 5; 22:5-7; 2 Kgs 3:11; 22:13-14), a prophet was usually sent by God to deliver his word (2 Sam 7:4-5). The prophetic formula "Thus says the LORD" (cf. 1 Sam 10:18; 2 Sam 7:4-5; 24:11-12; 1 Kgs 11:31; 12:22-24; 17:14; 2 Kgs 2:21; 3:16, 17; 4:43; 7:1; 22:14-22) was often, but not always (e.g. 1 Kgs 16:1-4; 17:1) used to deliver a prophetic utterance.[3]

Besides the individual prophets, prophetic bands or "sons of the prophets" appear to be widespread in Israel (1 Sam 10:5, 10-11; 19-20; 1 Kgs 18:4; 2 Kgs 2:3; 2:5, 7; 4:38). They are not mentioned by name but as a group, and were somehow associated with a prophetic leader-figure (1 Sam 19:20; 2 Kgs 2:15-16; 4:1, 38; 6:1; 9:1, 4). They seem to have received revelations from God about the things to come (2 Kgs 2:3, 5). Not much is known about their identity and ministry, except that they were recognised as "prophets of the LORD" (1 Kgs 18:4, 13; 19:14) and are even

---

[1] The term "man of God" was occasionally used as a synonym for a prophet (e.g. 1 Kgs 12:22 [cf. 2 Chr 12:5]; 13:1 [cf. 18]; 1 Kgs 20:13 [cf. 28]).

[2] Cf. Turner, *Holy Spirit*, 189.

[3] Cf. Gaffin, *Perspectives*, 65.

avenged by God (2 Kgs 9:7). It appears they did not necessarily have the same authority status as did their masters or other established prophets (cf. 1 Sam 19:20; 2 Kgs 2:15-16; 4:1, 38; 6:1-3; 9:1, 4). Carson affirms that it is not clear in the OT that everyone who was called or recognised as "prophet" (particularly in the "schools of prophets") enjoyed the same level of status as other established prophets.[1] There is also no record of such groups in the latter prophets.[2] Moreover, unlike the humanward prophesying of the individual prophets above, the prophesying of the band or sons of prophets appears to be Godward, consisting of Spirit-inspired doxological praise to God accompanied by musical instruments (1 Sam 10:5-6, 10-12 [cf. 1 Sam 19:20-24]).[3] The prophesying of Saul and his men (1 Sam 10:10-13, 19:20-24) would also fall in this category of exceptions. They also serve as exceptions, like the 70 elders (Num 11:25-29), since they could prophesy (once or twice) though not recognised as prophets. The Chronicler's description of prophesying with musical instruments (1 Chr 25:1-7) consisting of "thanksgiving and praise to the LORD" (1 Chr 25:3) would also fall under the same category of Godward prophesying. Turner claims that such prophesying "consisted in some kind of invasively inspired worship rather than intelligible specifically oracular speech."[4] The content of such Godward prophesying is unknown but it does not necessarily suggest that it was either unintelligible or uncontrollable and frenzied.[5]

In summary, prophecy in the historical books, among the individual and established prophets, was always humanward as direct messages of exhortation and correction from God through an individual (mostly prophets) to kings, others, and occasionally

---

[1] Carson, *Showing the Spirit*, 100 (also Grudem, *Prophecy*, 275).

[2] Cf. Rendtorff, *TDNT* 6: 800.

[3] It could be similar to the Godward prophesying of Miriam (Exod 15:20-21) and the 70 elders (Num 11:25-29).

[4] Turner, *Holy Spirit*, 189.

[5] Cf. Grudem, *Prophecy*, 275; Rendtorff, *TDNT* 6: 797, 800. The incident in 1 Sam 19:20-24 is an exception and a complex phenomenon, and not the norm of OT prophecy.

to Israel. It was initiated by God and came as a revelation that was often based on or related to previous revelation (cf. 1 Sam 10:18; 15:1-2; 2 Sam 7:5-7),[1] but also had some new information in regard to the immediate future of others (1 Kgs 11:29-39; 20:13, 28). It is this humanward form of prophesy that is the dominant form of prophecy here. Godward prophecy appears as an exception (as in the Pentateuch), exercised mostly by the band or "sons of the prophets", or some temple musicians (1 Chr 25:1-7), and occasionally by those not known as prophets (e.g. 1 Sam 10:10-13, 19:20-24; cf. Num 11:25-29).[2]

There is also evidence of women prophets (Judg 4:4; 2 Kgs 22:14-22), though not many. There are no responses to prophets by way of tests or warnings against them except for two recorded occasions in 1 Kgs 13:18 and 22:6-12. In the former, a prophet of the LORD lies by falsely claiming to have received a word from the LORD. It shows that even a prophet of the LORD could become corrupt and sin (cf. Balaam). In the latter, it is probably the prophets of Asherah, who falsely prophesy to please the king.

In conclusion, prophecy in the historical books is in continuity with prophecy in the Pentateuch featuring a humanward form of prophecy by designated prophets. Godward prophesying is an exception and is not exercised by established, individual prophets.

3.1.3 The Prophetic Books (Latter Prophets)

There is continuity, along with development, between prophecy in the historical books and in the "latter" prophetic books. Continuity is seen in regard to the essential nature of prophecy as a direct revelation or message from God to people through prophets to exhort and correct them (cf. Isa 51:16; Jer 1:9; 14:14-15). Development is seen in regard to the main focus of the prophetic utterances of the writing prophets, which focuses primarily (if

[1] This is confirmed by the use of the prophetic formula "Thus says the LORD" by the established prophets.

[2] Samuel's prophesying in 1 Sam 19:20 could be of the same nature but happens in a group and not as an individual.

not exclusively) on addressing Israel as God's covenant people (e.g. Jeremiah 2-6; Hosea 1-3; Amos 2:6–3:8), telling them how to live their lives in the light of their covenant with God (cf. Jer 7:1-5; Hos 4:1-2; Amos 5:4-6, 14-15).[1] Therefore, the difference between the prophets who figure in the narratives of the historical books, such as Samuel and Nathan, is their targeted audience, and not in regard to their authority or infallibility or the origin of their message. The former addressed more individuals and so had more prophecies of a personal nature, while the prophetic books primarily addressed the nation of Israel.[2] Furthermore, development in the writing prophets is also seen in the addition of messianic and eschatological prophecies (cf. Isa 7:14; 9:6-7; 53; 65:17-25; 66:18-24).

The use of the prophetic formula "Thus says the LORD" continues here as well, but with more frequency in the 8th to 6th centuries prophets (Isa 7:7; 10:24; Jer 2:1, 5; Amos 1:3, 6, 9, 11, 13; Obad 1:1; Mic 2:3; 3:5; Nah 1:12; Hag 1:2, 5, 7; Zech 1:3-4). At the same time, it is neither always used of all prophetic utterances (cf. Isa 1:1-2; Jer 3:12) nor by every prophet (cf. Hos 2:1; 4:1; Joel 1:1-2; Jonah 3:4; Zeph 1:1; Mal 1:1).[3] This continues to bear witness to the origin of a prophecy in God and not in human initiative. Furthermore, the Pentateuch, particularly the Exodus and the Deuteronomic Covenant (Deuteronomy 28 [cf. Jer 11:1-17; Hos 8:1]) provide a framework for the content of most prophetic utterances (applying the covenant truths already revealed).[4] There is also new revelation given that was predictive of the immediate and the distant (messianic and eschatological) future.

It can be summarised that prophecy in the latter prophets was always humanward, and consisted of direct messages from God to his covenant people through prophets to exhort and correct them,

---

[1] Cf. Grudem, *Prophecy*, 22; Turner, *Holy Spirit*, 187.

[2] See Hilber, "Diversity of OT Prophetic Phenomenon," 244.

[3] Cf. Hill, *Prophecy*, 12-15; Rendtorff, *TDNT* 6: 800; Gaffin, *Perspectives*, 65.

[4] Cf. Hilber, "Diversity of OT Prophetic Phenomena," 251.

with promises of future restoration and salvation.[1] There is, at least, one female prophet mentioned in Isa 8:3 (Isaiah's wife). There is no indication of Godward prophesying by individuals (or groups) not known as prophets. There is a significant number of warnings against and examples of false prophets, many of whom were the prophets of the LORD but were corrupt and greedy, prophesying falsely in his name (e.g. Isa 9:15; Jer 5:13, 31; 6:13; 14:14-15; 23:9-22, 32; 27:15; 28:15; 29:24-32; Lam 2:14; Ezek 13:2-3, 9; 22:28; Mic 3:5, 11). They speak lies and not the words from the LORD's mouth (Jer 23:16, 21). Their life-style is ungodly (Jer 23:11, 14-15) and they must not be listened to (Jer 23:16).

3.1.4 Conclusion

It can be concluded from the data presented that the norm of OT prophecy was humanward prophesying, limited to those recognised as prophets.[2] Prophecy was rooted in revelation from God, which, as Rendtorff says, was the decisive feature in OT prophecy because a prophet does not have God's word "at his disposal" and has to wait until it comes (cf. Jer 28:11, 12; cf. Jer 1:9), delivering as it is given.[3] The content of prophecy was diverse including previous and new revelation with predictions of immediate and distant future. There was progression in prophetic revelation with new content added to the old. The over-all purpose of OT prophecy was to exhort and correct God's people as individuals and as a people, Israel. There was also a Godward form of prophecy, generally seen among the "sons of the prophets", temple musicians, and occasionally among those not known as prophets. It was rare, and was neither inscripturated nor practised (so far as it appears) by the writing prophets. There were women prophets but not many. False prophets and prophecies were expected and were to be tested. The main test was the fulfilment of their prophecies but also loyalty

---

[1] Cf. Hill, *Prophecy*, 17-18.

[2] Cf. Turner, *Holy Spirit*, 184-85 (also Aune, *Prophecy*, 339; Forbes, *Prophecy*, 219).

[3] Rendtorff, *TDNT* 6: 810.

to God and their personal character.[1] In brief, OT prophecy was distinct from Corinthian congregational prophecy in many ways.

3.2 Prophecy in the Intertestamental Period

The nature and function of prophecy in the OT is quite clear and certain, but there are debates about OT type prophecy continuing during the intertestamental period. The traditional view argues that prophecy ceased in Israel after Malachi until John the Baptist (cf. Mal 3:1; 4:5) for almost 400 years, also known as the silent years.[2] The OT itself does not state it[3] but some apocryphal books (1 Macc 4:45b-46; 9:27; 14:41 [cf. Psa 74:9]) and Josephus, the Jewish historian (ca. A.D. 90), are quoted to support this view.[4] Waltke argues for the decline of prophecy in the post-exilic period, pointing out that neither Ezra not Nehemiah were called prophets, nor were there prophets to encourage or direct them on their mission as had always been the case before this (cf. Haggai and Zechariah). He further argues that neither Ezra nor Nehemiah makes mention of prophets in his writing. Waltke claims that the focus in Second Temple Judaism was on the study and teaching of the Law (cf. Ezra 7:10) with the decline of prophecy prompting an emphasis on the exegesis of the OT Scripture.[5] Sommer argues that while the Second Temple Jews did not continue to believe in

---

[1] Cf. Hilber, "Diversity of OT Prophetic Phenomena," 252-53.

[2] Cf. Farnell, "Gift of Prophecy," 387-90.

[3] Though, texts like Ezek 13:9; Zech 13:2-6; Dan 9:24 are used to support the cessation of prophecy during the exilic and post-exilic period, Aune argues that both Ezekiel and Zechariah "refer, not to the general deterioration in the credibility of prophets, but to the eschatological elimination of false prophets. Similarly, Dan 9:24 probably refers not to the historical cessation of prophecy but to the eschatological climax of the predictions of all the prophets up to and including Daniel" (Aune, *Prophecy,* 105 [also Meyer, *TDNT* 6: 812-13]).

[4] Cf. *Against Apion,* 1:37-41; *2 Baruch* 85:3; *Prayer of Azariah*, 15; *Tosephta Sotah*, 13:2-4.

[5] Bruce Waltke, *An Old Testament Theology: An Exegetical, Canonical, and Thematic Approach* (Grand Rapids: Zondervan, 2007), 848-49.

the continued existence of prophecy, they were looking forward to its renewal with the coming of the Messiah.[1]

Contrary to the traditional view above, some have argued that the texts have been misunderstood.[2] Aune suggests that the rabbinic texts are to be evaluated carefully since some of the texts are not only relatively late but they only express the views of those particular segments of Judaism which produced them. There are significant variations, even contradictions among them. Some rabbis held that prophecy had ceased but other rabbis claimed the gift of prophecy. The assertion that there was a cessation of prophecy during the Second Temple period was only "one view among many."[3] Sandmel claims that, "Outside the circle of the Rabbinic sages the view that prophecy had ended simply did not exist."[4] Other Jewish sects did not see that either prophecy or the Holy Spirit completely ceased to function in Jewish religious life. The Qumran community believed the Holy Spirit to be present and active among them (cf. *4 Ezra* 14:22; *1 En.* 91:1).[5] Aune argues that 1 Macc (cf. 4:45b-46; 9:27; 14:41) does not point to the complete cessation of prophets (or prophecy) but only to what he refers to as the temple or clerical and eschatological prophet. He considers that the prophecy reflected in 1 Macc 4:45b-46 and 14:14 is "'clerical' type prophecy," which, like early Jewish prophecy, saw prophetic gifts as "coextensive with the priestly-political leadership of the nation."[6] Moreover, the oft-quoted Rabbinic text of *Tosephta Sotah* 13:2 affirms the cessation of the work of the Holy Spirit with the last of the prophets (i.e. Haggai, Zechariah, and Malachi) in Israel,

---

[1]. Benjamin D. Sommer, "Did Prophecy Cease? Evaluating a Re-evaluation," *JBL* 115 (1996): 46.

[2] Cf. Aune, *Prophecy*, 103-106; F. E. Greenspahn, "Why Prophecy Ceased," *JBL* 108 (1989): 37-49; J. R. Levison, "Did the Spirit Withdraw from Israel? An Evaluation of the Earliest Jewish Data," *NTS* 43 (1997), 35-57; Turner, *Holy Spirit,* 190-92.

[3] Aune, *Prophecy*, 103-104.

[4] S. Sandmel, *Judaism and Christian Beginnings* (New York: Oxford, 1978), 174.

[5] Cf. Aune, *Prophecy*, 104.

[6] Aune, *Prophecy*, 105.

but not the cessation of all revelation by means of oracles ("a heavenly voice or sound" known as בת קל [*bat kol*] i.e. 'daughter of a voice') and through the words of the sages.[1] Levison also argues that such a text "does not imply a long-term or ubiquitous absence of the Spirit" since this same passage (13:3-4) speaks of Hillel and Samuel the Small upon whom the Spirit rested.[2] Aune further points out in the famous passage of *Against Apion* 1.37-41 that Josephus nowhere says that prophecy ceased in Israel but only that there was no longer an "exact succession" of the OT prophets.[3] Aune, therefore, affirms that prophecy was "alive and well" during the Second Temple period (516 B.C. – A.D. 70) but in a different form to what it had been in the OT since "it underwent a number of far-reaching and even radical changes …in form and function."[4] However, he maintains that such "alternate forms of revelation" were subordinate to "the Mosaic revelation codified in the Torah and expounded as oral law by the sages."[5]

Cousland has similarly argued that within the milieu of Second Temple Judaism, "the writings of Josephus, Philo and Dead Sea community reveal that prophecy had not died out but continued as a viable, if diverse, phenomenon."[6] He refers to the Dead Sea Scrolls (1QpHab 7:1-5 and CD 1:12-13) where "charismatic exegesis" of the OT prophets by "the Teacher of Righteousness" to whom God reveals the mysteries of the prophets, is to be identified as prophecy. The inspired insight of this teacher into the OT writings qualifies him to be considered as a prophet.[7] Cousland also refers to the records of the tests employed to identify false prophets and prophecy (4Q375) that support the continuation of prophecy during this time.[8]

---

[1] Aune, *Prophecy*, 103-104.

[2] Levison, "Did the Spirit Withdraw," 35-57.

[3] Aune, *Prophecy*, 106.

[4] Aune, *Prophecy*, 103-104.

[5] Aune, *Prophecy*, 105.

[6] J. R. Cousland, "Prophets and Prophecy," *DNTB*, 831.

[7] Cousland, "Prophets," 833.

[8] Cousland, "Prophets," 833.

Further evidence in support of continuing prophecy is also found in Josephus who, though he appears to distinguish between the special status of the OT prophets and modern prophetic figures,[1] regards the Essenes as gifted with prognostication.[2] Gray argues that for Josephus "the differences between ancient and modern prophetic figures were differences of degree, not of kind."[3] Josephus himself claimed to have prophesied as a prophet that included prediction.[4] There were also claims of prophecy by the self-proclaimed so-called "Sign Prophets,"[5] whom Josephus declares to be "deceivers" or "false prophets" since their prophecies of deliverance and redemption did not come true.[6] Cousland, therefore, concludes that "for Josephus prognostication is one of the distinguishing hallmarks of prophecy in Second Temple period."[7] Like Josephus, Philo recognises the unquestionable authority of Moses and the OT prophets, but also regards the prophetic experience as ecstatic and open to "every good man."[8] Based on his Platonic view of prophecy, he too seems to refer to himself as a prophet.[9]

Turner points out that claims to prophetic revelations during this period have been too many that even those who held the traditional view have had to modify it.[10] He refers to Grudem as an example of one who tries to solve this tension by proposing a

---

[1] Josephus, *Against Apion* 1.8: 41.

[2] Josephus, *Jewish War* 2.8.12: 159 (cf. 1.3.5: 78-80; *Jewish Antiquities* 13.11.2: 311-13; 15.10.5: 373-79).

[3] R. Gray, *Prophetic Figures in Late Second Temple Palestine: The Evidence from Josephus* (New York: Oxford, 1993), 167.

[4] Josephus, *The Jewish War* 3.8.9: 399-408 (cf. Meyer, *TDNT* 6: 819-21; Aune, *Prophecy*, 153.

[5] Cf. P. W. Barnett, "The Jewish Sign Prophets – A.D. 40-70: Their Intentions and Origin," *NTS* 27 (1980-81): 679-97.

[6] Josephus, *The Jewish War* 6.5.2: 285-87; 6.5.3: 288.

[7] Cousland, "Prophets," 834.

[8] Philo, *Quis Rerum Divinarum Heres*, LII: 259; LIII: 265.

[9] Philo, *De Migratione Abrahami*, 35; *De Cherubim,* 27 (cf. Aune, *Prophecy,* 147-51).

[10] Turner, *Holy Spirit*, 190-91.

lesser form of prophecy distinct from OT prophecy occasionally operating during this period.[1] Turner, therefore, concludes that "while the 'intertestamental' period may not have produced prophetic figures of the calibre of the canonical prophets, prophecy was by no means extinct."[2] Hilber thinks that the debate "hinges on both the interpretation of intertestamental literature referring to prophetic speech, and one's opinion concerning the reliability of this literature as a testimony to what actually happened."[3]

This book holds that it is undeniable, in view of the evidence available from the sources mentioned above, that prophecy had not completely ceased in Israel. Just because such sources are not canonised does not mean they are altogether faulty and are of no value. These historical texts have often been used to support biblical data, and have been held in high regard by many scholars. Claims of prophetic revelations, along with the presence of false prophecy and prophets during this period, indicate that prophecy was still continuing in Israel whether as predictions or as an inspired reiteration of previous revelation. Hill regards it largely as charismatic exegesis,[4] but it is to be noted that even such expositions would only be achieved through Spirit-inspired revelation.[5] Since it was not a canonical form of prophecy, it could be similar (if not identical) to congregational prophecy exercised in the Corinthian and other NT churches, providing guidance and exhortation to the community of God's people.

3.3 Prophecy in the New Testament

The NT data on prophecy confirms the existence of congregational prophecy alongside canonical prophecy. There is both continuity and discontinuity between OT and the NT prophecy. Continuity is seen in the fact that NT prophecy, like OT prophecy, was also revelatory, based on revelation from the Holy Spirit (cf. 1 Cor

[1] Cf. Grudem, *Prophecy*, 26 (cf. 27-32).

[2] Turner, *Holy Spirit*, 191.

[3] Hilber, "Diversity of OT Prophetic Phenomena," 254 n. 42.

[4] See Hill, *Prophecy*, 21-43.

[5] Cf. Turner, *Holy Spirit,* 191.

14:30; Rev 1:1, 3; 22:7, 10, 18). The prophecies of Agabus (Acts 11:28 and 21:10) also have similar features to prophecies in the OT (i.e. prediction of immediate future, the phrase "Thus says the Holy Spirit" similar to the OT prophetic formula, and the use of symbolic action).[1] The book of Revelation also has apocalyptic prophecies of a similar type to those found in Ezekiel, Zechariah, and Daniel (discussed below).

There are also significant differences between OT and NT prophecy. Firstly, the NT has considerably fewer actual prophecies recorded than are in the OT. Apart from the book of Revelation, the NT does not have exclusively prophetic writings. Secondly, beside the few in Acts (cf. 11:27-28 [cf. 21:10]; 13:1; 15:32), most NT references to NT prophets in the epistles are to unknown individuals. In fact, while some NT prophets seem to be well-recognised and established in NT churches (Acts 11:27-28 [cf. 21:10]; 13:1; 15:32), there appear to be no NT prophets of the same calibre as OT established prophets. Furthermore, unlike many OT prophets, NT prophets in general are not said to have received a special call, nor to be sent on a mission (John the Baptist and Agabus being exceptions). Grudem argues that it is the NT apostles that stand as parallels to OT prophets, not the NT prophets.[2] Hodge also regards the apostles as permanently inspired and authoritative, while NT prophets are occasionally inspired and authoritative.[3] Moreover, though there is indication of canonical revelation given to some NT prophets (Eph 2:20; 3:5), there is no known NT prophet, beside the apostles (and Agabus), whose prophecies are said to be inscripturated as was the case for many OT prophets. A fourth significant difference between OT and NT prophecy is seen in the fact that OT prophecy (both humanward and Godward) was confined to a few individuals (mostly prophets and occasionally others), while in the NT, prophesying is not restricted to the few, but, as a gift of the Spirit, prophecy becomes a specific mark of the NT eschatological community given to many

[1] Cf. Friedrich, *TDNT* 6: 849.

[2] Grudem, *Prophecy,* ch. 2.

[3] Hodge, *I & II Corinthians,* 262.

NT believers (cf. Acts 2:4, 16-18; 1 Cor 14:1, 5, 12, 39; Rom 12:6; 1 Thess 5:20).[1] In the NT, anyone could potentially be granted the gift of prophecy, at least occasionally. This book labels this form of prophecy congregational prophecy, exercised particularly in the Corinthian church. The NT data on prophecy below confirms the existence of congregational prophecy, operating alongside canonical prophecy in the NT.

3.3.1 The Gospels and Acts

Of the four canonical Gospels, Luke records the most material on prophecy. His second composition, Acts, also records some data on NT prophetic activity in the early church. Therefore, the focus here will be on the Lukan material with occasional excursions to other books where appropriate.

Only a few individuals are described as prophets in the Gospels, while fewer seem to have received and uttered a prophetic revelation. Luke mentions Zechariah, a priest and not explicitly referred to as a prophet, who prophesied (Luke 1:67-79) once when "filled with the Holy Spirit" (v. 67). His prophesying consisted of spontaneous doxological praise to God based on the OT revelation that was delivered through the OT prophets (v. 70). As a result of being filled with the Holy Spirit, Zechariah obtains by this experience a greater understanding of the fulfilment of the OT prophecies regarding the coming of Christ. His prophesying is Godward (no humans are present), similar to the OT phenomenon of Godward prophesying. The Spirit-inspired utterances of Elizabeth (Luke 1:41-45), Mary (Luke 1:46-55), and Simeon (Luke 2:25-32), though none is described as a prophet, appear to be similar to Zechariah prophesying and can be seen as a Godward form of prophecy similar to the OT phenomenon.[2] Luke describes Anna as a prophetess (Luke 2:36-38) who is given a spontaneous prophetic revelation by the Holy Spirit about Christ's presence in the Temple, seeing Jesus as the eschatological Saviour. As a result, she gives "thanks to God" for Christ and speaks "of him to all who

---

[1] Cf. Friedrich, *TDNT* 6: 849.

[2] Cf. Friedrich, *TDNT* 6: 835-36; Baker, "Prophecy," 972.

were waiting for redemption" (v. 38). Anna's prophesying is seen in her reception and proclamation of the revelation about Christ to others.

The above examples show that Luke regards prophesying as a Spirit-inspired activity consisting of both Godward and humanward forms of prophecy. It consisted of a spontaneously Spirit-inspired deeper understanding of what had been previously revealed in the OT, which results in doxological praise to God, as well as in its proclamation to others (in Anna's case). Luke particularly shows that the Spirit's role is deeply connected and crucial in both giving prophetic revelations to individuals and in inspiring prophetic praise to God in individuals.

Others described and seen as prophets in the Gospels are John the Baptist (Matt 11:9-10, 14; 4:5; 21:26 [cf. Mark 11:32; Luke 20:6]; Luke 1:76) and Jesus (Matt 16:14 [cf. 21:11; Mark 6:15; 8:28; Lk 7:16, 39; 9:8, 19; 24:19; John 4:19; 6:14; 7:40; 9:17]; Matt 26:68 [Luke 22:64]). John is never said to have prophesied as such but his message and ministry (Matt 3:1-12) are recognised as in line with OT prophets, in particular Elijah (Matt 11:14; 17:12-13; [cf. Mal 3:1, 5-6]).[1] Though his preaching is primarily a reiteration and application of OT prophecies, there is prediction present as new revelation. The prophetic and revelatory elements in his preaching can be seen in his prediction about the coming of the Messiah, his baptism with the Holy Spirit and fire, and his judgment (Matt 3:11-12).

Jesus as a prophet is an exception and not comparable to other NT prophets.[2] He occasionally referred to himself as a prophet (Matt 13:57 [cf. Mark 6:4]) and saw his destiny with OT prophets (Luke 13:33). Some saw him as the eschatological prophet *par*

---

[1] Cf. Friedrich, *TDNT* 6: 836-41; Baker, "Prophecy," 972; F. Schnider, "προφήτης," *EDNT* 3: 184; Hilber, "Diversity of OT Prophetic Phenomenon," 254.

[2] For a detailed discussion on the prophetic role of Jesus, see Aune, *Prophecy*, chs. 6-7.

excellence promised in Deut 18:15 [cf. Acts 3:22; Acts 7:37]).[1] Like John, Jesus too is never said to have prophesied but his messages contained features of OT prophecies (e.g. prediction of future events as new revelation [Mark 9:1; 10:33-34; 13:2, 28-31; Matt 24:2; Luke 21:6], calls to repentance, threats of coming judgment [Matt 23:37-39; Luke 13:34-35; 23:28-31], promises and invitations of salvation [Mark 1:15; 13:26-27; Luke 12:8-9], supernatural knowledge of the thoughts and conditions of others and of the future [Luke 7:39-40; John 4:16-19]).[2] At the same time, he is more than an OT prophet (cf. Matt 12:41) as "the One who fulfils the prophecies."[3] He is not just God's messenger but God himself who brings the perfect revelation (cf. Heb 1:1-2). Jesus, instead of saying "Thus says the LORD," says "I say to you" (Matt 5:28, 32, 44), which shows a remarkable difference between Jesus and OT prophets.[4] Christ also warns of false prophets in the future (Mark 13:22 [cf. Matt 24:11, 24]). The test of their prophecies would be their character since they will be known "by their fruits" (Matt 7:15, 20). Similarly, Christ also predicts that many false disciples would prophesy in his name yet they never belonged to him and are really "workers of lawlessness" (Matt 7:22-23). The context of this passage is eschatological and suggests that Christ did not see the cessation of all prophecy in the near future. In other words, Christ's prediction of such false disciples prophesying was for the future until the Day of Judgment (i.e. *parousia*), and was not limited to the first century church.

The prediction by the High Priest Caiaphas, of Christ's death and the gathering of all God's children into one, is described as prophesying (John 11:51-52). The passage indicates that this

---

[1] Baker sees Christ as more than the eschatological prophet of Deut 18:15 since he also sends out other prophets (cf. Matt 23:34), and not only declares "the words of God, but is himself the Word" (Baker, "Prophecy," 973 [also Grudem, *Prophecy*, 283]).

[2] Cf. Friedrich, *TDNT* 6: 841-48; Schnider, *EDNT* 3: 184-85; Aune, *Prophecy,* 171-88.

[3] Friedrich, *TDNT* 6: 843.

[4] Grudem, *Prophecy*, 283.

revelation was not from Caiaphas' own reflection ("he did not say this of his own accord," v. 51) but was revealed to him.[1] It also appears to be a one-time prophetic activity rather than a regular ministry of foretelling. In brief, it appears that the prophetic activity of John the Baptist, Jesus, and Caiaphas, are in continuity with the OT prophetic phenomenon with similar features of reiteration and application of previous revelation, along with predictions of the immediate and distant (in Jesus' case) future.

Acts introduces to a whole new era of prophesying (along with tongue-speaking) from Pentecost onwards (Acts 2:17-18). Luke and Peter describe the Pentecost event as the fulfilment of Joel 2:28-29. God had promised His Spirit to be poured upon the whole church under the new covenant that would result in many believers prophesying and having dreams and visions.[2] Stott affirms that "In the post-Pentecost era all God's people receive the Holy Spirit and all may therefore 'prophesy'" (Acts 2:17 [cf. Num 11:29]).[3]

It is worth noting that speaking in tongues (Acts 2:4) is evidence of the Spirit having being poured out on the NT church (Joel 2:28), indicating a connection between tongues and the prophesying foretold in Joel. Peter O'Brien suggests that this could be because "the range of phenomena covered by the prophesy word-group in the NT, let alone the first-century world, was considerable," suggesting that the broad semantic range of terminology could see speaking in tongues as a form of prophesying.[4] This might suggest the reason for Luke and Peter to consider speaking in tongues as a

---

[1] Caiaphas' prophesying is more like Balaam's case (Num 22:38) since he did not believe in Christ but was used as the Spirit's instrument to prophesy.

[2] Cf. K. N. Giles, "Prophecy, Prophets, False Prophets," *DLNT*, 970; James Greenbury, "1 Corinthians 14:34-35: Evaluation of Prophecy Revisited," *JETS* 51 (2008): 724. Baker ("Prophecy," 973) adds that the coming of the Spirit of prophecy on Pentecost should be understood in relation to the promise of the Spirit already made by Jesus (Luke 24:48-49; John 14:26; 15:26-27; Acts 1:8).

[3] John Stott, *The Message of Thessalonians*, BST (Nottingham: IVP, 1991), 127.

[4] Peter T. O'Brien, *The Letter to the Ephesians*, PNTC (Grand Rapids: Eerdmans, 1999), 215.

form of prophesying. The content of speaking in tongues in Acts is described as τὰ μεγαλεῖα τοῦ θεοῦ (*ta megaleia tou theou*, "the mighty acts of God" in Acts 2:11 [cf. 10:45]), which is directed to God rather than to people. In addition, it appears that since Luke in his Gospel (Luke 1:67-79; 2:25-32, 36-38) already sees similar content as Acts 2:11 present in the Godward prophesying of Zechariah and others, he identifies speaking in tongues in Acts 2 (cf. 10:45) as a Godward form of prophecy. It could also be that since Luke was also already familiar with the Godward form of prophecy in the OT (cf. Exod 15:20-21; Num 11:25-29; 1 Sam 10:5-6, 10-12 [cf. 19:20-24]), he identifies the speaking in tongues on the Day of Pentecost as similar to that (if not identical).

Furthermore, while Luke seems to distinguish speaking in tongues from prophesying in Acts 19:6 (ἐλάλουν τε γλώσσαις καὶ ἐπροφήτευον [*elaloun te glossias kai epropheteuon*, "they were speaking in tongues and prophesying"]), the pattern in Acts 10:46 (λαλούντων γλώσσαις καὶ μεγαλυνόντων τὸν θεόν [*lalounton glossais kai megalunonton ton theon*, "speaking in tongues and exalting God"]) indicates that Luke uses ἐπροφήτευον (*epropheteuon,* ""prophesying") as synonymous with μεγαλυνό ντων τὸν θεόν (*megalunonton ton theon*, "exalting God"). Bruce also affirms that μεγαλυνόντων τὸν θεόν (*megalunonton ton theon*, "exalting God" in 10:45) is synonymous with τὰ μεγαλεῖα τοῦ θεοῦ (*megaleia tou theou*, "the mighty acts of God") in Acts 2:11.[1] Thus, the content of speaking in tongues and prophesying in Acts 19:6 appears to be the same as in Acts 2:11 and 10:45. It is also worth noting that in all three incidents prophesying and speaking in tongues are all Godward activities (Acts 2:11; 10:45; 19:6). This suggests that Luke does not always maintain a strict distinction between the two in his writings since they share similar content (i.e. τὰ μεγαλεῖα τοῦ θεοῦ [*megaleia tou theou,* "the mighty acts of God"]). Forbes suggests that Luke regards "virtually any speech inspired by the Spirit" as prophetic,[2] and

---

[1] F. F. Bruce, *The Book of Acts,* NICNT (Grand Rapids: Eerdmans, 1988), 217 n. 71.

[2] Forbes, *Prophecy,* 219.

so identifies speaking in tongues with prophesying in Acts 2:17-18. It is also noteworthy that Godward prophesying in Acts is seen among believers who were not necessarily designated as prophets (cf. Acts 2:17-18; 19:6). This is similar to the Godward prophesying in Num 11:25-29 and 1 Sam 10:5-6 [cf. vv. 10-12; 19:20-24]) of the OT.

There appears to be a good number of individuals in Acts recognised as prophets.[1] From the small amount of data recorded, it is clear that their prophetic activity was humanward, consisting of few predictions (Acts 11:28; 21:4, 10-11), specific guidance to the church (Acts 13:1-3) for special tasks, and words of encouragement for the strengthening of the church (Acts 15:32 [cf. 1 Cor 14:3]).[2] Therefore, while prophecy in Acts appears to be wide-ranging in content, with humanward and Godward forms of prophesying, it was always revelatory as an activity of the Spirit.[3]

In summary, prophecy in the Gospels was in continuity with the OT prophetic phenomenon (including humanward and Godward forms); in Acts prophecy becomes a widespread activity of the Spirit in post-Pentecost church. Though, Luke occasionally identifies speaking in tongues with Godward prophesying, humanward prophesying remains the norm for those recognised as prophets. There are also a few women prophets (Luke 2:36-38; Acts 21:9) and those not called prophets could also prophesy, at least Godward form of prophecy (Acts 2:17-18; 10:45-46; 19:6). There is also an inscripturated form of prophecy (Acts 11:28;

---

[1] There is Agabus and the unnamed prophets (Acts 11:27-28; 21:10), Judas and Silas (Acts 15:32), Barnabas, Symeon, Lucius, Manean and Paul (Acts 13:1) also known as teachers, the four daughters of Philip in Caesarea (Acts 21:9). It is suggested that though the title "prophetess" is not used for Philip's daughters, the present participle of the verb προφητεύουσαι (*propheteuousai*) means they prophesied regularly (see Giles, "Prophecy," 970; Dunn, *Jesus and the Spirit*, 175).

[2] Whether the activity of Judas and Silas in encouraging and strengthening the Antioch church should be seen as prophesying is not clear. But in view of 1 Cor 14:3, prophecy can produce such results. The fact that Luke particularly describes them as prophets (v. 32) would support prophesying.

[3] Cf. Turner, *Holy Spirit*, 200; also Forbes, *Prophecy*, 221.

13:1-3; 21:10-11) but it does not appear to be consisting of new doctrinal revelation in content. The distinguishing feature of prophecy in Acts is that it becomes a congregational phenomenon unlike in the OT and the Gospels.

3.3.2 Pauline Material

Paul's extended discussion on prophecy is recorded in 1 Corinthians 12-14. However, he does mention the gift of prophecy and prophets in his other epistles as well (cf. Rom 12:6; Eph 2:20; 3:5; 4:11; 1 Thess 5:20; 1 Tim 4:14). This confirms that prophecy was also functioning in other Pauline churches beside Corinth.[1] Since the next chapter will look at Corinthian prophecy in detail only brief comments on prophecy in Paul's other epistles are necessary here.

In Rom 12:6, Paul exhorts believers in general to exercise the gift of prophecy in proportion to their faith. The fact that Paul addresses the whole church, and not a particular group (prophets), suggests that Paul expected anyone in the church to be able to prophesy if gifted by the Spirit (cf. 1 Cor 14:1, 39) and further, that prophecy was common among NT believers. Such prophesying would be unlike canonical prophecy of the OT and parts of the NT since there is no record of it being inscripturated. It is also worth noting that Paul makes a distinction between the gift of prophecy and the gifts of teaching and exhortation (vv. 7-8) showing that they are not the same gifts (cf. 1 Cor 14:6, 26).

In 1 Thessalonians, Paul asks the church not to "despise prophecies but test everything" (1 Thess 5:20). Morris suggests that the Thessalonian church experienced "prophetic outbursts in connection with second advent expectations,"[2] which caused many to look down on prophecies. Morris' assessment of Thessalonian prophecy suggests that prophesying was not only common but was also prone to be incorrect and misleading, which in turn caused the church to undermine its value. Despising of prophecies suggests a large number of prophetic claims made

---

[1] Stott, *Thessalonians,* 127.

[2] Leon Morris, *1 & 2 Thessalonians*, TNTC (London: Tyndale, 1956), 104.

by many Thessalonian Christians. Once again, it is unlikely that such prophesying was like OT canonical prophecy which was always infallible and would not be treated this way. Thessalonian prophecy was congregational prophecy as in Rom 12:6.

The prophecy referred to in 1 Tim 4:14 (cf. 1:18) consisted of guiding the church (elders) in confirming the gift given to Timothy by the Spirit. It is similar to Acts 13:1-3 where the church is also guided through a prophetic revelation about appointing Paul and Barnabas for a special task. Knight also affirms that the term προφητείας (*propheteias*, "prophecies") in 1 Tim 1:18 "is used uniformly in the NT of revelations (supernatural communications) from God" (cf. Rom 12:6; 1 Cor 12:10; 14:6, 22; 1 Thess 5:20) and is parallel to Acts 13:1-4.[1] It is important to note that such prophecy (or prophecies) is not necessarily given to prophets but to anyone, such as the elders (4:14) who are not called prophets but serve as leaders. It confirms that this refers to the same phenomenon of congregational prophecy as in 1 Thess 5:20 and Rom 12:6 above. One of the main functions of such prophesying was to provide guidance to the church in specific matters.

In the Ephesians passages (Eph 2:20; 3:5), Paul (accepting Pauline authorship) has in mind particularly those recognised as NT prophets who are distinct from OT prophets and the apostles.[2] Not only the word order (ἀποστόλων καὶ προφητῶν [*apostolon kai propheton*, "of apostles and prophets"]) confirms this but also other references to προφηταί (*prophetai*, "prophets") in the letter itself (Eph 3:5; 4:11).[3] Neither are they OT prophets since "the salvation-historical νυν (*nun*) definitely forbids us interpret them as OT prophets."[4] It is important to note that these NT

[1] George W. Knight III, *The Pastoral Epistles*, NIGTC (Grand Rapids: Eerdmans, 1992), 108.

[2] See O'Brien, *Ephesians*, 214-15 (contrary to Grudem who suggests that the prophets are the apostles who are prophets [cf. Grudem, *Prophecy*, 45-47]).

[3] O'Brien, *Letter to the Ephesians*, 214 n. 244.

[4] O'Brien, *Letter to the Ephesians*, 214 (cf. K. O. Sandnes, *Paul – One of the Prophets? A Contribution to the Apostle's Self-Understanding* [Tubingen: J. C. B. Mohr (Paul Siebeck), 1991], 233).

prophets mentioned seem to enjoy an authority and role like the apostles not found elsewhere in the Pauline letters. They had a foundational role like the apostles (Eph 2:20) and were entrusted with "the mystery of Christ," not made known in the previous generations (Eph 3:4-6).[1] This mystery was of a doctrinal nature and concerned the gentiles becoming "partakers of the promise of Christ Jesus through the gospel" (v. 6). This implies that the group of prophets mentioned is given a canonical form of prophecy that contained "the revelation of the gospel."[2] Hence, it was distinct from congregational prophecy, which did not bring new doctrinal revelation.

Before briefly commenting on Corinthian prophecy below, the data above confirms that, except for Eph 2:20 and 3:5, all of Paul's references to prophecy in his writings, refer to congregational prophecy and not to canonical prophecy. The data in 1 Corinthians 12-14 also confirms this assertion.

Paul describes prophecy as one of the gifts (χαρίσματα [*charismata*, "grace gift"]) of the Holy Spirit, sovereignly administered (1 Cor 12:4-7, 11) but open and commended to all Christians (1 Cor 14:1, 5, 39) indiscriminately, including women (1 Cor 11:5). Paul expected prophecy to be a widely practised gift among believers (1 Cor 14:29-31 [cf. Rom 12:6; 1 Thess 5:20; 1 Tim 4:14]), apart from those known as prophets (1 Cor 12:28-29 [Eph 2:20; 3:5; 4:11]). Paul saw Corinthian prophecy primarily as humanward (1 Cor 14:3, 6, 19, 24-25, 31), consisting of revelations from God to the church (1 Cor 14:30 [cf. v. 6, 26]) for her edification, encouragement, and consolation (1 Cor 14:3-5, 26, 31). He expresses an expectation that prophecy be a controlled phenomenon (1 Cor 14:29-32) and yet revelatory and spontaneous (v. 30). It was distinct from other forms of speech (1 Cor 12:8, 28-29, 34 [cf. 1 Tim 2:11-12]) but had a didactic or instructive function (1 Cor 14:19, 31). From the reaction of the unbeliever, it appears that Corinthian prophecy could also consist of a Spirit-inspired gospel proclamation, exposing sin, convicting

[1] Cf. Gaffin, *Perspectives,* 61.

[2] O'Brien, *Ephesians*, 216.

and converting the unbeliever (1 Cor 14:24-25). Despite Paul's high estimation of prophecy, he not only requires prophecy to be weighed or discerned by the church (1 Cor 14:29), but he also places the authority of any Corinthian prophet under his apostolic authority (1 Cor 14:37). This shows that the Corinthian prophets (and others who prophesied) did not carry an unquestionable authority like OT prophets and the apostles (and the prophets of Eph 2:20; 3:5). Since, Paul puts Corinthian prophecy and prophets under his own authority, it suggests that Corinthian prophecy was congregational prophecy, and not canonical. As a result, Paul also did not anticipate the cessation of Corinthian type congregational prophecy before the coming of the new heaven and earth at the *parousia* (13:8-12).

The Corinthian material on prophecy, summarised above, shows some differences between Luke and Paul.[1] Since, Luke's view of prophecy "is relatively broad and less precisely laid out than that of Paul,"[2] Luke regards speaking in tongues as parallel to Godward prophesying. Paul's view, on the other hand, is more specific and narrower, particularly because there is no indication of Godward prophecy in 1 Corinthians. Paul not only sharply distinguishes prophecy from glossolalia but also from other speech gifts (cf. 1 Cor 12:8; 14:6, 26). Another distinction between Paul and Luke, pointed out by some scholars, concerns whether Paul's view of prophecy included prediction of the future.[3] There is no evidence of prediction in 1 Corinthians 12-14. Forbes suggests that since Paul's view of prophecy was based on prophecy in Judaism, Corinthian prophecy could occasionally be predictive. In addition, Paul had experienced prediction first hand in NT prophecy (cf. Acts 21:10-11).[4] Prediction of the future could be a possibility in

---

[1] Often differences between the two are seen by scholars on various grounds (cf. Friedrich, *TDNT* 6: 851; Grudem, *Prophecy*, 150-77; Aune, *Prophecy*, 19-21; Callan, "Prophecy and Ecstasy," 127).

[2] Forbes, *Prophecy,* 221.

[3] Cf. Friedrich, *TDNT* 6: 829.

[4] Forbes, *Prophecy*, 222-25 (also Aune, *Prophecy*, 253, 258-59; C. M. Robeck, "The Gift of Prophecy in Acts and Paul," *SBT* 5 [1975]: 50; idem,

congregational prophecy but the text does not indicate it clearly, and so no certain conclusions can be reached.

It can be argued that any distinction between Luke and Paul is not necessarily due to their different understandings of the phenomena of prophecy but due to their differing situations and purposes of writing. Luke writes Acts to provide a salvation-historical account of the early church (Acts 1:1-2), not to provide a theological-biblical description or comparison of the phenomenon of prophecy and tongues. Paul, on the other hand, writes 1 Corinthians as a polemical-pastoral response to issues related to tongues and prophecy in the church. Forbes affirms that with the exception of Godward prophesying in the Lukan material (cf. Luke 1:67-79; 2:25-32; Acts 2:4, 11 [vv. 16-18]; 10:45-46; 19:6), both Paul and Luke essentially see prophecy as "the declaring of a revelatory experience"[1] and "a matter of speaking under the inspiration of the Holy Spirit" (cf. 1 Cor 12:4-11, 30).[2]

3.3.3 Non-Pauline Epistles and Revelation

Outside of the Pauline corpus, while the book of Revelation is called a prophecy (Rev 1:3; 22:7, 10, 18, 19), other non-Pauline writings only have warnings against false prophets and teachers (cf. 1 John 4:1-6; 2 Pet 2:1; Jude 4, 8, 11-16). Though such warnings provide little help in ascertaining the nature of NT prophecy, they do confirm that prophecy was common in the NT churches and always required testing. The main standard for the testing of false prophets is their doctrine (i.e. Christological confession [1 John 4:2]).

The book of Revelation is an exception in NT prophecy due to its apocalyptic nature. The writer John repeatedly calls it a prophecy (Rev 1:3; 22:7, 10, 18, 19) based on revelation from God with many predictions and a series of message of consolation and exhortation

---

"Prophecy, Prophesying," *DPHL,* 755).

[1] Turner, *Holy Spirit,* 194 (cf. Dunn, *Jesus and the Spirit*, 228).

[2] Forbes, *Prophecy*, 219 (cf. 219-21).

(e.g. Revelation 2-3).[1] Giles points out that though it "reflects the influence of the Jewish apocalyptic tradition," it also differs from it in many ways.[2] Beale affirms that "the most preferable view is that Revelation is "'a prophecy cast in an apocalyptic mold and written down in a letter form.'"[3] Its apocalyptic nature is to be understood "as an intensification of prophecy," and not different from it "though it contains a heightening and more intense clustering of literary and thematic traits found in prophecy."[4] Such apocalyptic prophecy is also present in the OT prophets (e.g. Daniel 7-12, Ezekiel 37-48, and Zechariah 4-6, 14).[5] Though, Revelation is seen as a recapitulation of the OT history and contains prophetic messages similar to that of OT prophets such as warnings of coming judgment, restoration, exhortations, it also features new eschatological revelation.[6] It reflects an "already and not yet" approach to end-time salvation, incorporating both prophetic and apocalyptic themes. Thus, Beale concludes that "Revelation can be defined as God's revelatory interpretation (through visions and auditions) of his mysterious counsel about past, present, and future redemptive-eschatological history."[7] As such, Revelation is not only "unique among prophecies"[8] but almost unparalleled among the NT prophecies. The closest to it is probably Matthew 24 (cf. Mark 13). Since it has been inscripturated, it is the canonical form of prophecy, distinct from Corinthian congregational prophecy.

---

[1] Cf. G. K. Beale, *The Book of Revelation,* NIGTC (Grand Rapids: Eerdmans, 1999), 37; Grudem, *Prophecy,* 290; Farnell, "When Will the Gift," 178.

[2] Giles, "Prophecy," 974.

[3] Beale, *Revelation*, 37-38 (cf. Carson and Moo, *Introduction to the New Testament*, 479).

[4] Beale, *Revelation*, 37.

[5] Cf. Beale, *Revelation*, 37.

[6] Cf. Beale, *Revelation*, 37-38.

[7] Beale, *Revelation*, 38.

[8] J. Ramsey Michaels, *Interpreting the Book of Revelation* (Grand Rapids: Baker Press, 1998), 30-32.

3.3.4 Conclusion

It concludes that OT prophecy was consistently humanward and was largely confined to those designated as prophets. The content of humanward prophesying was both based on previous revelation and was also new, of both a personal and doctrinal nature. Much of this form of prophecy also became inscripturated for the future generations. There were also occasional occurrences of Godward prophesying among some individuals and bands of prophets early in the OT (the Pentateuch and the historical books) but not in the latter prophetic writings.

There is some evidence in the extra-biblical sources that prophecy was still alive during the intertestamental period in some form, while no new doctrinal revelation appears to have come through it.

While there is continuity between OT and NT prophecy, this book shows that there is also some discontinuity and development in prophecy in the NT from the OT. There are occurrences of Godward prophesying in the Lukan material alongside humanward prophesying but the former is absent in the rest of the NT writings, including 1 Corinthians. It is the latter that serves as the norm of NT prophecy. Moreover, though there is some prophecy that brought new doctrinal revelation and became inscripturated in the NT (cf. Eph 2:20; 3:5; the book of Revelation), there is a form of prophecy that was quite extensive among NT believers and served for edification and guidance of the NT church rather than for canonisation. It is this congregational form of prophecy that was practised in the Corinthian and other NT churches. The following chapter defines the specific features of Corinthian congregational prophecy in detail, narrowing the focus of investigation in this book to that proposed at first.

Chapter 4

The Nature of Corinthian Prophecy

It was noted in chapter two that many, if not all, evangelical scholars agree that a non-canonical form of prophecy operated in the NT, alongside canonical prophecy. They also agree that such prophecy was to guide and edify the church, and was not for canonisation. They all agree that canonical prophecy ceased with the NT having being completed. There were also few scholars, outside the continuationist camp, who acknowledge prophecy to continue as preaching and teaching.

In chapter three, it was observed that prophecy in the OT was mostly humanward and only occasionally Godward. It was largely confined to those recognised as prophets. Much of it was also canonised. In the NT, while prophecy in the Gospels was like OT prophecy, in Acts it becomes common and consisted of both canonical and congregational prophecy. Luke also records both humanward and Godward forms of prophecy in Luke-Acts.

In the Corinthian correspondence, it has been maintained in this book from the beginning, there is no canonical prophecy but only congregational prophecy is referred to. There is also no sign of Godward prophecy but only humanward (as Paul maintains distinction between prophecy [being Godward] and tongues [being humanward] unlike Luke in Acts). It is also important to note the level of authority given to Corinthian prophecy as Paul subjects Corinthian prophets to his own apostolic authority (1 Cor 14:37 [cf. v. 29]), something he would never do for OT canonical prophecy or prophets in his writings. In this chapter, this book seeks to define Corinthian prophecy as Paul describes in the text of 1 Corinthians 12-14. In Chapter 1, a methodology was outlined where it was asserted that the text must define Corinthian prophecy. Therefore, this chapter approaches prophecy in 1 Corinthian 12-14 thematically under appropriate categories to determine what congregational prophecy looked like and how it functioned in the Corinthian church. This will be divided into six categories drawn from the text itself.

4.1 Distribution: A Widely Distributed Gift of the Spirit (1 Cor 12:10 [cf. v. 7], 29; 14:1 [cf. v. 39], 3, 24, 29-31 [cf. 11:4-5])

One of the main features of Corinthian prophecy was its availability as a gift of the Spirit to all believers, and not just to a few individuals. It was discussed in chapter three that in the OT, it was primarily the prophets who prophesied regularly, but others, not called prophets, also prophesied occasionally (cf. Num 11:25-26; Josh 7:13; 24:2; 1 Sam 10:10-13; 19:20-21, 23-24; 2 Chr 20:14-20, 37; 24:20).[1] The Gospels also record a few similar cases (Luke 1:67-79; Luke 2:25-32; John 11:51-52). In Acts, prophesying appears to have become a widespread gift of the Holy Spirit among believers from Pentecost onwards (Acts 2:17-18 [cf. v. 4, 11]; 19:6; cf. 10:45-46; 21:9). Forbes affirms that due to the endowment of the Holy Spirit upon the NT church at Pentecost, prophecy became common and all believers were considered prophets in some way, "fulfilling the prophecy of Joel."[2] There

---

[1] However, note that such cases were exceptions and not the common experience of all OT believers. Moreover, in most cases it was Godward prophesying.

[2] Forbes, *Prophecy,* 244-45 (also Gaffin, *Perspectives,* 59; Horton, *Christian Faith* , 883; Stott, *Thessalonians*, 127; Friedrich, *TDNT* 6: 849; Fee, *First Epistle*

were prophets present in several places (Acts 11:27-28; 21:10; Acts 15:22-32; Acts 13:1; Acts 21:9; 1 Cor 12:28-29; Eph 2:20; 3:5; 4:11) and other believers prophesied in most NT churches (1 Cor 11:4-5; 12:10; 14:24, 31; Rom 12:6; 1 Thess 5:20; 1 Tim 1:18; 4:14). Hence, the main question here is: "Did Paul also consider prophecy in Corinth to be strictly confined to the prophets alone (1 Cor 12:28-29), or also occasionally exercised by other believers as one of the Spirit's gifts available to anyone (1 Cor 12:10 [cf. v. 7]; 14:24, 31 [11:4-5])?" The text of 1 Corinthians 12-14 indicates the latter, which is also agreed upon by most scholars.[1]

The term προφητεία (*propheteia*, "prophecy") in 1 Cor 12:10 (cf. 13:2; 14:22; Rom 12:6) refers to the gift of prophecy or prophesying (BDAG, 722) and is recognised by Paul as a φανέ ρωσις (*phanerosis*, "manifestation" in 1 Cor 12:7) of the Spirit. προφητεία (*propheteia*, "prophecy") here appears without the mention of προφῆται (*prophetai*, "prophets") who are mentioned only later in the text (1 Cor 12:28-29). In fact, προφητεία (*propheteia*, "prophecy" [and its plural form προφητεῖαι, *propheteiai,* "prophecies"]) often occurs in the Pauline corpus without necessarily being associated with προφήτης (*prophetes*, "prophet") or προφῆται (cf. 1 Cor 13:2, 8; 14:6, 22; Rom 12:6; 1 Thess 5:20; 1 Tim 1:18; 4:14). This suggests that Paul saw the gift of προφητεία (*propheteia*, "prophecy") in 1 Cor 12:10 as not just confined to the προφῆται (*prophetai*, "prophets") but including a wider circle of those who exercised it. As one of the gifts of the Spirit, it was "potentially available to all since all now possessed the Spirit in fullness (cf. Acts 2:17-18)."[2] In other words, the Spirit

---

to the Corinthians, 595).

[1] Cf. Friedrich, *TDNT,* 6: 849; Forbes, *Prophecy*, 219-21, 252-53; Grudem, *Prophecy*, 235; Hill, *Prophecy*, 96; Robeck, "Prophecy, Prophesying," 757, 759; Ferguson, *Holy Spirit*, 210; Ciampa and Rosner, *First Letter to the Corinthians*, 611; Garland, *1 Corinthians,* 599. On the contrary, those who see prophecy confined to formally designated prophets alone, see Aune, *Prophecy*, 199-200, 402 n. 36; Hans Conzelmann, *1 Corinthians* (Philadelphia: Fortress Press, 1975), 245; Greenbury, "1 Corinthians 14:34-35," 724-25.

[2] Fee, *First Epistle to the Corinthians*, 595 (cf. 586 n. 12e).

is "free to choose anyone through whom to speak."[1] Morris affirms that though prophecy might be an occasional or a settled office (1 Cor 12:28), in 1 Cor 12:10b it is possible that Paul includes both.[2] Gaffin similarly argues that "the designation *prophet* is applied to those who exercise the gift frequently or with some regularity (e.g., Acts 21:10; 1 Cor 12:28), while the gift itself can function temporarily in others on particular occasions" (cf. Acts 19:6; 21:9; 1 Cor 11:4-5; 12:10).[3] Even Aune, who sees NT prophecy as ordinarily confined to "those designated as prophets," accepts the occasional exercise of the gift of prophecy by other believers (not formally called prophets) as repeatedly present in Acts (2:1-21; 8:14-17; 10:44-46; 19:1-6) and 1 Corinthians (12:14). He calls it "congregational prophecy."[4] Further support to the exercise of congregational prophecy by believers comes from Paul's instructions about head covering (1 Cor 11:4-5). Here too Paul mentions προφητεία (*propheteia*, "prophecy") without προφήτης (*prophetes*, "prophet") or προφῆτις (*prophetis*, "prophetess") but in connection with men and women in general, prophesying and praying in a worship service. This indicates that a good number of believers, beside prophets, were able to prophesy during a worship service as gifted by the Spirit.

Paul's exhortation to ζηλοῦτε τὸ προφητεύειν (*zeloute to propheteuein*, "be zealous to prophesy" in 1 Cor 14:1, 39) indicates the same expansion, addressed not to prophets or a small group but to the whole church. Fee argues that Paul addresses the entire community from the very beginning (cf. 1 Cor 14:1) and not the prophets alone or he would make it clear as he does in

[1] Forbes, *Prophecy*, 258 (also C. K. Barrett, *The First Epistle to the Corinthians*, BNTC [London: Adam & Charles Black, 1971], 329).

[2] Leon Morris, *1 Corinthians,* TNTC (London: Tyndale, 1958), 172.

[3] Gaffin, *Perspectives*, 59.

[4] Aune, *Prophecy,* 199-200. While he also argues that in the rest of the outside of Acts and 1 Corinthians there is little or no evidence for congregational prophecy, this book argues that prophecy in Rom 12:6, 1 Thess 5:20, 1 Tim 1:18 and 4:14 was congregational prophecy.

other places.[1] Paul's exhortation to the whole church implies that he assumed every Corinthian believer to be eligible to prophesy occasionally when enabled by the Spirit, whether previously known as a prophet or not.[2] Robeck affirms that it was a genuine possibility, in continuity with Moses' wish (Num 11:29) and Joel's prediction (Joel 2:28; cf. Acts 2:14-18), and not just "a vapid rhetorical wish."[3]

Paul's usage of the adjectival pronoun πάντες (*pantes,* "all or every") in 1 Cor 14:24, 31 also refers to the same inclusive nature.[4] In both verses Paul presents a hypothetical scenario, which is "impressionist rather than numerical."[5] In other words, πάντες (*pantes*) does not mean every individual believer. Paul already indicated earlier (cf. 1 Cor 12:28-29 [vv. 8-11]) that not every Christian is a prophet nor could they prophesy since prophecy, as a gift, is sovereignly administered by the Spirit's will (1 Cor 12:11) and is given to whomever the Spirit wants to give it. Then to whom does πάντες (*pantes*) refer? Ciampa and Rosner suggest that it refers to "a variety of speakers (with different styles, themes, and sensibilities)" who minister to the different needs of those present in the church.[6] Garland suggests that it could refer "to every person without distinction (social status, gender, race) rather than every person without exception" since Paul also seeks to correct "any selfish monopoly of prophecy" by some who esteemed themselves higher than others, who dominated worship services.[7] While either is possible, both interpretations hold that,

---

[1] When addressing a specific group, Paul makes it explicitly clear (cf. 1 Cor 7:1-5, 8, 10, 12; 1 Timothy 3, 5; Titus 2). See Fee, *First Epistle to the Corinthians,* 694 (also Forbes, *Prophecy*, 306, 319).

[2] Cf. Garland, *1 Corinthians,* 661.

[3] Robeck, "Prophecy, Prophesying," 759 (also Ciampa and Rosner, *First Letter to the Corinthians*, 716).

[4] See Forbes, *Prophecy,* 259; Garland, *1 Corinthians,* 632.

[5] Thiselton, *First Epistle to the Corinthians*, 1128 (also see Conzelmann, *1 Corinthians*, 243 and 243 n. 5; Fee, *First Epistle to the Corinthians,* 693-94; Ciampa and Rosner, *First Letter to the Corinthians,* 706).

[6] Ciampa and Rosner, *First Letter to the Corinthians,* 716.

[7] Garland, *1 Corinthians,* 660 (also see Carson, *Showing the Spirit*, 123-24).

though πάντες (*pantes*) does not mean every single Christian, it is inclusive of others not known as prophets. Here too (vv. 24, 31) the term προφῆται (*prophetai,* "prophets") is missing, while the act of prophesying is attributed to the whole congregation. Fee argues that "the nature of this argumentation seems to exclude the option that this gift was limited to a group of authoritative people who were known in the community as 'the prophets,'" rather πά ντες (*pantes*) expresses Paul's view of the Spirit of prophecy not limited to a few men and women, but potentially available to all.[1]

The προφῆται (*prophetai,* "prophets") mentioned in 1 Cor 12:28-29 are those who prophesied more frequently and regularly, and so came to be known as προφῆται (*prophetai,* "prophets").[2] Paul mentions such individuals in Eph 4:11 [cf. 2:20; 3:5]), suggesting that some individuals did come to be recognised as prophets in an official sense (cf. Acts 11:27-28; 13:1; 15:32; 21:10).[3] Ferguson even suggests that the lists of ministries in 1 Cor 12:28 and Eph 4:11 indicate that "the gift involved in fulfilling these ministries spread beyond those who were recognised in the church in a quasi-official way."[4] It is important to note that the emphasis in 1 Cor 12:28-29 is more on the function of prophets ("to build up the community") than on establishing an office.[5] In other words, the term προφῆται (*prophetai,* "prophets") refers not to specific persons but to the ministry that finds expression

---

[1] Fee, *First Epistle to the Corinthians,* 685, 695 (contra Conzelmann, *1 Corinthians*, 245; Aune, *Prophecy*, 198-200, 402 n. 36).

[2] Cf. Fee, *First Epistle to the Corinthians*, 595-96; Garland, *1 Corinthians*, 599; Forbes, *Prophecy,* 246; Ciampa and Rosner, *First Letter to the Corinthians*, 611.

[3] Cf. Gaffin, *Perspectives,* 59.

[4] Ferguson, *Holy Spirit*, 210.

[5] See Fee, *First Epistle to the Corinthians*, 620-21. Fee even suggests that the prophets in 14:29 do not necessarily refer to a "special group of authoritative persons" in church since the emphasis in v. 29 is on the function of prophecy. The noun "prophets" should be seen "as functional language, similar to the use of 'interpreter' in v. 28, and means, as in v. 3, 'the one who is prophesying'" (694-95).

in various persons.[1] Whether there was an established office of prophet in the NT is debatable. Robeck argues that Paul never used the term *office* to describe the position of the prophet but rather seems "to alternate between using the noun for 'prophet' and a substantive participle, 'the one who prophesies" (1 Cor 14:3).[2] Barrett similarly contends that since prophecy is a gift from the Spirit, it is not dependent on any human decision that makes a person a prophet (or prevents him/her from being a prophet). He concludes that "prophecy is a function rather than an office."[3]

Alternatively, others see the possibility of an office of prophet in the NT to be substantiated.[4] Support for this can be seen in the fact that like προφητεία (*propheteia,* "prophecy"), προφῆται (*prophetai,* "prophets") are also "given or granted" as gifts (ἔδωκεν, *edoken,* "bestowed") to the church from God (Eph 4:8, 11). Hence the person is the gift. Moreover, the fact that God ἔθετο (*etheto*, "placed/established/set" 1 Cor 12:28 [v. 18], BDAG, 816) prophets in the church probably indicates an office, like that of the apostles. The scope and space of this book do not allow venturing further into this debate; however, neither view denies the gift of congregational prophecy being exercised beyond those recognised as prophets, which is the main focus here.

A further support for the congregational prophecy being exercised by believers is also seen in Paul's limitation on the number of individuals prophesying (1 Cor 14:29), which assumes a proportionately significant or large number of individuals eager to prophesy in a gathering. In view of the usage of the term προφητεία (*propheteia,* "prophecy") discussed above, it is unlikely that such a large number of individuals prophesying would only include formally designated προφῆται (*prophetai,* "prophets"). Forbes suggests that while the "two or three" in 1 Cor 14:29 are the

---

[1] Cf. Fee, *First Epistle to the Corinthians*, 619 (cf. 619 n 15); Barrett, *First Epistle to the Corinthians*, 295.

[2] Robeck, "Prophecy, Prophesying," 757.

[3] Barrett, *First Epistle to the Corinthians,* 329.

[4] Cf. Hodge, *I & II Corinthians*, 263; Morris, *1 Corinthians,* 172; Gaffin, *Perspectives,* 59.

elitist prophets, Paul extends the invitation to prophesy to πάντες ([*pantes,* "all or every"] v. 31) in general.[1] This is also supported by the fact that a prophetic revelation could come to anyone (ἄλλῳ [*allo,* "to other or another"]) sitting in the congregation (v. 30). Though, the meaning of ἄλλῳ (*allo*) is debated whether it refers to another prophet[2] or anyone in the church, in the neutral sense ἄλλῳ (*allo*) can refer to "several others" or "additional persons" beside the speaker mentioned in the context.[3] Fee's comment in regard to οἱ ἄλλοι ([*hoi alloi,* "the others"] v. 29) also applies to ἄλλῳ ([*allo*] v. 30). He suggests that οἱ ἄλλοι (*hoi alloi*) basically means "others different from the subject" and not necessarily "the rest of the same class," in which case it would only mean other prophets and the more appropriate term would be οἱ λοίποι ([*hoi lopoi,* "the others"] 1 Cor 9:5).[4] Hence ἄλλῳ (*allo*) would refer to a larger group than other prophets. Besides, the πάντες (*pantes,* "all or every") in v. 31, as discussed above, suggests that ἄλλῳ (*allo*) is not restricted to προφῆται (*prophetai,* "prophets") alone but includes the whole church. In fact, ἄλλῳ (*allo*) "could be anyone, a learned or a simple person, an eloquent or an unpolished speaker" from among the members.[5]

The fact that prophecy in Corinth needed to be regulated (cf. 14:29-32) also indicates that a larger number of individuals were eager to prophesy in a gathering. Forbes claims that vv. 29-30 imply that there were either too many prophets wishing to speak at the same time or there were certain individuals "'holding the

---

[1] Forbes, *Prophecy,* 250-65 (also Richard B. Hays, *First Corinthians* [Interpretation; Louisville: Westminister John Knox Press, 1997], 243).

[2] See Aune, *Prophecy*, 221; Gillespie, *First Theologians,* 163; Farnell, "Fallible New Testament Prophecy," 44-45.

[3] K. Weiss, ἄλλος, *EDNT* 1:64.

[4] Fee, *First Epistle to the Corinthians,* 694 n. 30 (also see Cf. Greenbury, "1 Corinthians 14:34-35," 728; Carson, *Showing the Spirit,* 120; Grudem, *Prophecy,* 60).

[5] Garland, *1 Corinthians,* 661.

floor' for long periods," not letting others prophesy.[1] This would not only have created confusion and disorderliness in a gathering (cf. vv. 33, 40) but would have overlooked the essential requirement of prophecies being weighed (v. 29). It is debated whether Paul's restrictions on the number of individuals prophesying refers to two or three prophets per gathering or two or three prophets at a time before the weighing would take place. Fee argues that 1 Cor 14:24 and v. 31 indicate "no more than three at a time" before others have weighed what has been prophesied (v. 29).[2] This can be supported by the absence of τὸ πλεῖστον ([*to pleiston,* "the most"] cf. v. 27) for regulating the number of glossolalists, which indicates more than two or three prophets per gathering.[3] On the other hand, Ciampa and Rosner suggest that Paul most likely has in mind "three prophetic messages per meeting, whether the speakers were previously known as prophets or not."[4] So while any three might prophesy in a gathering, "others would have their turn as well, presumably at future meetings."[5] While the former view is preferred by this book, either view supports the main argument that prophecy was being exercised by many others beside the προφῆται (*prophetai,* "prophets").

By weight of the evidence presented, this book proposes that Paul held all Corinthian Christians as capable of prophesying occasionally since prophecy is a gift from the Spirit available to anyone (1 Cor 14:29). While those who prophesied frequently came to be known as προφῆται ([*prophetai,* "prophets"] 1 Cor 12:28-29), the gift of prophecy was not limited to them alone. This implies that Corinthian congregational prophecy also became the dominant form of prophecy in other NT churches (e.g. Rom 12:6; 1 Thess 5:20; 1 Tim 1:18; 4:14) with the Spirit of prophecy poured

---

[1] Forbes, *Prophecy*, 262 (also Garland, *1 Corinthians,* 662 n. 9 [cf. 269]; Fee, *First Epistle to the Corinthians*, 695).

[2] Fee, *First Epistle to the Corinthians*, 693.

[3] Garland, *1 Corinthians,* 661.

[4] Ciampa and Rosner, *First Letter to the Corinthians,* 714.

[5] Ciampa and Rosner, *First Letter to the Corinthians*, 716 (also Robertson and Plummer, *I Corinthians*, 322).

out on NT believers indiscriminately under the new covenant on the day of Pentecost (Acts 2:3-4, 17-18 [cf. Joel 2:28-29]).[1] Moreover, because congregational prophecy became widely distributed and practised among NT believers, it can be argued that it was distinct from canonical prophecy that was limited to only a few individuals.

4.2 Origin: Rooted in Revelation (14:30 [cf. vv. 6, 26])

In Paul's view Corinthian congregational prophecy was deeply rooted in revelation. Divine revelation is one of the most important features, not only of Corinthian congregational prophecy, but of all biblical prophecy. With the exception of some exegetes who identify prophecy as preaching/teaching, the majority of scholars agree that prophecy in the Bible, including Corinthian prophecy, was always based on revelation from God.[2] In fact, there could be no prophecy without revelation.[3] All prophecy, whether canonical or congregational, can be defined as a "proclamation of divine revelation"[4] or a "declaration of Spirit-inspired revelation" by an intermediary chosen by God.[5] As was discussed in chapter one, the type of revelation experienced within congregational prophecy was distinct in nature and authority from the revelation that was received through canonical prophecy as recorded in Scripture. Congregational prophecy was neither meant for inscripturation nor did the Corinthian believers receive and proclaim it through

---

[1] Cf. Forbes, *Prophecy,* 219-21, 252-53; Robeck, "Prophecy," 756; Dunn, *Jesus and the Spirit*, 171-72, 281; J. Reiling, "Prophecy, the Spirit and the Church," *Prophetic Vocation*, 67-68; Turner, *Holy Spirit*, 207-208.

[2] See Gaffin, *Perspectives,* 59; Saucy, "An Open But Cautious View," 127; Friedrich, *TDNT* 6: 853; Aune, *Prophecy,* 195; G.F. Hawthorne, "Prophets, Prophecy," *DJG*, 636; Robeck, "Prophecy," 755; Boring, "What Are We Looking For?," 152, (cf. 44); Hill, *Prophecy*, 8-9; Edgar, *Miraculous Gifts*, 72; Garland, *1 Corinthians*, 583; Grudem, *Prophecy*, 95-96; Storm, "A Third Wave View," 207-209; Greenbury, "1 Corinthians 14:34-35," 723.

[3] Cf. Farnell, "When Will the Gift" 181-82; Grudem, *Prophecy,* 123; Dunn, *Jesus and the Spirit*, 228.

[4] Cousland, "Prophets and Prophecy," 830.

[5] Greenbury, "1 Corinthians 14:34-35," 724.

direct speeches from God with the prophetic formula ("Thus says the LORD"). Nevertheless, congregational prophecy did bring specific revelations from God to the church for her edification. This is confirmed from the text below.

Paul's use of ἀποκάλυψις (*apokalupsis,* "revelation") in connection with Corinthian prophecy (1 Cor 14:30 [cf. vv. 6, 26]) confirms that in Paul's view Corinthian prophecy was revelatory.[1] Explicit evidence of this can be found in 1 Cor 14:30 which refers to Corinthian prophecy as a reception and subsequent proclamation of a revelation from God. The verse pictures a situation where someone has had something revealed to them spontaneously (but quietly) from the Spirit during the worship service (or at home) and is prompted by the Spirit to share it with the whole assembly.[2] Fee claims that "the verb 'reveal' in this context (cf. 1 Cor 14:30) points to the essential character of prophecy in Paul's view."[3] Similarly, Robeck asserts that "Paul clearly links prophecy and revelation by mentioning revelation in the midst of his very specific discussion of prophecy."[4] Since the verb ἀποκαλυφθῇ (*apokalufhthe,* "was revealed") is passive, it confirms that a prophetic revelation is revealed to (or received by) an individual spontaneously by the Holy Spirit.[5] The root verb of ἀποκαλυφθῇ (*apokalufhthe,* "was revealed") is ἀποκαλύ πτω (*apokalupto*, "to reveal") which generally refers to "divine revelation of certain supernatural secrets" (BDAG, 92) revealed by the Holy Spirit that cannot be known otherwise.[6] For this very reason, Paul also saw Corinthian prophecy having its source and origin in the Spirit and not in a reflection or intuition of one's own mind or deductions from other human sources.[7] This also

[1] See T. Holtz, "ἀποκαλύπτω," *EDNT* 1: 130; Friedrich, *TDNT* 6: 853.

[2] Cf. Grudem, *Prophecy*, 62; Robertson and Plummer, *I Corinthians,* 322.

[3] Fee, *First Epistle to the Corinthians,* 695.

[4] Robeck, "Prophecy, Prophesying," 759.

[5] See Garland, *1 Corinthians*, 662; Grudem, *Prophecy*, 96.

[6] For more on the meaning of the verb ἀποκαλύπτω and noun ἀποκά λυψις, see below.

[7] Cf. Grudem, *Prophecy,* 96; Storm, "A Third Wave View," 207-209.

means that the Spirit's role in prophecy is both essential and foundational since a prophetic revelation comes to an individual according to the sovereign will of the Spirit (cf. 1 Cor 12:11). The Spirit reveals only whenever he wishes to reveal something to an individual for prophesying.[1] One cannot prophesy until and unless the Spirit reveals. In other words, prophets or those with the gift of prophecy could go without prophesying for an indefinite time if the Spirit chose not to reveal anything to them. Therefore, Robeck concludes that prophecy always comes by way of revelation from the Spirit and when that revelation is spoken, it forms the basis of prophecy.[2]

Further evidence of the revelatory nature of Corinthian prophecy is seen in Paul's use of the term ἀποκάλυψις (*apokalupsis,* "revelation") in connection with prophecy in 1 Cor 14:6 (cf. v. 26). Here Paul lists four terms, namely, α ποκαλύψει (*apokalupsei,* "revelation"), γνώσει (*gnosei,* "knowledge"), προφητείᾳ (*propheteia,* "prophecy"), διδαχῇ (*didache,* "teaching").[3] The main question is: Did Paul consider them as four distinct gifts or as interrelated and overlapping with each other in some way? In other words, if prophecy is always based on revelation (as argued above), why does Paul list them separately in 14:6 as if distinct gifts? A number of opinions exist among scholars regarding this but the one that has gained much acceptance is Calvin's proposal. Calvin puts revelation with prophecy into one class and suggests that "the latter is the administration of the former."[4] Calvin applies the same rule to the relation between knowledge and teaching.[5]

[1] Garland, *1 Corinthians,* 662 (cf. 583).

[2] Robeck, "Prophecy, Prophesying," 759.

[3] All Greek dative case.

[4] John Calvin, *Commentary on the Epistles of Paul the Apostle to the Corinthians* (Grand Rapids: Baker Press, 2009), 438 (also Grudem, *Prophecy,* 138-39; Hodge, *1 Corinthians,* 268; Conzelmann, *1 Corinthians,* 235 n. 20; Carson, *Showing the Spirit,* 106; Robertson and Plummer, *I Corinthians,* 308; Robeck, "Prophecy," 759; W. Schrage, *Der erste Brief an die Korinther,* vol 3 [Zurich: Benziger, 1991-2001], 390; Garland, *1 Corinthians,* 635).

[5] Calvin, *Corinthians,* 438.

Here ἀποκαλύψει (*apokalupsei,* "revelation") and γνώσει (*gnosei,* "knowledge") "relate more directly to the perception of truth," while προφητεία (*propheteiai,* "prophecy") and διδαχῇ (*didache,* "teaching") "relate more directly to the modes by which each of those kinds of truths are communicated."[1] So that which is received through revelation is communicated in prophecy and that which is perceived through knowledge is communicated in teaching. This pairing is further confirmed in 14:26 (see below), where only revelation and teaching appear without prophecy and knowledge, indicating that prophecy subsumes revelation and teaching subsumes knowledge.

Despite such a logical explanation, doubts have been raised regarding this arrangement of the four terms. Ciampa and Rosner claim that, though such pairing is possible, "Paul's use of the terminology is not consistent enough to be dogmatic." The dilemma, they point out is that sometimes knowledge is associated with prophecy (cf. 1 Cor 13:2)[2] while at other times it is distinguished from it (1 Cor 12:8, 10; 13:8-9; 14:6). They conclude that it is not clear "whether Paul always has a clear distinction in mind between teaching and prophecy or whether he sometimes thinks of them as interrelated gifts or ministries, perhaps ones that have to do with the communication of (different kinds of) knowledge."[3] While this still remains an unresolved question, perhaps it goes too far to say that Paul did not see a clear distinction between prophecy and teaching (discussed below in length).

Fee points out the same dilemma and thinks that since the list here, like previous lists (1 Cor 12:8-10, 28, 29-30; 13:1-2, 8), is *ad hoc*, it is hard to find out what content Paul has in mind by "revelation" and how it would differ from "knowledge" or "prophecy." He further argues that "there is a general lack of precision in Paul with regard to these various items"

[1] Ciampa and Rosner, *First Letter to the Corinthians,* 679 (also Robeck, "Prophecy," 759).

[2] See Hodge's comments below on 13:2 to resolve this dilemma.

[3] Ciampa and Rosner, *First Letter to the Corinthians*, 679.

(cf. 1 Cor 14:30) and the data are insufficient to come to any clear conclusions.[1] Barrett also asserts that "all these activities ... shade too finely into one another for rigid distinctions."[2] At the same time, Fee recognises that such lack of precision is expected since Paul's main concern is not to define the terms specifically but "to specify various kinds of Spirit-inspired utterances that have intelligibility as their common denominator" and result in the edification of the whole assembly.[3]

While it is true that "how the terms differ from one another is open to speculation"[4] due to possible over-lapping between revelation (prophecy) and knowledge, it is worth noting that Paul particularly connects revelation with prophecy (v. 30) and not with knowledge or teaching directly (cf. vv. 6, 26). Moreover, if Hodge's explanation of 13:2 is followed (see below), then even 13:2 maintains the distinction between prophecy and knowledge and only μυστήρια ([*musteria*, "mystery"] 13:2) is connected with prophecy. The over-lapping between the two can be explained as prophecy naturally subsuming the knowledge of mysteries revealed through revelation.[5]

In 1 Corinthians 14:26, although the term ἀποκάλυψιν (*apokalupsin,* "a revelation") appears, προφητεία (*propheteia,* "prophecy") is missing. The same applies for διδαχήν (*didachen,* "a teaching") since γνῶσις (*gnosis,* "knowledge") is also missing. Once again the list of the gifts (ψαλμόν [*psalmon,* "a psalm"], διδαχήν [*didachen,* "a teaching"], ἀποκάλυψιν [*apokalupsin,* "a revelation"], γλῶσσαν [*glossan,* "a tongue"], ἑρμηνείαν [*hermeneian,* "an interpretation"]), like all previous lists, is *ad hoc* and neither intends to provide an order of the gifts nor to define the nature of each gift. The list primarily represents

---

[1] Fee, *First Epistle to the Corinthians,* 662-63 (cf. 593).

[2] Barrett, *First Epistle to the Corinthians*, 317.

[3] Fee, *First Epistle to the Corinthians,* 662 (also Garland, *1 Corinthians,* 636).

[4] Garland, *1 Corinthians,* 635.

[5] Cf. Barrett, *First Epistle to the Corinthians*, 243; Calvin, *Corinthians,* 438.

the types of verbal manifestations of the Spirit that should be occurring in the assembly.[1] However, the very absence of the term προφητεία (*propheteia,* "prophecy") assumes that ἀποκάλυψιν (*apokalupsin,* "a revelation") here subsumes the gift of prophecy, just like διδαχήν (*didachen,* "a teaching") subsumes γνῶσις ([*gnosis,* "knowledge"] cf. 14:6). Garland claims that even though προφητεία (*propheteia,* "prophecy") is missing in the list (v. 26), ἀποκάλυψιν (*apokalupsin,* "a revelation") refers to "something divinely disclosed and presented in comprehensible language" through prophecy.[2] Gaffin also argues that in the light of 14:30, prophecy is also indicated in v. 26 since "revelation is a variant reference to prophecy" (v. 6).[3] He further explains that in the list, ἀ ποκάλυψιν (*apokalupsin,* "a revelation") is "followed directly by 'a tongue, or an interpretation,' reflecting the correlation between prophecy and tongues that dominates the chapter."[4] Gaffin's argument also finds support in the immediate context (vv. 27-31) that focuses on Paul's specific instructions about regulating tongues and prophecy, indicating that ἀποκάλυψιν (*apokalupsin,* "revelation") serves as a synonym for prophecy before tongues in v. 26 (cf. 1 Cor 12:10).[5]

Having established that in Paul's view Corinthian congregational prophecy was deeply rooted in revelation, it becomes essential to define how Paul understood and applied the term ἀποκάλυψις (*apokalupsis,* "revelation") in connection with prophecy. Though, it was noted above that there appears to be a general lack of precision in regard to Paul's use of ἀποκάλυψις (*apokalupsis,* "revelation"),[6] there are indications in the Pauline

---

[1] See Ciampa and Rosner, *First Letter to the Corinthians,* 709; Fee, *First Epistle to the Corinthians,* 690.

[2] Garland, *1 Corinthians*, 658.

[3] Gaffin, *Perspectives,* 60 (also see Hodge, *1 Corinthians,* 300; Holtz, "ἀ ποκάλυψις," *EDNT* 1: 131).

[4] Gaffin, *Perspectives,* 60 (cf. Fee, *First Epistle to the Corinthian,* 663).

[5] Cf. Greenbury, "1 Corinthians 14:34-35," 727.

[6] Cf. Fee, *First Epistle to the Corinthians,* 662-63 (cf. 593).

corpus that help identify the possible content that came in ἀποκά λυψις (*apokalupsis,* "revelation") through Corinthian prophecy.

Uncertainty about the meaning of the term ἀποκάλυψις (*apokalupsis,* "revelation") in 14:6 and 26 [cf. 30]) is due to Paul's varying use of the verb ἀποκαλύπτω (*apokalupto,* "to reveal") and noun ἀποκάλυψις (*apokalupsis,* "revelation") in his writings. The verb appears 13 times and the noun 10 times in the Pauline corpus.[1] The noun sometimes refers to visible disclosures associated with Christ's return (1 Cor 1:7, 2 Thess 1:7; Rom 2:5; 8:19), while in other places, it refers to the revelation of the gospel from Christ to Paul (Gal 1:12, Eph 3:3) or of God's will in Paul's life (Gal 2:2). Similarly, the verb form refers to divine eschatological disclosure about various things (cf. Rom 1:17, 18; 8:18), or to God's act of revealing his mysteries/secrets to his chosen people (Eph 3:3-5; 1 Cor 2:10), or to God's revealing of Christ to Paul (Gal 1:16; 2 Cor 12:1). Both the verb and the noun forms also refer to the Spirit's work of illumination in all Christians (Eph 1:17; Phil 3:15). Fee concludes that in most cases they refer to "the disclosure of divine 'mysteries,' either about the nature of the gospel itself (cf. 1 Cor 2:10) or perhaps about things otherwise hidden to the 'natural man.'"[2]

From the examples above, it is to be noted that in their various usages, both ἀποκάλυψις (*apokalupsis,* "revelation") and ἀποκαλύπτω (*apokalupto,* "to reveal") always refer to divine activity – either of God (cf. Gal 1:16; Phil 3:15) or of Christ (cf. Gal 1:12) or of the Holy Spirit (cf. Eph 3:5; 1 Cor 2:10). Grudem claims that in the NT, both the noun and the verb forms never refer to human activity.[3] Secondly, they do not always refer to inscripturated or new canonical revelation (cf. Gal 2:2; Eph 1:17; Phil 3:15). This confirms, as has been stated above, that though

[1] See Holtz, *EDNT* 1: 130; Robeck, "Prophecy," 759; Fee, *First Epistle to the Corinthians,* 662 n. 14.

[2] Fee, *First Epistle to the Corinthians* 663 (also see, Thiselton, *First Epistle to the Corinthians,* 1101).

[3] Grudem, *Prophecy,* 96.

Corinthian congregational prophecy was revelatory, it was not about new canonical revelation for inscripturation.

In regard to the content of revelation in 1 Cor 14:6, 26, and 30, the examples above provide multiple possibilities. As has already been discussed, new canonical revelations were given to some prophets in the NT (Eph 2:20; 3:5; Rev 22:18), but it is unlikely that such was the case in Corinth since there is no inscripturated record of Corinthian prophecies. This entails that the content of Corinthian prophetic revelation was non-canonical and had a qualitative difference from canonical revelation. Fee advises that in 1 Cor 14:6, revelation indicates "some kind of utterance given by the Spirit for the benefit of the gathered community."[1] This means the focus of Corinthian prophecy was to provide guidance and edification to the church in both specific and general matters. The idea of edification is also present in v. 26 and v. 31 (cf. 14:3) as the primary goal of revelation and is the overriding theme of Paul's teaching on spiritual gifts in the whole of chapter 14 (vv. 3, 4, 5, 6, 12, 17, 19, 26, 31). Thus in general, prophetic revelation in Corinthian prophecy was expected to consist of a wide range of content(s), both specific and general, that would serve the edification of the whole church (see below discussion on 14:3). Robeck proposes that in the context of prophecy, ἀποκάλυψις (*apokalupsis,* "revelation") and ἀποκαλύπτω (*apokalupto,* "to reveal") "appear to have a more specific nuance, one which may form the basis of the content to be revealed."[2] Grudem also affirms that Corinthian prophetic revelations were not "magical disclosure or mysterious insight," rather they were putting matters and issues "in a heavenly or divine perspective."[3] As was seen above, Fee's proposal is questionable, namely that ἀποκάλυψις (*apokalupsis,* "revelation") "could very easily be a cover word for all other forms of intelligible inspired speech" in 1 Corinthians 14,[4] since Paul does not directly apply the term ἀ

[1] Fee, *First Epistle to the Corinthians,* 662 n. 14.

[2] Robeck, "Prophecy," 759.

[3] Grudem, *Prophecy,* 99.

[4] As proposed by Fee, *First Epistle to the Corinthians,* 691.

ποκάλυψις (*apokalupsis,* "revelation") to any other gifts except to prophecy.

The revelatory nature of Corinthian prophecy magnifies two significant distinctions. These are spontaneity, and distinctiveness from preaching and teaching, which will be investigated in turn below.

4.2.1 A Spontaneous Phenomenon

Here, spontaneity refers to the sudden activity of the Spirit in revealing something to an individual whether the individual is expecting it or not. The fact that Biblical prophecy was always revelatory also implies spontaneity in prophecy, since the will or agency of the person is subject to the will or agency of the Holy Spirit declaring the revelation. First Corinthians 14:30 (ἐὰν δὲ ἄλλῳ ἀποκαλυφθῇ καθημένῳ [*ean de allo apokaluphthe kathemeno,* "But if a revelation is made to another sitting"]) suggests that Corinthian prophecy was also spontaneous in nature since a revelation is given to an individual by the Holy Spirit spontaneously during worship. In other words, prophecy happens when and where the Spirit decides, not at the behest of the individual.[1] The spontaneous character of Corinthian prophecy is well recognised and supported by most scholars. Turner affirms that "for Paul prophecy is the reception and subsequent communication of spontaneous, divinely given ἀποκάλυψις (*apokalupsis,* "revelation")."[2] Similarly, Fee upholds that for Paul, prophecy consisted of "spontaneous, Spirit-inspired, intelligible messages, orally delivered in the gathered assembly, intended for the edification or encouragement of the people."[3] Farnell (a cessationist) also asserts that the elements of prediction and revelation confirm the spontaneous nature of NT prophecy.[4] The spontaneous character of Corinthian prophecy is also supported

[1] Cf. Garland, *1 Corinthians*, 660; Ciampa and Rosner, *First Letter to the Corinthians*, 715.

[2] Turner, "Spiritual Gifts Then and Now," *VoxEv* 15 (1985): 10; cf. 7-64.

[3] Fee, *First Epistle to the Corinthians,* 595.

[4] Farnell, "When Will the Gift," 182-84.

by prophetic revelations in the OT (see Chapter 3), the Gospels (Luke 1:67-79; 2:27; 2:36-38), and Acts (11:28; 13:2).

It must be noted that spontaneity does not limit the reception of a prophetic revelation to worship gatherings alone as one might misinterpret 1 Cor 14:30. While 14:30 suggests that a prophetic revelation could come spontaneously during a gathering, Paul's instructions in vv. 26-29 assume that some believers would bring into worship prophetic revelations received any time prior to the worship gathering (cf. v. 6). Paul assumes that when the Corinthian church comes together, each member comes prepared with something that they have received already from the Spirit as a gift to contribute to the edification of the church, prior to the gathering (14:26 [cf. v. 6]). Furthermore, the limitation on the number of individuals prophesying in a gathering (v. 29) also suggests a good number of individuals are already ready to share their prophetic revelations received earlier. It is unlikely that the whole church would sit in silence for extended periods expecting or waiting for the Spirit to give a prophecy to some individuals during worship. Ciampa and Rosner suggest that a revelation "may be given during the time of worship, but there is no reason to assume that people would not bring to the service a revelation that they had received during the week."[1] In fact, spontaneity or its lack in the exercise of prophecy is not the major focus in Paul's discussion of gifts. Paul's emphasis in 1 Corinthians 14 is on the intelligibility and proper function of prophecy (and tongues) that must always result in the church's edification (cf. 1 Cor 14:3-6,12, 19, 24, 26, 31). The spontaneous nature of prophecy does not refer to the exact time of its reception and subsequent proclamation; rather it refers to the Spirit's initiative in giving a prophecy to an individual. It also means that prophecy does not originate in an individual's desire or effort but in the Spirit's sovereign will and power. It is immediate in the sense that it involves a "revelation

---

[1] Ciampa and Rosner, *First Letter to the Corinthians,* 710 (also Garland, *1 Corinthians,* 658).

which could not be known through ordinary human means," except through the Spirit's initiative in revealing it.[1]

Spontaneity in prophecy can be qualified by Paul's expectation of order. It does not mean a frenzy where the Holy Spirit takes absolute control or possession of the one prophesying (1 Cor 14:30-32).[2] Paul expected the Corinthian prophets to be in control of their minds and prophetic activity, willing to stop or discontinue from prophesying when needed.[3] Grudem affirms that in 1 Cor 14:29-33 both the first prophet (already prophesying) and the second prophet (who spontaneously receives a revelation) could control their speech. The former could stop (v. 30b) in the middle of prophesying, the latter could wait while the first stops (v. 30a). They could prophesy in an orderly fashion one by one (v. 32). The term ἀκαταστασίας ([*akatastasias*] v. 33) meaning "disorder/confusion" (BDAG, 30) implies self-control on the part of the prophet. Paul's demand for prophecies to be weighed (v. 29) also shows that they were not only intelligible to the speaker and the listeners, but under the control of the speaker to stop for such evaluation whenever asked.[4] Paul makes it clear in the text that "Christian prophets do not lose control in some ecstatic trance or as though possessed by some foreign spirit."[5] Even when "the impulse to speak may still be present … the speaker can restrain those impulses."[6] So while the content of prophetic utterance is

---

[1] Farnell, "When Will the Gift," 184.

[2] See Fee, *First Epistle to the Corinthians*, 595; Farnell, "When Will the Gift," 179 n. 28; Dunn, *Jesus and the Spirit*, 243; Carson, *Showing the Spirit,* 75-77; Grudem, *Prophecy,* 103-104.

[3] Thiselton, *First Epistle to the Corinthians,* 1084 n. 18, confirms that since Paul's view of prophecy was shaped by the OT prophetic phenomenon, it had nothing to do with the prophetic phenomenon in the Greco-Roman world, which was characterised by frenzied and uncontrollable behaviour. Grudem, *Prophecy,* 104-105, suggests that it was probably the Corinthians, not Paul, who saw Christian prophecy (and tongues) in the light of their pagan religious background (cf. 1 Cor 12:1-3).

[4] Cf. Grudem, *Prophecy,* 105.

[5] Ciampa and Rosner, *First Letter to the Corinthians,* 716.

[6] Garland, *1 Corinthians,* 661.

"the product of the Divine Spirit … the utterances are subject to the speakers in terms of timing."[1]

Thiselton plays down and deemphasises the spontaneous nature of Corinthian prophecy. He argues that though the term ἀποκαλυφθῇ (*apokaluphthe,* "was revealed" in 14:30) suggests "an act of divine disclosure on the spot" (i.e. spontaneous revelation), it "does not exclude the communication of what came to be revealed by God through some experience or through biblical reflection prior to the act of worship itself."[2] He contends that prophecy could also occur during "sustained reflection" on Scripture and could be "prepared with judgement, decision, and rational reflection."[3] Thus he views all of biblical prophecy (including Corinthian prophecy) as "prophetic preaching" (though distinct from teaching) that "addressed issues of moment" by providing "pastoral insight into needs of persons, communities, and situations." He contends that spontaneity in prophecy does not mean "unprepared or *ad hoc*" but only that it is "not merely self-induced."[4] With this understanding of spontaneity, he agrees that "spontaneous prophecy may occur" though not necessarily or always.[5] This presents a loose understanding of spontaneity in prophecy because it fails to notice the essential revelatory nature of prophecy which highlights its origin in the Spirit and not in a human effort or experience. It was already argued above that prophecy is always revelatory, and not only occasionally.

This book agrees with Thiselton's view only regarding the fact that the Spirit would give prophetic revelations to individuals about specific needs and situations of persons and communities during times of personal reflection upon Scripture. As such, Corinthian prophecy could consist of pastoral insights with specific applications of biblical truths to current situations. However, Thiselton does not clarify or elaborate on the claim that

[1] Fee, *First Epistle to the Corinthians,* 696.

[2] Thiselton, *First Epistle to Corinthians,* 1135.

[3] Thiselton, *First Epistle to Corinthians*, 1091-92 (cf. 964).

[4] Thiselton, *First Epistle to Corinthians*, 964 (cf. 961).

[5] Thiselton, *First Epistle to the Corinthians*, 1077.

such pastoral insights or applications of biblical truths to specific situations come only as revelations from the Holy Spirit. While he sees spontaneity in prophecy as "not merely self-induced," his view seems to imply that prophecy could happen purely *as a result* or *product* of a "rational reflection," rather than the Spirit spontaneously revealing something during such a reflection. Overemphasising sustained reflection as a basis of prophecy tends to make prophecy more of a human activity, controlled by human efforts rather than by the Holy Spirit, whereas Paul views Corinthian prophecy entirely as a Spirit-inspired activity (cf. 1 Cor 12:11; 14:30). It can be observed that Thiselton's emphasis on sustained reflection resulting in prophecy is due to his particular view of prophecy as pastoral preaching that identifies illumination from the Spirit with prophecy. This requires a further comment on the difference between prophecy and the Spirit's work of illumination. Even though, illumination (Eph 1:17; 2 Tim 2:7) and prophecy (Acts 11:27-28; 21:10-11; 1 Cor 14:30) are both activities of the Holy Spirit, they are not the same. While all believers could have ongoing experiences of illumination from the Spirit (Eph 1:17; 1 Cor 2:14-15), prophecy (though potentially available to all) is confined to some believers as a gift of the Spirit (1 Cor 12:7, 10, 28-29). Furthermore, illumination consists of a general working of the Holy Spirit in believers to understand spiritual things better and is personally edifying. Prophecy, on the other hand, consists of a special and specific working of the Holy Spirit in revealing particular truth which is indented to be edifying to the whole church (1 Cor 14:31). Gaffin explains that "revelation" in 14:30 (cf. vv. 26 and 30) "does not result from the general working of the Spirit as the 'Spirit of wisdom and revelation' (Eph 1:17), given to all believers (cf. Phil 3:15), it is a specific revelation given by inspiration to one for the edification of others."[1] Ferguson further argues that although the same terminology "revelation" is used by Paul "to refer to both the giving of the truth and the illumination of its meaning ... the conceptual distinction is a biblical one (Ps 119:18; 2 Tim

[1] Gaffin, *Perspectives,* 60.

2:7)."[1] He clarifies that "revelation" in prophecy was given in a special sense to certain individuals (i.e. apostles also prophets, Eph 3:5), whereas Paul's prayer for the Spirit of revelation to know God better is for all believers (Eph 1:17; cf. Matt 16:17). Saucy concurs with this assertion and similarly insists that the use of the term "revelation" in connection with "the Spirit's work of illuminating one's understanding of Scripture and giving personal insight (Matt 16:17; Eph 1:17; Phil 3:15)" should not be equated with prophecy.[2] So, even if both share common terminology (i.e. revelation), it does not mean "a single concept but either of two related ideas which have certain analogous characteristics."[3] Ferguson continues to differentiate the two by explaining that canonical revelation is objective revelation and the illumination of its meaning is subjective revelation which is common to all believers through the Spirit. As a result, he sees illumination continuing today, consisting of subjective revelation, while prophecy ceased since it consisted of objective revelation.[4]

While Ferguson's distinction above between prophecy and illumination has merit, he seems to overlook the fact that biblical prophecy, at times, also consisted of subjective revelation (2 Sam 12:1-15; 1 Kgs 13:11-28; Acts 20:4, 10-11). As discussed in chapter three, not all prophecy became objective revelation recorded in Scripture (e.g. Num 11:25-29; 1 Sam 10:10-13, 19:20-24; Acts 19:6; 21:9). In fact, none of the Corinthian prophecies was recorded in Scripture and it is unlikely that any Corinthian prophets ever wrote any part of Scripture. Thus, the primary distinction between prophecy and illumination, beside the ones already pointed out by Ferguson above, is that while illumination is directed toward understanding Scripture better; prophecy can happen without Scripture since it involves specific knowledge that might or might not necessarily be based on previous written revelation. Hence, it

[1] Ferguson, *Holy Spirit,* 230.

[2] Saucy, "An Open but Cautious View," 127-28.

[3] Ferguson, *Holy Spirit,* 230.

[4] Ferguson, *Holy Spirit,* 230.

concludes that while both share the same terminology, revelation in prophecy originates from the Holy Spirit more directly than in illumination which is always derivative from the written Word.[1]

In either case, the spontaneous nature of Corinthian prophecy is affirmed by Paul (14:30) and cannot be ruled out completely by the cessationist view nor by someone like Thiselton who sees prophecy as prophetic preaching. This also leads to the further distinction of prophecy from preaching and teaching, which is also rooted in its revelatory spontaneous character.

4.2.2 Distinct from Preaching and Teaching

As discussed in chapter two, both cessationist and continuationist scholars maintain that the spontaneous revelatory character of Corinthian prophecy distinguishes it from other forms of speech (e.g. a sermon or teaching). Grudem argues that since prophecy happens at the "prompting of the Holy Spirit," it is unlike a sermon or teaching that is derived from already existing sources and results from one's own reflection and study, even when such reflection or study is guided under the general illuminating work of the Holy Spirit.[2] Similarly Dunn asserts, "For Paul prophecy is a word of revelation. It does not denote a previously prepared sermon … it is a spontaneous utterance" (1 Cor 14:30).[3] Friedrich has also argued that because "all prophecy rests on revelation" (1 Cor 14:30) the prophets do not declare what is taken from tradition or their own thoughts but only what is revealed to them (1 Cor 14:26).[4] He further distinguishes prophecy from teaching, arguing that "whereas teachers expound Scripture, cherish

---

[1] Gaffin, *Perspectives,* 60.

[2] Grudem, *Prophecy,* 96 (cf. P. Schaff [ed.], "The homilies of St John Chrysostom on the Epistles of Paul to the Corinthians," *A Select Library of the Nicene and Post-Nicene Fathers* [Edinburgh: T & T Clark, 1889], 256).

[3] Dunn, *Jesus and the Spirit*, 228 (see also Fee, *First Epistle to the Corinthians,* 595; Storm, "A Third Wave View," 207).

[4] Friedrich, *TDNT* 6: 853 (cf. Greenbury, "1 Corinthians 14:34-35," 723). On the other hand Friedrich identifies proclamation of a divine revelation by a prophet as preaching (see 852). Thus, there appears to be a little confusion about terminology in Friedrich's view.

the tradition about Jesus and explain the fundamentals of the catechism, the prophets, not bound by Scripture or tradition, speak to the congregation on the basis of revelations."[1] This implies that prophecy "deals with specific situations" with focus on future action, while teaching concerns itself primarily with instruction and is always based on past revelation.[2] Greenbury, similarly, argues that since prophets receive their messages "by direct revelation, under the impulse of the Holy Spirit (1 Cor 14:6, 26, 30; Rev 1:1, 3) … prophecy articulates God's otherwise unknowable will and purpose concerning issues of the moment (1 Cor 13:2; Rev 2-3)."[3] Paul prefers and commends prophecy because the revelatory nature of prophecy "allows it to be suited to the specific needs of the moment, needs that may be known only to God."[4] It is this specific spontaneous revelation that makes prophecy different from other forms of speech gifts. Therefore, it can be argued that, because revelation is an inseparable and essential element of prophecy, without direct revelation from God, any edification through exhortation and comfort is based on the words of others (i.e. preachers or teachers), which is the gift of exhortation (cf. Rom 12:8) or teaching (cf. 1 Cor 12:28), not prophecy.[5] Turner contends that teaching in the NT "included exposition that related Scripture and tradition to the immediate needs of a congregation … prophecy primarily denoted the declaration by a person of material revealed to him or her *directly* by supernatural source, rather than mediated through consideration of Scripture."[6] Farnell also has provided an extended argument against identifying prophecy with preaching/teaching. He summarises that "it is unlikely that a

---

[1] Friedrich, *TDNT* 6: 854 (also Storm, "A Third View,"207; Turner, *Holy Spirit*, 203-204; Farnell, "When Will the Gift" 182; Keener, *Gifts and Giver*, 120-21).

[2] Friedrich, *TDNT* 6: 854.

[3] Greenbury, "1 Corinthians 14:34-35," 724.

[4] Grudem, *Prophecy,* 128.

[5] Cf. Walvoord, *Holy Spirit,* 42-43; Thomas R. Edgar, *Miraculous Gifts: Are they for Today?* (Neptune, NJ: Loizeaux Brothers, 1983), 70.

[6] Turner, *Holy Spirit*, 203.

proclamation made apart from immediate revelation may strictly be termed 'prophecy'"[1] since no human speech "is ever said to be based on revelation ... instead teaching is put in contrast to divine 'revelation.'"[2] The same argument applies against identifying preaching as prophecy since "preaching is essentially a merging of the gifts of teaching and exhortation."[3]

Paul maintains this distinction in his listing of Spiritual gifts (1 Cor 12:8-11, 28-29, 14:6, 26; Rom 12:6-8, and Eph 4:11).[4] In all lists, Paul distinguishes the gift of prophecy (and prophets) from other speech gifts, particularly teaching/teachers and pastors (cf. Rom 12:6 [cf. vv. 7-8]; 1 Cor 14:6; Eph 4:11).[5] The term διδαχήν (*didachen,* "teaching") in 1 Cor 14:26, means a word of "instruction or teaching" (BDAG, 192), or "speech and exhortation in the form of teaching,"[6] and "reflects time in reflection and study"[7] rather than something spontaneous.[8] Similarly, διδαχῇ (*didache,* "teaching") in 1 Cor 14:6, refers to "speaking in the form of teaching" (BDAG, 192) and carries the same idea as in 14:26. It is also worth noting that the preaching of the apostles and of Paul is called διδαχή (*didache,* "teaching") by the high priests (Acts 5:28) and others in Athens (Acts 17:19). No strict distinction is applied here between teaching and preaching, and in both places διδαχή (*didache,* "teaching") carries the same idea as in 1 Cor 14:26 (cf. 6). Furthermore, in Acts 2:42 and in Titus 1:9 (cf. 2 Tim 4:2; Rom 6:17; 16:17), διδαχή (*didache,* "teaching")

---

[1] Farnell, When Will the Gift," 179 (cf. 173 n. 9).

[2] Farnell, When Will the Gift," 183.

[3] Farnell, When Will the Gift," 183-84 (cf. 184 n. 41; also see Saucy, "An Open but Cautious View," 127; Dunn, *Jesus and Spirit*, 228; also Robeck, "Prophecy," 761, who seems to agree with Dunn but is open to the other possibility.

[4] Contra Hays, *First Corinthians,* 237 (cf. Ciampa and Rosner, *First Letter to the Corinthians,* 679).

[5] See Grudem, *Prophecy*, 119.

[6] K. Weiss, "διδαχή," *EDNT* 1:319.

[7] Ciampa and Rosner, *First Letter to the Corinthians,* 710 (also Thiselton, *First Epistle to the Corinthians,* 1135).

[8] Garland, *1 Corinthians,* 658.

refers to the tradition of instruction in church where one has to learn the "definite traditions of faith."[1] This indicates that these traditions were already available in oral and probably written form and were not to be received through spontaneous revelation as in prophecy. Neither prophecy nor revelation is connected with teaching anywhere in these passages.

Though, the origin and revelatory nature are distinct, prophecy does have a teaching and preaching function whereby, being edifying to the church (1 Cor 14:19), the church can learn from it and be encouraged (14:31). However, functional similarities between prophecy and other speech gifts (1 Cor 14:3; cf. vv. 6, 26) do not mean conceptual or phenomenological similarity since, as noted previously, the source of each is rooted in different objects. While prophecy always originates in a revelation from the Spirit, preaching/teaching is always derived from Scripture.

In conclusion, it can be summarised that for Paul prophecy is distinct from teaching and preaching. While both were gifts of the Spirit, Paul saw prophecy always rooted in revelation and consisting of spontaneously delivered knowledge in contrast to teaching, whereas knowledge was normally acquired through study and reflection. The effort to identify prophecy with preaching and teaching misunderstands and misrepresents Paul's teaching regarding the fundamental nature of biblical prophecy as a revelatory phenomenon. Such an effort may be to build a bridge between the continuationist and the cessationist views by suggesting the continuation of prophecy today in preaching and teaching based on written Scripture without threatening the sufficiency and finality of Scripture or perhaps even secondarily, to bolster the esteem of preaching and teaching.

4.3 Content: A Diverse and Responsive Phenomenon (1 Cor 14:3 [cf. 4b], 19 [v. 31], 24-25; 13:2)

The discussion below seeks to identify specifically the possible content that Corinthian prophecy brought through revelation.

[1] Weiss, *EDNT* 1:320.

Several scholars agree that NT prophecy was often a responsive phenomenon; it was an address to present situations, relating to current issues, providing guidance and encouragement to the church by applying previously revealed biblical truths.[1] This means that prophecy required "the necessity of God revealing particularistic knowledge" through the Holy Spirit to address specific situations.[2] Farnell defends the view that NT prophecy provided "immediate and temporal advice to local congregations" based on the revelations received from the Holy Spirit. As such, "many NT prophets gave oral rather than canonical revelation."[3] The main question is whether Corinthian congregational prophecy also had the same feature. The text of 1 Corinthians 12-14 does not answer this question directly because there is no record of the content of Corinthian congregational prophecy. Nevertheless, there is enough material in the text to provide information regarding content.

It was discussed in Chapter 3 that while NT prophecy did bring some new doctrinal canonical revelation (Eph 2:20; 3:5; the Book of Revelation),[4] it mostly consisted of occasional predictions (e.g. John 11:49-52; Acts 11:28; 21:10-11), spontaneous doxological praise (Luke 1:67-79; Acts 10:46; 19:6) and words of guidance to the church to deal with specific local situations (cf. Acts 13:2; 1 Tim 4:14). It was also pointed out that in Acts, prophecy became a congregational phenomenon from Pentecost onward (cf. Acts 2:17-18), with prophecy available to many believers not designated as prophets (Acts 10:45-46; 19:6; 21:9). As such, unlike in the Gospels, Acts has examples of both canonical (Acts 11:28; Acts

---

[1] Cf. Thiselton, *First Epistle to the Corinthians*, 956, 961; Garland, *1 Corinthians,* 583.

[2] Turner, *Holy Spirit*, 38.

[3] Farnell, "Gift of Prophecy," 409 (also Gaffin, *Perspectives*, 99-100).

[4] The prophetic utterances of Zechariah, Anna and Simeon were also doctrinal in nature (Luke 1:67-79; 2:25-32, 36-38). While they were based on previous OT revelations, there was predictive element added to them (as new doctrinal revelations [cf. Luke 1:76-79]).

21:10-11) and congregational prophecy (Acts 2:11; 10:46; 13:2; 19:6; 21:9).

Since, Corinthian prophecy was primarily congregational prophecy, it was distinct from prophecy in the Gospels and the Apocalypse of John. The latter consisted of canonical prophecy alone. Corinthian prophecy was also distinct from canonical prophecy in Acts but similar to congregational prophecy in Acts. There are indications in the text of 1 Corinthians 12-14 that Corinthian prophecy as congregational prophecy also addressed present situations and provided guidance and encouragement to the church through diverse contents (1 Cor 14:3). It even included didactic content (cf. 1 Cor 14:19, 31) and gospel proclamation (14:24-25).[1] Unlike in Luke/Acts, there is no indication of either predictions (cf. Acts 11:28; 21:10) or the Godward form of prophecy (Luke 1:67-80; Acts 19:6). Moreover, Corinthian prophecy was subject to weighing (1 Cor 14:29), which is not indicated of prophecy in Luke/Acts nor in Revelation.

Thus, having clarified the difference between canonical and Corinthian congregational prophecy, it is appropriate now to identify the main function and content of the latter.

4.3.1 Its General Function: οἰκοδομὴν καὶ παράκλησιν καὶ παραμυθίαν (1 Cor 14:3 [cf. 4, 31])

Carson and Edgar confirm that οἰκοδομὴν καὶ παράκλησιν καὶ παραμυθίαν (*oikodomen kai paraklesin kai paramuthian,* "edification, exhortation, encouragement") does not provide a specific definition but only a function of Corinthian prophecy since other gifts also share the same virtues.[2] Godet also asserts that "one may edify, comfort, encourage without deserving the title of prophet or prophetess."[3] Thus, Thiselton calls the three terms

[1] Cf. Packer, *Keep in Step* 214-17; Grudem, *Prophecy*, 15; Gaffin, *Perspectives,* 99-100; Farnell, "Gift of Prophecy," 409.

[2] See Carson, *Showing the Spirit*, 105; Edgar, *Miraculous Gifts,* 69-70 (also Grudem, *Prophecy,* 126).

[3] F. Godet, *Commentary on St. Paul's First Epistle of St. Paul to the Corinthian,* vol. II (trans. A. Cusin; Edinburgh: T. & T. Clark, 1887), 267-68.

"proleptic accusatives" referring more to what the speaker wants or hopes to achieve through their speech than to the essential nature of the gift itself.[1] While it is true that other gifts can also produce the same results as prophecy (cf. 1 Cor 14:3, 26 [cf. Col 3:16; Eph 4:29]), Paul uses the three terms particularly to describe the key functions of Corinthian prophecy that may inform of its content to some extent. Grudem claims that such general statements about the purpose and function of Corinthian prophecy give a better understanding of the gift than examples of actual prophecies themselves since they reflect what prophecy accomplishes and intends to do.[2] Thus, determining the meaning of οἰκοδομὴν καὶ παράκλησιν καὶ παραμυθίαν (*oikodomen kai paraklesin kai paramuthian,* "edification, exhortation, encouragement") is the first step to get a clue as to the content of Corinthian prophecy.[3]

Scholars have had varying opinions and proposals in regard to the meaning of the three terms (cf. 14:3).[4] Fee points out that these terms function grammatically as the compound direct object of the verb λαλεῖ (*lalei*, "to speak" in 14:3); they are therefore, the results of prophesying and not the prophetic content.[5] Scholars, however, agree that among the three, οἰκοδομήν (*oikodomen,* "edification") governs the whole chapter (1 Cor 14:3, 4, 5, 12, 17, 26) and is central to Paul's whole discussion of spiritual gifts and to his argument.[6] In fact, this particular feature of prophecy is what makes prophecy superior to speaking in tongues (vv. 4-5) and is also the ultimate goal of all spiritual gifts (cf. vv.

[1] Thiselton, *First Epistle to the Corinthians,* 1087.

[2] Grudem, *Prophecy*, 126. This may, perhaps, appear to be an overstatement since actual prophecies themselves (as seen in chapter 3) help form a better understanding of the phenomenon of prophecy than the general statements about its function.

[3] Cf. Ciampa and Rosner, *First Letter to the Corinthians,* 672.

[4] See Thiselton, *First Epistle to the Corinthians,* 1087-1090 for a detailed discussion on these terms.

[5] Fee, *First Epistle to the Corinthians*, 657 n. 28.

[6] Cf. Thiselton, *First Epistle to the Corinthians*, 1094; Ciampa and Rosner, *First Letter to the Corinthians*, 672; Fee, *First Epistle to the Corinthians*, 657-58.

12, 17, 26). Garland calls edification the "benchmark by which to measure what goes on in public worship."[1] It usually carries the idea of "building/construction" (BDAG, 558 [cf. 1 Cor 3:10; 8:1, 10; 10:23]),[2] but in 14:3 it particularly refers to "spiritual strengthening" (BDAG, 559 [cf. 1 Cor 14:5, 12, 26])[3] or "people being stronger in their faith and walk with Christ."[4] Thus, it refers more to "the qualitative growth of the church," than quantitative (cf. 2 Cor 10:8; Rom 14:19; 15:2; Eph 4:29).[5] It is also a general term for "any kind of help toward growth in Christian maturity" and is not characteristic of prophecy alone. In fact, "any legitimate activity" (e.g. a hymn, a teaching, a revelation, a tongue, an interpretation) can bring edification in a church context (1 Cor 14:26)," and prophecy is one of such activities as contributes to that.[6] This means that the content of Corinthian congregational prophecy could be overlapping with or similar to the content of other gifts since they all aim to produce the same result (i.e. edification). This leads Thiselton to argue that because οἰκοδομήν (*oikodomen,* "edification") is "closely associated with gospel preaching itself, whether to unbelievers or to believers," prophecy is identical to gospel proclamation (preaching).[7] While there is an indication in 14:24-25 that congregational prophecy could contain Spirit-prompted gospel-proclamation (as discussed later in this chapter), it will be argued below that gospel proclamation was only one of the contents that Corinthian prophecy would produce. Gospel-proclamation in preaching does not originate in revelation as it does in prophecy. Paul, in 1 Corinthians 12-14, nowhere refers

---

[1] Garland, *1 Corinthians,* 633.

[2] Cf. Ciampa and Rosner, *First Letter to the Corinthians*, 672; Fee, *First Epistle to the Corinthians*, 675 n. 29.

[3] Contra Fee, *First Epistle to the Corinthians,* 657 n. 29.

[4] Ciampa and Rosner, *First Epistle to the Corinthians,* 672 (also see Garland, *1 Corinthians,* 634; Robertson and Plummer, *1 Corinthians,* 306).

[5] Garland, *1 Corinthians,* 633 (also Grudem, *Prophecy,* 126).

[6] Grudem, *Prophecy,* 127.

[7] Thiselton, *First Epistle to the Corinthians*, 1076 (cf. 1088; Gillespie, *First Theologians*, 144).

to prophecy as merely gospel-proclamation even if its content was based on or included gospel truths (cf. Eph 2:20; 3:5). At best, the term οἰκοδομήν (*oikodomen,* "edification") indicates that prophecy produced intelligible utterances that would edify God's people though the content of such utterance could be varied and overlapping with other speech gifts.

The precise meanings of παράκλησιν (*paraklesin,* "exhortation") and παραμυθίαν (*paramuthian,* "encouragement") are uncertain since they could not only be "near synonymous,"[1] but could also cover a broad range of meanings.[2] Various possibilities exist in the NT regarding the meaning of παράκλησις (*paraklesis,* "exhortation or consolation or admonition") and the verb παρακαλέω (*parakaleo,* "to exhort or comfort or rebuke/ admonish").[3] παράκλησις (*paraklesis*) could refer to comfort from sorrows (Luke 2:25; 6:24; 2 Cor 1:3-7), encouragement to those who are discouraged (Rom 15:4, 5; 2 Cor 7:4, 13), and exhortation or appeal or encouragement for someone to do something (2 Cor 8:17; 1 Thess 2:4; Heb 12:5; 13:22).[4] Ciampa and Rosner propose that in 14:3, παράκλησιν (*paraklesin*) could be an "'act of emboldening another in belief or course of action'" but may also mean essentially the same as παραμυθίαν (*paramuthian,* "encouragement") "that which serves as encouragement to one who is depressed or in grief").[5] This is possible since παρά κλησις (*paraklesis*) also appears with παραμυθία (*paramuthia,* "encouragement") in other places as the combination of cognate verbs (cf. 1 Thess 2:12) and cognate adjectives (cf. Phil 2:1). Therefore, it is difficult to ascertain whether they are used in 14:3 as in other places, as "near synonymous, meaning to encourage

---

[1] Fee, *First Epistle to the Corinthians,* 658.

[2] See J. Thomas "παρακαλέω, παράκλησις," *EDNT* 3: 23-27.

[3] Cf. Conzelmann, *1 Corinthians,* 233-34; Ellis, *Prophecy and Hermeneutics*, 132 n. 13.

[4] See Grudem, *Prophecy,* 127.

[5] Ciampa and Rosner, *First Letter to the Corinthians,* 672 (also Garland, *1 Corinthians,* 634; Thiselton, *First Epistle to the Corinthians,* 1089; Robertson and Plummer, *1 Corinthians*, 306; Dunn, *Jesus and the Spirit*, 229-30).

or comfort, or whether they embrace the broader categories of exhorting and comforting."[1] Grudem concludes that since the context of 14:3 (cf. v. 31) does not define the exact meaning, it might "encompass a variety of speech activities which could include any or all of these elements," bringing "the hearers at times 'comfort,' at times 'encouragement,' and at times 'exhortation."[2] Paul's use of παράκλησις (*paraklesis*) also gives weight to the consideration that Corinthian prophecy consisted of content that was multiform and could address multiple situations and issues. Garland contends that παράκλησις (*paraklesis*) has a broad range of meanings with pastoral dimension since in Acts 15:32, it is used of the activity of Judas and Silas (παρεκάλεσαν [*parekalesan,* "they exhorted"] and ἐπεστήριξαν [*epesterixan,* "they strengthened"]) who are described by Luke as prophets. On this basis he argues that it "epitomises what Paul means by prophecy."[3] Even though, Judas and Silas are identified as prophets and it is possible that encouragement resulted from teaching and preaching contained in their speeches, the text (Acts 15:32) does not define this activity as prophecy. Many of the NT prophets were also called teachers (Acts 13:1 cf. 15:35) and could teach and preach without necessarily prophesying. Moreover, even if Judas and Silas did encourage the Antioch church through prophetic revelations, it still does not support the premise that prophecy is identical with preaching or teaching just because it produces similar effects or results as other speech gifts. In addition, Acts 15:32 does not necessarily present Paul's view of prophecy but that of Luke, which was much broader, perhaps more loosely defined, than Paul's view (as discussed in Chapter 3).

Gillespie and Thiselton have also emphasised the pastoral and the multiform character of the term παράκλησις (*paraklesis*) to

---

[1] Fee, *First Epistle to the Corinthians*, 658 (also see Grudem, *Prophecy,* 127 [cf. G. Stalin, "παράκλησις," *TDNT* 5: 821]).

[2] Grudem, *Prophecy,* 127.

[3] Garland, *1 Corinthians,* 634. For others with similar approach to prophecy based primarily on παράκλησις, see Hill, *Prophecy*, 122-32; Gillespie, *First Theologians*, 142-50; Ellis, *Prophecy and Hermeneutic*, 131-32 (cf. 129-44).

conclude that Corinthian prophecy included "gospel preaching, ethical instruction, and applied theology."[1] Once again, while these may consist in the contents of Corinthian prophecy, they resulted from revelatory experience, which is the core character of prophecy. Grudem also makes clear that while the three terms help define the content and function of Corinthian prophecy, they do not distinguish prophecy from other speech activities "for there is no one function that will serve as a distinguishing characteristic" of prophecy. This is where the revelatory character of prophecy becomes the defining and unique element of Corinthian prophecy.[2]

It can be briefly summarised that while it is difficult to ascertain any particular content of Corinthian prophecy on the basis of the three terms alone, they do suggest that Corinthian prophecy encompassed a variety of speech activities that would produce οἰκοδομὴν καὶ παράκλησιν καὶ παραμυθίαν (*oikodomen kai paraklesin kai paramuthian,* "edification, and exhortation and encouragement").[3] The terms also indicate prophetic content that was directed more to situations in the present rather than to those in the future. Fee claims that the three terms basically "set forth parameters of the divine intent of prophecy," indicating "that in Paul's view the primary focus of a prophetic utterance is not future, but the present situations of the people of God" since the three terms are particularly used in Scripture in relation to current situations.[4]

4.3.2 Its Teaching Aspect (1 Cor 14:31 [cf. v. 19])

It has been argued earlier that though Paul makes a distinction between prophecy and teaching (12:28-29; 14:6, 26), he sees prophesying as having a teaching function (1 Cor 14:31 [cf. v. 19]). Paul affirms that the church could learn ("μανθάνωσιν"

---

[1] Gillespie, *First Theologians,* 144-48 (cf. Thiselton, *First Epistle to the Corinthians,* 1088-89).

[2] Grudem, *Prophecy,* 127.

[3] Cf. Grudem, *Prophecy,* 126.

[4] Fee, *First Epistle to the Corinthians,* 657.

[*manthanosin,* "may learn"]) and be encouraged from the prophesying of believers (v. 31). Prophecy could also instruct (κατηχήσω [*katecheso,* "might instruct"]) the church for her edification (v. 19) as does teaching. Such *learning* from and *instruction* through prophecy is directed to the edification of the whole assembly (vv. 19, 31). This means it would require the type of prophetic content that is not personal or specific to only a few believers but is relevant to all ("πάντες" [*pantes*] v. 31). As such the content of congregational prophecy could include a Spirit-inspired reiteration of doctrinal material and its applications to Christian life in general.[1] Even Hodge (a cessationist) recognises this function of prophecy, involving "an immediate impulse and aid from the Holy Spirit, in presenting truth already known."[2] However, this does not reduce prophecy or the one prophesying to the level of mere teaching or a teacher. The difference between the two still stands since, as argued earlier, the latter is derived from a pre-existing text or oral tradition, while the former is received through a direct revelation from God.[3]

Ciampa and Rosner translate μανθάνωσιν ([*manthanosin,* "may learn"] v. 31) as "be instructed,"[4] and they argue that since the term is usually more associated with teaching (cf. Deut 4:10; Jer 12:16; Rom 16:17; Eph 4:20-21; 1 Tim 2:11-12), "its usage here suggests that the prophetic ministry should not be radically distinguished from teaching, even if the two have different emphases."[5] Grudem provides a correction to such a view by pointing out that, in the NT, the term is not always used of "formal

[1] Cf. Gaffin, *Perspectives,* 60.

[2] Hodge, *I & II Corinthians*, 247.

[3] See Gaffin, *Perspectives,* 60; Greenbury, "1 Corinthians 14:34-35," 726 (cf. Schaff, "The Homilies of St John Chrysostom," 256; Keener, *Gifts and Giver*, 120-21).

[4] The translation "be instructed" (passive) probably reflects the effort of Ciampa and Rosner to identify prophecy with teaching as closely as possible, since the more preferable translation is "to learn" (cf. UBS, Reader's Edition with Textual Notes, 471). It is κατηχήσω (v 19) that is to be translated as "instruct" or "inform" (See Fee, *First Epistle to the Corinthians,* 676).

[5] Ciampa and Rosner, *First Letter to the Corinthians,* 716.

Bible teaching or doctrinal instruction" but could also often mean "'to learn how to act, to learn knowledge that will affect one's manner of life' (Matt 11:29; 1 Cor 4:6; Eph 4:20; Phil 4:9, 11; 1 Tim 5:4; Titus 3:14; Heb 5:8)."[1] Nebe similarly suggests that in 1 Cor 14:31, μανθάνωσιν (*manthanosin,* "may learn") has "an ethical and consoling use."[2]

Hence, Paul's use of μανθάνωσιν (*manthanosin,* "may learn") in connection with prophecy does not necessarily suggest that prophecy consisted of a rigid formal-teaching/instruction or was identical to it. It simply means that prophecy could bring doctrinal material along with its applications revealed by the Spirit from which the church can learn and be encouraged more practically than intellectually. Similarly, the term cannot be used to suggest that a prophet had the same function as a teacher. μανθάνωσιν (*manthanosin,* "may learn") simply indicates that people could learn from both activities.[3] Fee also explains that μανθάνω ([*manthano,* "to learn"] cf. v. 35 [1 Tim 2:11]) means "to *receive* instruction (=to learn) as over against giving it (=to teach)," which emphasises that "all" should be willing to learn from and be encouraged or exhorted by one another as the Spirit leads each believer.[4] This fits more with prophesying than with teaching where the emphasis is on instruction from the teacher to others rather than on mutual learning. Usage of the same term (μανθάνω [*manthano,* "to learn"]) for teaching and prophesying in the NT does not make prophecy identical to teaching. The weakness of Ciampa and Rosner's argument is that they seem to identify prophecy with teaching primarily on the basis of one term (i.e. μανθάνωσιν [*manthanosin,* "may learn"]). It was already discussed above at length that while there is overlap between prophecy and other speech gifts in terms of the similar results or their contents that they can produce, the distinction between them remains, due to the source of their content.

---

[1] Grudem, *Prophecy,* 129 (cf. *BDAG*, 490).

[2] G. Nebe, "μανθάνω," *EDNT* 2: 383.

[3] Grudem, *Prophecy,* 129.

[4] Fee, *First Epistle to the Corinthians,* 696 (cf. n. 59).

Paul does not explicitly mention κατηχήσω (*katecheso,* "might instruct" in v. 19) in relation to the function of prophecy. In the light of v. 6, it can be connected to all intelligible gifts (e.g. revelation, knowledge, prophecy, and teaching) in a general sense since all such gifts can "instruct" the church. Paul's comparison of the unintelligible nature of tongues with the intelligible nature of other gifts for the edification of the whole church shows that κατηχησω (*katecheso,* "might instruct") applies to other gifts as well and not prophecy alone.[1] Fee asserts that κατηχησω ([*katecheso,* "might instruct"] cf. Gal 6:6; Rom 2:18) is not an ordinary word for "teach." It rather means "informing" or "instructing" another in religious matters.[2] Thus, the term could include all intelligible gifts in v. 6 since all of them can inform and instruct the church in religious matters. It is also argued that the term is related to the noun "catechesis" and was used in early Christian literature of instruction in theological matters. This would imply that the content of such instruction would be of a doctrinal nature for the general edification of the church.[3] It also means πέντε λόγους τῷ νοΐ (*pente logous to noi,* "five words with mind" in v. 19)[4] does not necessarily refer to prophecy in particular but to the content of any intelligible gift in general (vv. 6, 26) since it corresponds to κατηχήσω (*katecheso,* "might instruct").[5] The important fact, is that Paul includes prophecy among such intelligible gifts. It is quite possible that since the context of chapter 14, and vv. 22-24 in particular, shows that Paul's overall discussion in chapter 14 focuses on comparing prophecy and tongues, κατηχήσω (*katecheso,* "might instruct") is being applied by Paul to prophecy in particular or, at least, as a leading

---

[1] Ciampa and Rosner, *First Letter to the Corinthians*, 695.

[2] Fee, *First Epistle to the Corinthians,* 696 n. 59 (cf. G. Schneider, "κατηχέω," *EDNT* 2: 273).

[3] *BDAG,* 423.

[4] Or "with my understanding" as in vv. 14-15 (see Fee, *First Epistle to the Corinthians*, 675).

[5] See Ciampa and Rosner, *First Letter to the Corinthians,* 694 n. 119 (cf. *BDAG,* 423).

gift among others. In either case, two things are made clear that are important to this book:

1) Prophecy has a function to instruct others since it is included among the gifts that share the same function (v. 19 [cf. vv. 6, 26]);

2) Any effort to define prophecy exclusively on the basis of κατηχήσω (*katecheso,* "might instruct") alone is not convincing since, like μανθάνωσιν (*manthanosin,* "may learn") above, instruction could also result from other intelligible gifts.

In summary, therefore, both μανθάνωσιν (*manthanosin,* "may learn" in v. 31) and κατηχήσω (*katecheso*, "might instruct" in v. 19) only inform us of one of the main functions and some possible content of Corinthian congregational prophecy rather than defining it. Additionally, they confirm that the content of Corinthian prophecy could also contain similar content found in other intelligible gifts (e.g. teaching, knowledge, preaching) that was primarily doctrinal in nature. However, none of this overlap of function and content between prophecy and other gifts makes prophecy identical to any of them.

4.3.3 As Gospel Proclamation (1 Cor 14:24-25)

Some scholars see 1 Cor 14:24-25 as referring to the evangelistic nature of Corinthian prophecy, consisting of gospel-proclamation.[1] They also affirm that prophecy as gospel proclamation was addressed to unbelievers and not only to believers (vv. 24-25).[2] Thus, a conclusion is drawn that overall NT prophecy, including Corinthian prophecy, was primarily gospel proclamation of the NT prophets. The content of Corinthian prophecy is understood as exclusively consisting of the *kerygma*.[3]

While this book agrees that 1 Cor 14:24-25 could support Spirit-inspired gospel proclamation being part of Corinthian congregational prophecy, it does not see gospel proclamation as

---

[1] Cf. Hill, *Prophecy,* 123-24; Gillespie, *First Theologians*, 134-50; Thiselton, *First Epistle to the Corinthians,* 1128.

[2] Thiselton, *First Epistle to the Corinthians,* 1128-29.

[3] Gillespie, *First Theologians*, 134-50.

the defining feature of Corinthian prophecy or congregational prophecy as exclusively confined to gospel proclamation in the NT. The text of 1 Corinthians 12-14 shows that Corinthian prophecy was a church phenomenon, primarily directed to the church and had effects on unbelievers only indirectly (14:22-25).

In the text (14:24-25), Paul presents a hypothetical situation[1] where an unbeliever happens to visit a Christian gathering and overhears many believers prophesying, which leads to the unbeliever's conversion in being ἐλέγχεται (*elegchetai,* "convicted") and ἀνακρίνεται (*anakrinetai,* "examined") by what they hear.[2] Note that Paul's focus, here, is not on the number of individuals prophesying but on the content of prophecy, being intelligible and relevant even to an unbeliever (cf. v. 23). The key terms here are ἐλέγχεται (*elegchetai,* "convicted") and ἀνακρί νεται (*anakrinetai,* "examined"), which shed some light on the content and function of Corinthian prophecy. Though, the verb ελέγχω (*elegcho,* "to convict") can mean, in classical contexts, "to bring to the light, to expose, to set forth" (BDAG, 249), in the NT and often in the papyri, "it denotes both 'conviction of sin' and 'conviction of truth'" (e.g. John 8:9, 46; 16:8).[3] Calvin and Barrett both point out that in 14:24 ἐλέγχεται (*elegchetai,* "convicted") is closely parallel to the work of the Holy Spirit in convincing the world of sin described in John 16:8.[4] Its usage in v. 24 confirms that the content of Corinthian prophesying was relevant and intelligible to visiting unbelievers, convincing them of their sins. The second verb ἀνακρίνω (*anankrino*) could generally mean, in

---

[1] Thiselton, *First Epistle to the Corinthians,* 1127, points out that ἐὰν δέ, with the "present subjunctive προφητεύσωσιν projects a scenario," which means "suppose" or "by contrast." The use of πάντες (as discussed above) also confirms this (cf. Ciampa and Rosner, *First Letter to the Corinthians,* 706).

[2] Thiselton, *First Epistle to the Corinthians,* 1129 (also Garland, *1 Corinthians,* 652), suggests that grammatically ὑπὸ πάντων, most probably, refers to "'all that is said' in the most inclusive sense (both prophets and prophetic message) … especially since Paul's antecedent is not the noun 'prophet' but the verb προφητεύσωσιν (indefinite present subjunctive)."

[3] Thiselton, *First Epistle to the Corinthians,* 1128 (cf. *BDAG,* 249).

[4] Calvin, *Corinthians*, 457; Barrett, *First Epistle to the Corinthians,* 326.

judicial settings, "to question, to examine" or "to judge, to discern, to call to account" (BDAG, 56). Here, it refers to bringing the unbeliever under an examination/account and judgment regarding his or her sin, unbelief, and conduct.[1]

Therefore, it has been argued by some, on the basis of ελεγχεται (*elegchetai,* "convicted") and ἀνακρίνεται (*anakrinetai,* "examined"), that Corinthian prophecy enacted "judgment and grace in the mode of warning and promise," consisting of "gospel promise with pastoral exhortation," addressed to both believers and unbelievers.[2] From Paul's usage of ἐλέγχεται (*elegchetai,* "convicted") and ἀνακρίνεται (*anakrinetai,* "examined"), it does appear that Paul teaches that prophecy could consist of the messages of judgment and grace for an unbeliever, which may include the content of the gospel. This is also supported by the discussion above on vv. 19 and 31 that Corinthian prophecy could involve instruction and learning about biblical truths, including the gospel, previously revealed. However, this does not mean that the primary function of Corinthian prophecy was evangelism. The prophesying of v. 24 is not evangelistic preaching, specifically aimed at unbelievers as in evangelism. Here, neither a prophet is going out to prophesy to an unbeliever, nor is the church holding an evangelistic meeting for visiting unbelievers. This was a usual church gathering of Corinthian Christians where outsiders were welcomed. Carson points out that "the unbeliever comes in and *overhears* what is going on in the assembly, and by that means is brought to recognition of need, and to repentance and worship."[3] In other words, the Corinthian believers do not start prophesying specifically and directly to the unbeliever when they

---

[1] Thiselton, *First Epistle to the Corinthians*, 1128 (cf. *BDAG*, 56).

[2] Thiselton, *First Epistle to the Corinthians*, 1128-29 (cf. Muller, *Prophetie und Predigt,* 24-26; Hill, *Prophecy,* 123-24; Gillespie, *First Theologians*, 134-50). This function of NT prophecy is also seen in continuance with the pattern of prophetic speech in the OT (see Thiselton, *First Epistle to the Corinthians,* 1128-29).

[3] Carson, *Showing the Spirit*, 122-23 (cf. Ciampa and Rosner, *First Letter to the Corinthians,* 708).

enter the assembly. Rather the unbeliever only overhears what was already being prophesied in the assembly when they enter (v. 24). Hence, Corinthian prophecy was firstly addressed to believers in the church and only indirectly to visiting unbelievers. Paul's instruction regarding prophecy and other spiritual gifts in 1 Corinthians 12-14 also advocates that Paul saw prophecy as a church phenomenon, primarily exercised among and to the believing community for its edification (cf. 1 Cor 12:11-12, 27-28; 14:3-6, 12, 23, 26, 28, 33).[1] Moreover, Paul makes it explicitly clear in v. 22 that prophecy was a sign for believers and not for unbelievers because it was a sign of God's presence and favour among believers (even if it brings a message of warning or judgment) for their edification.[2] Robeck affirms that prophecy served as a positive sign for the church of "God's presence and of eschatological reality that the new age was inaugurated."[3] Calvin confirms that prophecy was not primarily given to unbelievers since they are unable to "see the light which shines forth from it" (Isa 28:11-12).[4] At the same time, the reaction of the unbeliever to prophecy resulting in their conversion shows that it could

---

[1] Even in the OT, as discussed in Chapter 3, prophecy was primarily addressed to God's people (as a nation or individuals) and only rarely to unbelievers (cf. the book of Jonah and probably Daniel 2). There were prophecies *about* rather than *to* unbelieving nations (e.g. Isaiah 13-27; Jeremiah 46-51; Amos 1:2–2:5). The evidence in the Gospels, Acts, and non-Pauline epistles also indicate the same (see Chapter 3).

[2] Paul's reference to Isa 28:11-12 (cf. 1 Cor 14:21) as an analogy to Corinthian tongues shows that while the foreign language (unintelligible tongues) of the Assyrians represented God's judgment on the unbelieving Israel, the prophetic ministry of the church serves as a sign of God's presence restored to his redeemed people (See Ciampa and Rosner, *First Letter to the Corinthians,* 701-703; Garland, *1 Corinthians,* 650; Dunn, *Jesus and the Spirit,* 230-32; Carson, *Showing the Spirit,* 119-20; Forbes, *Prophecy*, 181). In 1 Cor 14:22, tongues serve as a negative sign of judgment to the visiting unbelievers since it alienates them from the believing community; whereas, it is a positive sign for believers since it edifies them personally (1 Cor 14:4).

[3] Robeck, "Prophecy," 758 (cf. Garland, *1 Corinthians,* 651; Fee, *First Letter to the Corinthians,* 683).

[4] Calvin, *Corinthians,* 457.

also benefit the visiting unbelievers due to its intelligible and relevant content. Carson elucidates that "although prophecy serves as a sign to believers, it also has more positive effect on unbelievers than does the gift of tongues."[1] At the same time, such prophesying with gospel content does not make prophecy identical to preaching of the gospel. Any gospel proclamation in congregational prophecy happens at the prompting of the Spirit in an individual, and not by one's own human desire as is often the case in preaching. The prophet (or the one prophesying) declares what the Spirit reveals, even if the revelation was familiar or already revealed prior to the time of the prophetic utterance.

The phrase τὰ κρυπτὰ τῆς καρδίας αὐτοῦ φανερὰ γί νεται ([*ta krupta tes kardias autou fanera ginetai*, "the hidden things of his heart become manifest"] v. 25) is debated among scholars as to whether it refers to particular and private sins of the unbeliever brought into the open by prophecy,[2] or the secrets common in the hearts of all people as fallen.[3] Fee settles for a middle ground and affirms that it is difficult to know whether the nature of these prophecies would be same as in v. 3 that edify believers, "or whether some of the prophecies would be more specifically directed toward the unbelievers as such."[4] However, in his conclusion, he leans towards the former view suggesting that since "the emphasis here is on the revelatory aspect of the prophetic utterance," it could imply that a prophet (or the one prophesying) could be given specific knowledge about the

---

[1] Carson, *Showing the Spirit,* 122-23 (also Ciampa and Rosner, *First Letter to the Corinthians*, 708; Garland, *1 Corinthians,* 651).

[2] Forbes (contra Carson, *Showing the Spirit,* 122-23), *Prophecy,* 181 n. 69, suggests that it could certainly be a possibility "as in the case of Jesus and the Samaritan woman at the well" (John 4).

[3] Garland, *1 Corinthians,* 652-53, argues that "in this case, prophecy must be gospel proclamation" of general nature (cf. Hill, *Prophecy,* 124-25; Gillespie, *First Theologians,* 157).

[4] Fee, *First Epistle to the Corinthians,* 686.

unbeliever that penetrates "deeply into the moral consciousness" of the hearer.[1]

There are certain cases in the Bible where prophets were given prophetic revelations of specific and personal knowledge about individuals (Saul and Samuel [1 Sam 9:15-16, 19-20]; David and Nathan [2 Samuel 12]; Ahab and Elijah [1 Kings 21]; Elisha and the king of Syria [2 Kings 6:12]; Christ [John 4:19; Luke 7:39]; Agabus and Paul [Acts 21:10-12]).[2] However, it was neither a common feature of biblical prophecy nor was it common to all prophets unless God revealed such to them for some special purpose. In fact, in all the cases referred to above such knowledge is associated with and confined to only a few of the canonical prophets whose prophecies became a part of the Scriptures. Since, Paul does not indicate anything like this in 1 Corinthians 12-14, it is unlikely to be expected in Corinthian congregational prophecy. Moreover, publicly prophesying about the private sins of others would not only create many difficult pastoral situations but would also cause much anger, embarrassment, envy, quarrelling, disorder, and divisions in the church instead of unity and edification that Paul expects prophecy to produce and promote (14:3-5, 31). Such prophesying would not be in accordance with the virtue of love that Paul so extensively defines and argues for in 1 Corinthians 13 as the only context for exercising spiritual gifts. Calvin wisely and pastorally advises that the prophesying of v. 25 does not mean an external or verbal manifestation of the personal sinfulness of the unbeliever by a prophet in the assembly. It is the unbeliever's own conscience that "is aroused, so that he perceives his sins which previously lay hid from his view."[3] It is more likely that while a prophet (or the one prophesying) is oblivious to the unbeliever's personal circumstances, the Holy Spirit gives them such prophetic

---

[1] Fee, *First Epistle to the Corinthians,* 686-87 (cf. Thiselton, *First Epistle to the Corinthians,* 1129).

[2] It also appears that a prophet was sometimes expected to have supernatural knowledge of the private lives of others (cf. John 4:19; Luke 7:39; Matt 26:68 [cf. Luke 22:64]). But such an expectation is not present in 1 Corinthians.

[3] Calvin, *Corinthians,* 456-57.

utterances that convince the unbeliever of sin (cf. John 16:8) and lead him or her to repentance and worship without embarrassment. The individual prophesying serves as an instrument of the Spirit and is not given a supernatural knowledge of the private life of the unbeliever. Garland advises that "the prophet does not know to whom the words he or she speaks apply, except as one might generally understand the human condition and its alienation."[1] Such prophecies are "designed by the Spirit to expose the secrets of [the unbeliever's] own heart and thereby to convict him of sin, bringing him to repentance and worship."[2] Hence, it concludes that τὰ κρυπτὰ τῆς καρδίας αὐτοῦ (*ta krupta tes kardias autou*, "the hidden things of his heart" in v. 25) does not refer to any specific sins or situation of the unbeliever visiting the Corinthian gathering, rather it refers to the general message of the gospel that exposes the universal sinful human condition and the resultant alienation from God. It is possible that the Spirit can specifically apply even such general proclamation of the gospel to the unbeliever's personal life, but the one prophesying is not aware of that.

4.3.4 Its Relation to μυστήρια (*musteria,* "mysteries") and γνῶσιν ([*gnosin*, "knowledge"] 13:2)

Some of the content of Corinthian congregational prophecy identified above includes: addressing immediate situations in church to provide guidance, reiteration and application of previous doctrinal revelations for edification, and Spirit-inspired gospel proclamation for edification and even conversion. Further clues are found in 1 Cor 13:2 where Paul associates prophecy with μυστήρια (*musteria,* "mysteries") and γνῶσιν (*gnosin,* "knowledge"). Two important questions to the inquiry are: What do these two terms mean here? How are they associated with Corinthian prophecy?

---

[1] Garland, *1 Corinthians,* 653.

[2] Carson, *Showing the Spirit,* 116 (cf. Ciampa and Rosner, *First Epistle to the Corinthians,* 708).

Paul did exercise the gift of prophecy (cf. 13:2, 9; 14:6) but it is unlikely that he claimed to know and understand all mysteries and all knowledge (cf. 1 Cor 13:9-12; Rom 11:33-35) as it might appear in 1 Cor 13:2. As in other places (14:24, 31), this is a hypothetical situation (cf. ἐάν [*ean,* "if"], 13:2),[1] which does not refer to a reality but a possibility: "what it would be like ... to have the most prophetic gift imaginable."[2] Note that Paul's purpose is to prove the shallowness of spectacular spiritual gifts (highly esteemed by the Corinthians) without love, and not to define the particular content that prophecy brings forth.

The term μυστήριον (*musterion,* "mystery") is often used by Paul (cf. 1 Cor 4:1; 14:2; 15:51; Rom 11:25; 16:25; 2 Thess 2:7; Eph 1:19; 3:3, 4, 6, 9; 5:32; 6:19; Col 1:26, 27; 2:2; 4:3; 1 Tim 3:9, 16) and carries the idea of something that is hidden from humans and is only revealed by God,[3] i.e., something "too profound for human ingenuity" (BDAG, 530).[4] In regard to the content that such mysteries contained, Paul's usage generally shows that it was often about or related to God's redemptive and eschatological plan and activity in Christ (cf. 1 Cor 2:1-2; 4:1; 15:51; Rom 11:25; 16:25; Col 1:26).[5] Its usage in Eph 3:3-6 suggests the type of content that would better suit canonical prophecy since it brought forth new doctrinal revelation for inscripturation.[6] Hodge has argued that since μυστήρια (*musteria,* "mysteries") refers to "secrets, things undiscoverable by human reason, which divine revelation alone can make known," prophecy consists of "the gift of revelation by

---

[1] Garland, *1 Corinthians,* 613 (also see Grudem, *Prophecy,* 102).

[2] Ciampa and Rosner, *First Letter to the Corinthians,* 631 (also Thiselton, *First Epistle to the Corinthians,* 1044; Fee, *First Epistle to the Corinthians,* 632).

[3] See H. Kramer, "μυστήριον," *EDNT* 2: 448.

[4] Or things or secrets "too profound for mere human discovery" (Thiselton, *First Epistle to the Corinthians,* 1039).

[5] See Kramer, *TDNT* 2: 448-49.

[6] Hodge, *I Corinthians,* 267, affirms that it refers to "all secret purposes of God relating to redemption."

which such mysteries were communicated" (cf. 1 Cor 14:30).[1] Morris, similarly, defines μυστήρια (*musteria,* "mysteries") as "truths that men could never penetrate for themselves, but know only because it has pleased God to reveal them."[2] However, since Corinthian prophecy is not canonical but congregational prophecy, it could contain reiteration of previously revealed μυστήρια (*musteria,* "mysteries) for the edification of the church. This means such prophetic revelations of μυστήρια (*musteria,* "mysteries") through congregational prophecy did not bring new redemptive truths for inscripturation but simply consisted of reiteration of previously revealed truths. At the same time, the precise content of μυστήρια (*musteria,* "mysteries") in 13:2 in relation to Corinthian prophecy cannot be stated with certainty.[3]

The relationship between prophecy and μυστήρια (*musteria,* "mysteries") can be seen in prophecy containing the revelation of μυστήρια ((*musteria,* "mysteries") that is beyond human discovery or initiation.[4] In other words, prophecy serves as a channel through which such μυστήρια (*musteria,* "mysteries") are made known or revealed to the church. This not only confirms the necessity of revelation in prophecy (as argued earlier),[5] but also explains the relationship between revelation and mysteries since the latter is made known through revelation in prophecy.

The term μυστήρια (*musteria,* "mysteries") is also used in 1 Cor 14:2 where it is associated with speaking in tongues (see below for more). However, there is a difference between its usage in 13:2 and 14:2. The former refers to the "ability to understand the things of God," while the latter is an ability to "utter divine mysteries" but without understanding what is uttered (unless

---

[1] Hodge, *1 Corinthians,* 267.

[2] Morris, *I Corinthians,* 182.

[3] Cf. Grudem, *Prophecy*, 103.

[4] However, as was discussed earlier, prophecy was not always about revealing a new doctrinal mystery. It could simply include a reiteration or applications of such mysteries previously revealed.

[5] Cf. Grudem, *Prophecy,* 103.

interpreted).[1] Moreover, as will be argued below, in prophecy μυστήρια (*musteria,* "mysteries") are revealed from God to humans, whereas in tongues (being essentially Godward) how μυστήρια (*musteria,* "mysteries") can be addressed to God is not clear.[2] Fee claims that μυστήρια (*musteria,* "mysteries") in 14:2 are not the same as in 13:2 since in the latter they refer to God's ways revealed by the Holy Spirit to his people, and such "'mysteries' would scarcely need to be spoken back to God" since tongues is addressed to God, not to people.[3]

Unlike the connection between prophecy and μυστήρια (*musteria,* "mysteries"), defining the connection between prophecy and γνῶσις (*gnosis,* "knowledge") is more challenging since Paul seems to connect it with prophecy in 13:2 and makes a distinction between the two elsewhere (1 Cor 12:8; 14:6). Consequently, some see the relationship between the two as prophecy subsuming γνῶσις (*gnosis,* "knowledge") of μυστήρια (*musteria,* "mysteries")[4] since the verb εἰδῶ (*eido,* "know") controls both nouns.[5] Fee finds support for this in the Jewish apocalyptic literature,[6] where both nouns appear together, "especially with regard to the unfolding of God's final eschatological drama." He proposes in 13:2 that Paul uses these words to "refer to God's present revelations of his ways, especially in the form of special revelations by means of the

---

[1] Ciampa and Rosner, *First Letter to the Corinthians,* 631.

[2] Thiselton, *First Epistle to the Corinthians*, 1085, concludes that its meaning in both places is controversial.

[3] Fee, *First Epistle to the Corinthians,* 656 (cf. Ciampa and Rosner, *First Letter to the Corinthians,* 671; Thiselton, *First Epistle to the Corinthians,* 1085).

[4] Cf. Barnett, *First Epistle to the Corinthians,* 243; Ciampa and Rosner, *First Letter to the Corinthians,* 633.

[5] Fee, *First Epistle to the Corinthians,* 632 n. 34 (also Thiselton, *First Epistle to the Corinthians,* 1039).

[6] E.g. Dan 2:19-23, 28 has in LXX σοφία, γνῶσις, μυστήρια, and ἀνακαλύπτω; also see *1 Enoch* (41:1; 52:2; 61:5; 63:3; 68:5; 71:4). See Fee, *First Epistle to the Corinthians,* 633 n. 35.

eschatological Spirit whom Christians have received (cf. 14:6)."[1] While such a connection is possible, there are difficulties with it as well. Hodge argues that in 13:2, prophecy is connected only with μυστήρια (*musteria,* "mysteries") and not with γνῶσις (*gnosis,* "knowledge"). He refers to the distinction Paul makes between the two (cf. 1 Cor 13:8 and 12:8-10) and affirms that "the result of the gift of prophecy" was "the understanding or apprehension of mysteries, and not the possession of knowledge."[2] He further clarifies that the absence of ἐάν (*ean,* "if") leads to the common mistake of combining the first two clauses. γνῶσιν (*gnosin,* "knowledge") is not grammatically dependent on εἰδῶ (*eido,* "know") like μυστήρια (*musteria,* "mysteries") since "this would make Paul use an unexampled phrase, 'to know knowledge.'"[3] Therefore, he suggests that it is appropriate to supply either "though I have" or "I may have" in front of γνῶσιν (*gnosin,* "knowledge"), reading "though I have or may have all knowledge." Hodge connects γνῶσις (*gnosis,* "knowledge") to teachers since it refers to "the intellectual apprehension or cognition of revealed truth," and concludes that it was the prerogative "of the teacher to know and to instruct," while the prophet's prerogative was "to reveal" (14:6).[4] Hence, Hodge's interpretation of 13:2 sees two separate clauses, referring to two different gifts (i.e. prophecy and knowledge).

This book prefers Hodge's view, particularly in view of the distinction that Paul makes between prophecy and γνῶσις (*gnosis,* "knowledge") later within the same chapter (cf. 13:8-9) and also in other places (1 Cor 12:8-10; 14:6). On the other hand, it is also indisputable that there is some overlap between the two and a rigid distinction cannot always be established. In Col 2:2, knowledge appears in connection with mystery, and the two appear together in connection with prophecy in Eph 3:5-6. It seems best to

[1] Fee, *First Epistle to the Corinthians*, 632-33.

[2] Hodge, *I & II Corinthians,* 267.

[3] Hodge, *I & II Corinthians,* 267.

[4] Hodge, *I & II Corinthians,* 267.

conclude that in prophecy the knowledge of mysteries is revealed to prophets who proclaim it to people.

4.4 Authority: Subject to διακρίσις (*diakrisis*, "judgment or discernment" in 1 Cor 14:29, 37-38 [cf. 12:10; 1 Thess 5:21; 1 John 4:1])

This book argues that Corinthian prophecy was qualitatively different in authority from canonical prophecy. This is indicated by Paul's subjecting Corinthian prophecy to evaluation (14:29) and to his own apostolic authority (14:37-38). This is a significant and distinctive feature of Corinthian prophecy because it highlights the level of authority attached to it. As was discussed earlier in Chapter 3, prophets and their prophecies in the Bible were to be discerned and tested since the danger of false prophets and prophecy was always present. In the OT God provided certain guidelines for this task (cf. Deut 13:1-5; 18:20-22) and severe punishment was to be imposed upon a false or lying prophet in extreme cases (Deut 18:20). It was also pointed out that even prophets of Yahweh could become corrupt and greedy, and falsely prophesy in his name (Isa 9:15; Jer 5:13, 31; 6:13; 23:11-16, 21). In the NT there are warnings recorded about false prophets in the gospels (Matt 7:15, 15-23; Mark 13:22 [cf. Matt 24:11, 24]) and in the non-Pauline epistles (1 John 4:1-6; 2 Pet 2:1; Jude 4, 8, 11-16).

Paul does not provide any specific standard for evaluating Corinthian prophecy but 1 Cor 14:29 and 1 Thess 5:20-21 show that Paul did require prophecies to be weighed in church.[1] The weighing in 14:29 (cf. 1 Thess 5:20-21) differs from the material in the OT and other parts of the NT for two primary reasons – 1) weighing in the Pauline material is about the evaluation of prophecies and not the prophets; 2) it deals with congregational prophecy and not with canonical prophecy. This will become clear from the discussion below.

---

[1] Paul also predicts about the coming of false teachers and probably false prophets (Acts 20:29-30; 1 Tim 1:6-7; 6:3-5; 2 Tim 4:3-4).

The main concern here is to find answers to the following questions related to the inquiry – What exactly is meant by διακρι νω (*diakrino,* "to judge or discern") in 14:29 and what process did it involve? Does the gift of διακρίσεις πνευμάτων (*diakriseis pneumaton*, "discerning of spirits" in 1 Cor 12:10) refer to the same activity as διακρίνω (*diakrino,* "to judge or discern") in 14:29? Who exactly are οἱ ἄλλοι (*hoi alloi,* "the others") in 14:29 who were to weigh prophecies?

Answers to these questions vary and are debated. Many see the task of διακρίνω (*diakrino,* "to judge or discern" in 1 Cor 14:29) limited only to those with the gift of διακρίσεις πνευμά των (*diakriseis pneumaton*, "discerning of spirits" in 1 Cor 12:10) since the same root word is used in both places, referring to the same activity.[1] It is suggested that διακρίνω (*diakrino,* "to judge or discern") is the verb for the gift of διακρίσεις πνευμά των (*diakriseis pneumaton,* "discerning of spirits" in 12:10) and is to be understood as "a form of 'testing the spirits.'"[2] Connection between the two is also sought in seeing διακρίσεις πνευμάτων (*diakriseis pneumaton,* "discerning of spirits") related to the gift of prophecy in 1 Cor 12:10 just as διακρίνω (*diakrino,* "to judge") is related to prophecies in 14:29.[3] This view also sees 1 Thess 5:21 and 1 John 4:1 as referring to the same activity as in 1 Cor 14:29 (cf. 12:10) despite different verb being used there.[4] Gaffin claims that the apostle John's exhortation to the church to test different spirits to see whether they are from God (δοκιμάζετε τὰ πνεύ ματα εἰ ἐκ τοῦ θεοῦ ἐστιν [*dokimazete ta pneumata ei ek tou*

---

[1] Cf. G. G. Findlay, *St Paul's First Epistle to the Corinthians*, W. R. Nicoll (ed.) EGT (Grand Rapids: Eerdmans, [1900] 1961), 913; J. Moffatt, *The First Epistle of Paul to the Corinthians,* MNTC (London: Hodder & Stoughton, 1938), 182; Robertson and Plummer, *I Corinthians,* 322; Calvin, *Corinthians,* 461; Friedrich, *TDNT* 6: 851; Conzelmann, *1 Corinthians,* 244-45; Hill, *Prophecy,* 133; Martin, *Spirit and the Congregation,* 14; Aune, *Prophecy,* 220-22; Gillespie, *First Theologians,* 163; Gaffin, *Perspectives,* 70; Keener, *Gifts and Giver,* 121.

[2] Fee, *First Epistle to the Corinthians*, 693.

[3] Cf. Fee, *First Epistle to the Corinthians,* 596-97; Barrett, *First Epistle to the Corinthians,* 286; Dunn, *Jesus and the Spirit*, 233; Gaffin, *Perspective*, 70.

[4] Cf. Fee, *First Epistle to the Corinthians,* 596.

theou estin, "test the spirits if they are from God"], 1 John 4:1) refers to the same activity as in 1 Cor 14:29. He supports this by arguing that Paul's instruction in 1 Thess 5:21, to test everything (including prophecies), refers to the same activity as in 1 Cor 14:29 but has the same verb (δοκιμάζω [*dokimazo*], "to prove or approve") as in 1 John 4:1 (δοκιμάζετε [*dokimazete,* "test"]). He further justifies this by pointing out that just as the Christological confession of Christ's full humanity serves as a standard for testing of spirits in 1 John 4:1-3, the Christological confession of Christ's lordship in 1 Cor 12:1-3 serves as a standard for the weighing of prophecies in 1 Cor 14:29. Gaffin, therefore, concludes that all three passages (1 Cor 14:29; 1 Thess 5:21; 1 John 4:1) refer to the same activity and require the same gift of 12:10 despite the usage of different verbs (i.e. δοκιμάζω [*dokimazo,* "to test"] in 1 Thess 5:21 and 1 John 4:1; διακρίνω [*diakrino,* "to judge"] in 1 Cor 14:29).[1]

Regarding the nature of this weighing or testing of Corinthian prophecies, Gaffin contends that the weighing in 14:29 (cf. 1 Thess 5:21; 1 John 4:1) is of prophecies and not of the prophets to establish their own veracity. He claims that weighing consisted of determining "the source of an alleged prophecy, whether or not it is genuine, whether it is from the Holy Spirit or some other spirit" (cf. 1 Cor 12:1-3; 1 John 4:1 [cf. 2 Thess 2:2]) rather than separating or sifting revelatory elements from non-revelatory elements in a prophecy.[2] Gaffin adds that such weighing or testing could also include "an interpretive function, assessing in some way the significance of the prophecy for the congregation."[3] Fee suggests that the weighing in 14:29 is not so much about whether a prophecy is made under the influence of "a foreign spirit" (cf. 1 John 4:1-6) but whether a "prophecy itself truly conforms to the

---

[1] Gaffin, *Perspectives,* 70-71 (cf. Fee, *First Epistle to the Corinthians,* 596, who sees the connection between 1 Cor 12:10 and 1 John 4:1 due to the common term "spirits").

[2] Gaffin, *Perspectives,* 70 (contra Grudem, *Prophecy,* 60).

[3] Gaffin, *Perspectives,* 70.

Spirit of God."[1] In other words, the weighing consisted of making sure that a prophecy was in accordance with the existing revelation (written or oral apostolic traditions) and had the potential of edifying the church (1 Cor 14:3).

This book proposes two particular arguments against the view discussed above. Firstly, if 12:10 is seen as the same activity as 14:29, it implies that only those with the gift of διακρίσεις πνευμάτων (*diakriseis pneumaton,* "discerning of spirits") could evaluate Corinthian prophecies, and not the whole church. This would also mean that Paul, in 14:29, is addressing a particular group of people with the gift of διακρίσεις πνευμάτων (*diakriseis pneumaton,* "discerning of spirits"); whereas the context of chapter 14 indicates that Paul addresses the whole church throughout the chapter (vv. 1, 5, 24, 26, 31, and 39), and not a special group.[2] Secondly, while 1 Thess 5:20-21 concerns weighing of prophecies as in 14:29, despite different verbs being used, 1 John 4:1 appears to be concerned particularly with the testing of false prophets on the basis of their Christological confessions (vv. 2-3) rather than with the prophecies of believers in church.[3] The context indicates that John is warning of false prophets rather than of believers in the church whose prophecies could contain errors. However, it is to be acknowledged that the difficulty still remains in affirming a strict distinction between 1 Thess 5:20-21 and 1 John 4:1 since they both use the same verb (δοκιμάζω [*dokimazo,* "to test"]). If Paul meant a strict distinction between διακρίνω (*diakrino,* "to judge") and δοκιμάζω (*dokimazo*, "to test") he would use the former in 1 Thess 5:21 rather than the latter. It appears that there is some overlap between these passages and the two verbs, and a strict distinction cannot be sustained in all contexts. Moreover, since δοκιμάζω (*dokimazo*) literally means "to put to test, examine"

---

[1] Fee, *First Epistle to the Corinthians,* 693. In fact, he suggests that it refers to both, but particularly to the latter (Fee, *First Epistle to the Corinthians*, 596; cf. Barrett, *First Epistle to the Corinthians,* 286; Dunn, *Jesus and the Spirit*, 233).

[2] Cf. Carson, *Showing the Spirit,* 127 (also Grudem, *Prophecy,* 55-56.

[3] See Grudem, *Prophecy,* 58.

something (BDAG, 202), it could include both the prophets and their prophecies in 1 John 4:1 since prophets are tested through their prophecies.

Contrary to Gaffin's view, discussed above, Grudem argues that the noun διακρίσεις (*diakriseis*, "judgment") and the verb διακρίνω (*diakrino*, "to judge") do not refer to the same activity since they have a wide range of meanings in the NT.[1] Grudem supports this by pointing out that even within 1 Corinthians Paul uses the terms differently.[2] On this basis, Grudem concludes that Paul means "distinguishing" (or "differentiation of good and evil," BDAG, 185) in 1 Cor 12:10 but "evaluate or judge" (in relation to prophecy) in 1 Cor 14:29.[3] He further explains that while διακρινω (*diakrino,* "to judge") is particularly related to the evaluation of prophecies, the gift of διακρίσεις πνευμάτων (*diakriseis pneumaton,* "discerning of spirits") is not restricted to the testing of prophets and prophecies but has a wider area of operation (cf. Acts 16:16-18; 1 John 4:1-6). It specifically refers to "the ability to recognise the influence of the Holy Spirit or of demonic spirits in a person."[4] Carson supports this and argues that "there is no evidence that this careful weighing of the content of Christian prophecy should be confused with the gift of discerning spirits (1 Cor 12:10)" since this would mean that only a few select individuals (with the gift of discerning spirits) had the responsibility to do the evaluation required of prophecies in 1 Cor 14:29.[5] Grudem, therefore, treats 14:29 as completely

---

[1] See Grudem, *Prophecy,* 59-61.

[2] In 11:31, the verb means to "evaluate," in 11:29 it means to "distinguish (or evaluate)," in 6:5 it means to "give a legal judgment," in 4:7 it means to "distinguish." Moreover, in Rom 14:1, the noun means "arguments" or "disputes" (see Grudem, *Prophecy,* 364 n. 1 [cf. 59-61]).

[3] Grudem, *Prophecy,* 54 (also Garland, *1 Corinthians,* 662; *BDAG,* 185). For a detailed discussion on this, see Wayne Grudem, "A Response to Gerhard Dautzenberg on 1 Corinthians 12:10," *Biblische Zeitschrift* 22 (1978): 253-70.

[4] Grudem, *Prophecy,* 55 (also A. Bittlinger, *Gifts and Graces: A Commentary on 1 Corinthians 12-14,* trans. H. Klassen [London: Hodder and Stoughton, 1967], 46; Robertson and Plummer, *1 Corinthians*, 267).

[5] Carson, *Showing the Spirit,* 127 (also Grudem, *Prophecy,* 55-56).

different from 1 John 4:1-6 (cf. Matt 7:15-20 [cf. 24:11, 24]; also *Didache* 11.5, 6) since unlike the latter, he argues, 14:29 is not dealing with the weighing or evaluation of false prophets from outside the church but with the prophecies of believers who are already accepted in the church (14:26, 39). The two or three prophets (v. 29) are not new prophets from outside, present in every worship service, who need to be declared as true or false. For Grudem, 1 Thess 5:21 is parallel to 14:29 since it also concerns the evaluation of prophecies and not prophets.[1]

Regarding the nature of weighing of prophecies (1 Cor 14:29), Grudem argues that it involves "making distinctions … among related things or ideas" or "carefully evaluating" what is prophesied.[2] It is "a process whereby every member of the congregation would listen carefully and evaluate each statement, distinguishing what he or she felt to be good from less good, what was thought to be helpful from the unhelpful, what was perceived to be true from the false."[3] Grudem concludes that in 14:29 Paul requires prophecies to be specifically evaluated and not simply accepted as totally true or totally false.[4] In other words, for Grudem, διακρίνω (*diakrino,* "to judge") is about separating the weed from the wheat or human from divine, and not about deciding whether a prophecy is to be fully accepted or rejected. This also provides the reason for Grudem's view of NT prophecy as a lower type of prophecy because it consisted of "mere human words to report something God brings to mind."[5] Consequently, he sees διακρίνω (*diakrino,* "to judge") as an activity of separating the true (i.e. divine) part of prophecy from the false (i.e. human) part since what a prophet reports has a mixture of human and divine elements.

This book with the following exception, prefers Grudem's view that regards 14:29 and 1 Thess 5:21 dealing with the evaluation of

---

[1] Grudem, *Prophecy,* 58.

[2] Grudem, *Prophecy,* 60 (cf. Garland, *1 Corinthians,* 662).

[3] Grudem, *Prophecy*, 60.

[4] Grudem, *Prophecy*, 58-59, 64-66.

[5] Cf. Grudem, *Prophecy*, 51.

prophecies, and 1 John 4:1 with the testing of prophets. However, it does not agree with Grudem's understanding of the weighing of prophecies as involving sifting the true from the false or the divine from the human. Such a view diminishes Corinthian prophecy to the same level as a sermon or illumination or Christian advice. Corinthian prophecy was still based on divine revelation even if it was qualitatively different from canonical prophecy. Grudem's suggestion is based on an assumption which he does not establish or support using the text.

This book finds Fee's proposal to be preferable, which recommends that the weighing of Corinthian prophecies included both determining the source of a prophecy and confirming that a prophecy was in accordance with the existing revelation (written or oral apostolic traditions) with the potential to edify the church (1 Cor 14:3). In other words, whether a "prophecy itself truly conforms to the Spirit of God."[1]

It has already been pointed out that the weighing in 14:29 was of prophecies and not of prophets or individuals prophesying. Most scholars agree on this despite variations on whether or not 12:10 refers to the same activity as 14:29.[2] Grudem argues that if Paul meant the prophets, he would have used the verb κρίνω (*krino,* "to judge") which was used for judgments where there are clear cut options, such as guilty or innocent, true or false, right or wrong (e.g. Matt 7:1; 19:28; John 5:51; 18:31; Acts 16:15; 25:10; Rom 2:1; 14:3, 4, 10, 13; 1 Cor 4:5; 5:3, 12; 6:1, 2, 3, 6; 10:15; 11:13).[3] It is also supported by the fact that the speakers are already from among the believers and do not need to be examined as true or false every time they prophesy. What is to be evaluated is only

---

[1] Fee, *First Epistle to the Corinthians,* 693 (cf. 596).

[2] Cf. Ciampa and Rosner, *First Letter to the Corinthians,* 715; Garland, *1 Corinthians,* 662; Fee, *First Epistle to the Corinthians,* 693.

[3] See 1 Cor 6:2-6 where Paul maintains this distinction by using κρίνω (to refer to legal judgments outside the church) and διακρίνω (to refer to informal decision inside the church). Thus, rather than declaring one party guilty and the other non-guilty (as in the case of κρίνω), the use of διακρίνω shows that "a careful evaluation" is to be made to find fault on both sides (Grudem, *Prophecy,* 60 [cf. 59-61]).

what they say.[1] Moreover, since congregational prophecy was potentially available to any believer, it would be their prophecies that would be evaluated rather than their status, whether they were eligible to prophecy or not.

Concerning οἱ ἄλλοι ([*hoi alloi*, "the others"] i.e., those who weigh prophecies), there are two views. Some suggest that they are the other prophets.[2] Others suggest that οἱ ἄλλοι (*hoi alloi,* "the others") refers to the whole church.[3] Support for the former view is sought in the parallels between Paul's instructions regarding the regulation of tongues and prophecy in 1 Corinthians 12-14. Gillespie argues that just as tongues are interpreted by the one with the gift of interpretation (cf. 1 Cor 14:5), so also prophecy is to be evaluated by those (i.e. the prophets) with the gift of discerning spirits (cf. 1 Cor 12:10).[4] Many objections stand against this view. Firstly, if Paul confined the activity of weighing to the prophets alone, it would incorrectly imply that all prophets necessarily had the gift of διακρίσεις πνευμάτων (*diakriseis pneumaton,* "discerning of spirits") by virtue of being a prophet. But Paul clearly affirms in 12:10 that the gift was available to any believer and not just to prophets. In fact, in Paul's list, prophecy and διακρίσεις πνευμάτων (*diakriseis pneumaton,* "discerning of spirits") are shown as two distinct gifts. A prophet was not necessarily given the gift of discerning spirits along with the gift of prophecy since the former was not only related to prophecy but had a wider function (as argued above). Secondly, it would create a strange situation in the church where the prophets only are evaluating or weighing

---

[1] Garland, *1 Corinthians,* 662.

[2] Findlay, "First Epistle to the Corinthians," 913; F. W. Grosheide, *The First Epistle to the Corinthians,* NICNT (Grand Rapids: Eerdmans, 1953), 338; Robertson and Plummer, *1 Corinthians,* 322; Calvin, *Corinthians,* 461; Friedrich, *TDNT* 6: 851; Conzelmann, *1 Corinthians*, 244-45; Hill, *Prophecy*, 133; Aune, *Prophecy,* 220-22; Gillespie, *First Theologians*, 163.

[3] Cf. Garland, *1 Corinthians,* 663; Barrett, *First Epistle to the Corinthians,* 328; Grudem, *Prophecy,* 55-57; Fee, *First Epistle to the Corinthians,* 694; Forbes, *Prophecy,* 265-68; Carson, *Showing the Spirit,* 126; Hays, *First Corinthians*, 242.

[4] Gillespie, *First Theologians,* 163.

prophecies during worship, while the rest of the congregation sits in silence waiting for the final verdict to come.[1] Thirdly, such understanding would also incorrectly suggest that "the whole text is intended to regulate the activities of the prophets,"[2] while, on the contrary, Paul addresses the entire church throughout chapter 14 (cf. vv. 1, 5, 24, 26, 31, and 39). Fee argues that "it is gratuitous to suggest that the first 'all' means 'all the prophets' while the next two refer to the whole community" (cf. v. 31).[3] In other words, it is unlikely that Paul would suddenly address a special group of prophets in v. 29 without any clarification. Moreover, οἱ ἄλλοι (*hoi alloi,* "the others"] cf. 12:8 and 10) "basically means 'others different from the subject,'" so if Paul really had in mind other or the rest of the prophets, he would rather use οἱ λοίποι ([*hoi loipoi*, "the remaining"] cf. 1 Cor 9:5), which is a more appropriate term, meaning the rest of the prophets.[4] Lastly, since prophecy was intelligible to the whole church, it could be evaluated by everyone (cf. 1 Thess 5:20-21; 1 Cor 2:12-16).[5]

As a clarification, this book suggests that while οἱ ἄλλοι (*hoi alloi,* "the others") includes the whole church in the process of the evaluation of prophecies, it "does not necessarily mean that everyone in the congregation should participate equally in the evaluating process."[6] It is more likely that while the whole church was to be involved in the evaluation process, it would be the leaders (elders) and other gifted individuals (with the gifts of

---

[1] Cf. Grudem, *Prophecy,* 56-57.

[2] Fee, *First Epistle to the Corinthians*, 694. However, Fee sees the weighing confined to those, if not prophets, with the gift of διακρίσεις πνευμάτων (*First Epistle to the Corinthians*, 596-97 [cf. 693-94]).

[3] Fee, *First Epistle to the Corinthians*, 694.

[4] Fee, *First Epistle to the Corinthians*, 694 n. 30 (cf. Barrett, *First Epistle to the Corinthians*, 328; Grudem, *Prophecy*, 60-62).

[5] Garland, *1 Corinthians,* 663 n. 12 (also Hays, *First Corinthians*, 242).

[6] Carson, *Showing the Spirit,* 126-27.

wisdom, knowledge, teaching, and distinguishing between spirits) who would play a leading role in the evaluation process.[1]

Regarding the norms or scale for the weighing and testing of prophecies, Paul does not explicitly recommend anything in particular in 1 Corinthians 12-14. Nevertheless, Garland infers from Paul's letters the following norms that would have been used for the weighting and testing of Corinthian prophecies – 1) whether the prophecies were in accordance with OT Scripture and the tradition and sayings of Jesus (1 Cor 7:10; 9:14; 11:23; 12:3; 15:3); 2) whether they agreed with what the apostles taught and handed on to the Corinthians (1 Cor 7:25; 11:2; 2 Thess 2:15-3:6); 3) whether they manifested sacrificial love for others (1 Cor 13:1-13; 8:1) and promoted the edification of the whole community (1 Cor 14:3-5, 12, 17, 26; cf. 12:7), including the outsiders (1 Cor 14:20-25).[2] Some also see 1 Cor 12:3 (cf. 1 John 4:2-3) as a criterion for discerning prophecies, which could also be a possibility.[3]

In conclusion, Paul expects the Corinthian prophecies to be subject to weighing. He also confirms that Corinthian prophecies, being a congregational form of prophecy, did not have independent authority in or over the church. They were subject to the scrutiny of the church that were to determine, under the guidance of the Spirit, their validity and the sense, in which they were to be accepted.[4] This was not the case with canonical prophecy since the NT church would be subject to the authority of OT canonical prophecy. In fact, the church used what had already been known through the OT (including OT canonical prophecies) and the apostolic teachings (and their prophecies) to evaluate Corinthian prophecies. This is also indicated from the fact that Paul places

---

[1] Cf. Gaffin, *Perspectives,* 70; Ciampa and Rosner, *First Letter to the Corinthians,* 715.

[2] Garland, *1 Corinthians,* 664 (cf. Fee, *First Epistle to the Corinthians,* 693-94; Carson, *Showing the Spirit,* 139; Grudem, *Prophecy,* 61).

[3] Cf. Gaffin, *Perspectives,* 70-71; Fee, *First Epistle to the Corinthians,* 693.

[4] Fee, *First Epistle to the Corinthians*, 694.

the authority of the Corinthian prophets under his own (1 Cor 14:37-38) where Paul asks the Corinthian prophets to accepts his words as absolutely authoritative since "they are a commandment of the Lord" (v. 37). He even warns the Corinthians that if anyone, claiming to be a prophet disregards Paul's words, that person would be disregarded in the church (v. 38). Paul would not do so for OT canonical prophets and their prophecies (e.g. 1 Cor 15:54b-55 [cf. Isa 25:8; Hosea 13:14]) or the NT apostles and canonical prophets (e.g. Acts 21:10-11; 1 Cor 4:9; 15:9; 2 Cor 11:13; Gal 1:17, 19). In other words, no Corinthian prophets or the ones prophesying spoke with unquestionable authority as did the canonical prophets in the Bible. The requirement for weighing of prophecies suggests that the Corinthian speakers were not to be regarded as infallible, like the canonical prophets. All these evidences further confirm that Corinthian prophecy was congregational prophecy and was qualitatively different from canonical prophecy both in content as well as in authority despite certain similarities with it. Paul's instructions in 1 Cor 14:29-32 indicate the same, since Paul is open to the possibility of prophecy being interrupted in the middle and left incomplete (v. 30). Had they consisted of canonical revelation or carried such authority, Paul would not have given such instruction to interrupt the reception of canonical revelation.[1]

4.5 Distinction from Tongues: Interpreted Tongues not Equivalent to Corinthian Prophecy

A further important issue that needs to be clarified about the nature and content of congregational prophecy is the question of whether Paul saw interpreted tongues as equivalent to congregational prophecy. It was discussed in Chapter 2 that some scholars see interpreted tongues as closely related to or as a form of prophecy that brought doctrinal revelations from God like canonical prophecy did, and so ceased with canonical prophecy.[2] Ellis has argued that since a mere act of exhortation "is a form of

[1] Cf. Carson, *Showing the Spirit*, 99; Grudem, *Gift of Prophecy*, 62-63.

[2] Cf. Ferguson, *Holy Spirit*, 212-13, 230; Clowney, *Church*, 255; Robertson, *Final Word*, 27-28; MacArthur, *Charismatic Chaos*, ch 2.

prophecy," tongues in Acts 2:4 (cf. 11, 17) and 19:6 (cf. 10:46) also produce the same result (i.e. exhortation) as prophecy. He therefore concludes that interpreted tongues are equivalent to or a form of prophecy.[1] Tongues in Acts are also mentioned along with prophesying in Acts 19:6 [10:46]) and are seen by Luke and Peter (Acts 2:14-18) as a fulfillment of Joel's prophecy about prophesying. However, contrary to Ellis' claim, nowhere in Acts are tongues connected with any type of "exhortation," but only with doxological praise to God. The content of tongues in Acts 2:11, is "the mighty works of God," being directed to God rather than to people. It is probably the same case in Acts 10:46 and 19:6 since there too tongues appear with prophesying. Ellis' effort to see tongues as identical to prophecy on the basis of their exhortatory nature cannot be supported from Acts since tongues in Acts are Godward doxological praise and not exhortations to humans from God. At best, tongues can be seen as containing similar content as Godward prophecy, which is not exhortatory.

In Chapter 3 too, it was noted that there were certain incidents in the OT where prophesying appeared to have consisted of doxological praise to God (Exod 15:20-21; Num 11:25-29; 1 Sam 10:5-6, 10-13 [cf. 19:20-24]). In the NT, Luke sees Zechariah's doxological praise to God (Luke 1:67-79 [2:25-32]) as prophesying. These exceptions suggest that in rare cases, spontaneous doxological praise to God was seen as a form of prophesying. The book of Acts showed earlier that Luke does not make a tight distinction between speaking in tongues and prophesying, since in his view, prophecy could be Godward doxological praise as was the case with tongues. He interprets the Pentecost tongues as prophesying due to their content, consisting of doxological praise directed to God (Acts 2:11). Hence, it is only the Godward prophesying in Acts that shares a common content with tongues.

---

[1] E. E. Ellis, "The Role of the Christian Prophet in Acts," in *Apostolic History and the Gospel*, ed. W. W. Gasque and Ralph Martin (Grand Rapids: Eerdmans, 1970), 55 n. 1, 56 n. 3, 57-58 (cf. H. Conzelmann, *Die Apostelgeschichte* [Tübingen: Mohr, 1963], 27).

The following distinctions must be highlighted here. Firstly, there is a difference between Godward prophesying in the OT (and the Gospel of Luke) and in Acts. In the OT (and in the Gospel of Luke) such prophecy is without the phenomenon of tongues and was fully intelligible. It was also rare and confined to a few individuals only, and was not the norm of OT prophecy. Secondly, Acts 2 is the only place in the NT where speaking in tongues is identified with Godward prophesying. Even in Acts 10:46 and 19:6, while prophesying is probably Godward, it is distinguished from tongues though mentioned together. Hence, Acts 2 is an exception even within Acts. Thirdly, the identification of tongues with prophesying in Acts 2, is only applied to Godward forms of prophecy and not to humanward prophecy. It is humanward prophecy that is the norm of prophecy in Acts. Fourthly, in all instances of tongues in Acts, it serves as a one-time evidence of the reception and the presence of the Spirit on both Jews and Gentiles alike, and does not appear to be an on-going phenomenon for the edification of individual Christians.[1]

This raises an important question related to the inquiry here, whether tongues in Acts is essentially the same as tongues in 1 Corinthians? Answers to this question are numerous,[2] and the response requires determining the nature of tongues in Acts and in Corinth. The various proposals are as following –1) Tongues were the ability to speak to God in unlearned human languages. This view argues that the necessity for interpretation of γλῶσσα (*glossa*, "tongue or language") in Corinth (1 Cor 14:5, 27-28) shows that it consisted of coherent and actual languages as in Acts 2:11. Moreover, the same term γλῶσσα (*glossa,* "tongue")

[1] Cf. Hodge, *I & II Corinthians,* 251, who also sees it as a symbol of the calling of the Gentiles (cf. Carson, *Showing the Spirit,* 154-55).

[2] See for a discussion on various views, Thiselton, *First Epistle to the Corinthians,* 970-88. For an extended bibliography on the issue, see W. E. Mills, *Glossolalia: A Bibliography* (New York: Edwin Mellen Press, 1989). Also note that due to space limitations, the focus is only on those aspects of tongues that are related to prophecy. As such, other issues regarding this phenomenon would not be covered here.

is used by Luke and Paul, to mean different human languages.[1] Garland argues that Paul's reference to Isa 28:11-12 (cf. 1 Cor 14:21) mentions "foreign languages," which means it was analogous to Corinthian tongues, if not identical[2]; 2) Tongues was the ability to speak to God mostly in unlearned human languages but also in angelic languages. While this view also agrees that since γλῶσσα (*glossa,* "tongue") appears in both Acts and 1 Corinthians and is most commonly used for normal and contemporary human languages, in view of 1 Cor 13:1 and the *Testament of Job* (where Job's three daughters are said to be speaking ecstatically in the angelic dialect), tongues could also be angelic languages;[3] 3) Tongues only consisted of angelic speech. Here, Paul (or the Corinthians) is seen as influenced by the role of angels in Jewish apocalyptic texts or at Qumran (Testament of Job 48-50);[4] 4) Tongues consisted of unintelligible and incoherent ecstatic speech;[5] 5) Tongues consisted of unspeakable "groanings or sighs too deep for words" (cf. Rom 8:26-27);[6] 6) Lastly,

---

[1] See Ferguson, *Holy Spirit*, 213 (also Calvin, *Corinthians,* 403; Hodge, *I & II Corinthians,* 249; R. H. Gundry, "'Ecstatic Utterances' [NEB]?," *JTS* 17 [1966]: 299-307; J. G. Davies, "Pentecost and Glossolalia," *JTS* 3 (1952): 228-31; Garland, *1 Corinthians*, 583).

[2] Garland, *1 Corinthians*, 584.

[3] Cf. Ciampa and Rosner, *First Epistle to the Corinthians,* 574, 583, 585-86; Forbes, *Prophecy*, 60-61.

[4] Cf. Fee, *First Epistle to the Corinthians,* 598; Barrett, *First Epistle to the Corinthians,* 286, 299-300; Conzelmann, *1 Corinthians*, 209; G. Dautzenberg, "Zum religionsgeschichtlichen Hintergrund der Διάκρισις πνευμάτων (1 Kor 12:10)," *Biblische Zeitschrift* 15 (1971): 93-104; Dunn, *Jesus and the Spirit*, 244; Ellis, *Prophecy and Hermeneutics,* 63-71; D. Martin, "Tongues of Angels and other Status Indicators," *JAAR* 59 (1991): 574 (cf. 547-89); Witherington, *Conflict and Community*, 258; Hays, *First Corinthians,* 212; R. Collins, *First Corinthians,* Sacra Pagina 7 (Collegeville, Minn.: Liturgical Press, 1999), 456; Paul W. Barnett, *1 Corinthians*, Focus on the Bible (Ross-shire: Christian Focus, 2000), 243.

[5] Cf. Morris, *I Corinthians,* 172-73.

[6] Cf. R. Bultmann, *The Theology of the New Testament,* vol 1, trans. K. Grobel (New York: Scribner, 1951), 223; K. Stendahl, "Glossolalia and the Charismatic Movement," in *God's Christ and His People: Studies in Honor of*

there is Theissen's innovative view that argues that tongues is "the language of the unconscious which becomes capable of consciousness through interpretation," and is likely to constitute "socially learned behaviour."[1]

This book affirms the first view that tongues, most probably, consisted of real human unlearned languages, not just in Acts 2 but also in 1 Corinthians. Paul's reference to "tongues of angels" is "a hyperbolic expression to denote what is singular or distinguished ... referring to the diversity of languages"[2] and "the Corinthians' estimation of this gift."[3] Garland supports this by pointing out that since the second ἐάν (*ean,* "if") is absent in 13:1, "speaking in the tongues of angels may be an exaggeration of speaking in the tongues of humans."[4] Wallace, likewise, argues that since Paul is building his argument from "the actual (he does have prophetic powers) to the hypothetical (he does not understand all mysteries nor have all knowledge) ... It is therefore probable that Paul could speak in the tongues of human beings, but *not* in the tongues of *angels* (v. 1). 1 Cor 13:1, then, offers no comfort for those who view tongues as a heavenly language."[5] Moreover, if tongues consisted of angelic dialects or heavenly language, it is not clear why they should cease at the *eschaton* (1 Cor 13:8-10).

This means that tongues in Acts and in 1 Corinthians were essentially the same phenomenon. In both places, they were Godward and shared similar content (i.e. doxological praise to

---

Nils Alstrup Dahl, eds., J. Jervell and W. A. Meeks (Olso: Universitetsforlaget, 1977), 111; F. D. Macchia, "Sighs Too Deep for Words: Toward a Theology of Glossolalia," *JPT* 1 (1992): 47-73.

[1] Gerd Theissen, *Pshychological Aspects of Pauline Theology,* trans. J. P. Galvin (Edinburgh: T & T Clark, 1987), 79, 292 (cf. 59-114; 276-341); also Thiselton, *First Epistle to the Corinthians,* 988, 1100.

[2] Calvin, *Corinthians,* 419 (also Carson, *Showing the Spirit*, 52-53; cf. Thiselton, *First Epistle to the Corinthians,* 1061).

[3] Craig Bloomberg, *1 Corinthians,* NIV Application Commentary (Grand Rapids: Eerdmans, 1994), 259.

[4] Garland, *1 Corinthians,* 610 n. 7.

[5] Daniel B. Wallace, *Greek Grammar beyond the Basics: An Exegetical Syntax of the New Testament* (Grand Rapids: Zondervan, 1996), 698.

God, Acts 2:11 [cf. 1 Cor 14:2, 15-17]). The only addition in 1 Corinthians is that Paul also sees tongues as a form of prayer, along with offering praise to God (14:14-15).[1] In both places, it is a gift for believers and is not an evangelistic tool. The audience in Acts 2 does not come to faith by hearing tongues speakers but by listening to Peter's preaching (Acts 2:37 [cf. 14-41]). Even in Acts 10:44-46 (and Acts 19:4-6) speaking in tongues happens only as a result of hearing and believing the gospel. Similarly, an unbeliever comes to faith through hearing prophecy, not through tongues (1 Cor 14:22-23).

A difficult difference between Acts and 1 Corinthians is the frequency of the phenomenon. In 1 Corinthians tongues is an ongoing phenomenon experienced by believers as a gift of the Spirit, whereas in Acts it appears to be a onetime experience of believers at the reception of the Holy Spirit. This suggests that tongues functioned differently in Acts than in Corinth. In Acts it primarily served as an initial confirmatory visible sign of the Spirit's reception and of Gentile inclusion, in 1 Corinthians it serves as a gift of the Spirit for an individual's personal edification. Another difference between the two is often seen in the fact that tongues in Acts 2 did not require interpretation as did tongues in Corinth. This can easily be explained. It can be argued that in Acts 2 there was no need for any interpretation since the believers there spoke in the various languages of those present from different nations (Acts 2:9-11). The audience could understand the tongues speakers. However, it does not mean that each of the spectators understood each of the tongues speakers, but only those who spoke in their particular native language. The tongues in Acts 10:46 and 19:6 also do not give any clues as to whether there was interpretation needed or available. They only tell that those present saw it as a sign of the Holy Spirit being poured upon new Christians.[2] The lack of the requirement of interpretation for tongues in Acts could also be due to its specific purpose since in Acts it does not appear to be an ongoing edifying activity as is the

---

[1] Carson, *Showing the Spirit,* 154.

[2] See Carson, *Showing the Spirit,* 154.

case in Corinth. Moreover, interpretation of tongues in Corinth was also needed only when the gift of tongues was to be exercised in public worship and not when exercised in private.

In regard to the question, whether Paul saw tongues as a form of prophecy, there is no indication of such in the text since Paul describes Corinthian congregational prophecy as humanward, not Godward. In fact, Paul makes a strict distinction between tongues and prophecy in 1 Corinthians 14. He describes tongues primarily addressed to God as prayer and praise/thanksgiving (14:2, 14-17, 28), consisting of μυστήρια ([*musteria,* "mysteries"] 14:3).[1] It was already seen that the nature or content of μυστήρια (*musteria,* "mysteries") in tongues is unclear,[2] but they were probably distinct from μυστήρια (*musteria,* "mysteries") associated with prophecy in 13:2.[3] Thiselton affirms there can be no doubt whatever that contrary to prophecy as addresses from God to the community or to individuals within the assembled church, tongues are discourses from believers to God.[4] Furthermore, unlike prophecy as completely intelligible and edifying to the whole church, even unbelievers (14:3, 4, 6, 31, 24-25), tongues were unintelligible both to the speaker (14:14) and the hearers (14:16, 23, 27) since the tongues speakers spoke in languages unknown to the hearers.

---

[1] Cf. Garland, *1 Corinthians*, 584; Fee, *First Epistle to the Corinthians,* 598 (cf. 656); Dunn, *Jesus and the Spirit,* 245; Thiselton, *First Epistle to the Corinthians,* 1085; Carson, *Showing the Spirit,* 107; Simon J. Kistemaker, *I Corinthians,* NTC (Grand Rapids: Baker, 1993), 477; Ciampa and Rosner, *First Letter to the Corinthian*, 670.

[2] Various suggestions have been made regarding the contents of such mysteries but without much success. However, most scholars agree that it has to do with secrets or hidden truths that only God and the speaker share but can be understood only by those with the gift of interpretation (See Carson, *Showing the Spirit*, 104; Ciampa and Rosner, *First Letter to the Corinthians*, 671).

[3] Cf. Ciampa and Rosner, *First Letter to the Corinthians,* 631 (cf. 671); Fee, *First Epistle to the Corinthians,* 656; Thiselton, *First Epistle to the Corinthians,* 1085).

[4] Thiselton, *First Epistle to the Corinthians*, 970-71 (also Forbes, *Prophecy*, 92-102).

Furthermore, tongues benefitted primarily the speaker (14:4, 17),[1] and only indirectly and rarely the hearers if interpreted (14:5). Fee points out that even "what is 'interpreted' is not speech directed towards others, but the 'mysteries' spoken to God."[2] In other words, interpreted tongues can edify the church, not because they are addressed to the church but simply because what the speaker has been speaking to God is now made intelligible so that others can also benefit from it indirectly. Ciampa and Rosner point out that "such edification presumably takes place as people are ministered to by the content of the prayer or praise that is offered, just as they are when people offer prayer or praise to God (in normal voice or in song) apart from any form of tongues."[3] This indirect edifying function of tongues does not make it identical to prophecy or as functioning the same as prophecy. The audiences in each activity are totally opposite: God is addressed in the former and humans in the latter. This also suggests that tongues and Corinthian prophecy contained different types of revelations. In the former, it was primarily praise and prayers (and some sort of mysteries), whereas in the latter it was always didactic. Nowhere in 1 Corinthians 12-14, does Paul suggest any resemblance or functional similarity between tongues and prophecy.[4] Garland's view (based on Godet) that through interpretation "glossolalia is transformed into prophecy,"[5] overlooks the fact that the audiences as well as the content of the two activities were complete opposites. Even Carson, who also suggests that "tongues can have the same functional significance as prophecy" with interpretation,

---

[1] It is hard to know how mysteries can edify the speaker if they are unintelligible to them (cf. 14:14). Thus, Fee suggests that "spiritual edification can take place in ways other than through the cortex of the brain" (Fee, *First Epistle to the Corinthians*, 656).

[2] Fee, *First Epistle to the Corinthians*, 598.

[3] Ciampa and Rosner, *First Letter to the Corinthians*, 677.

[4] See Fee, *First Epistle to the Corinthians*, 659.

[5] Garland, *1 Corinthians*, 635 (cf. Godet, *First Epistle of St Paul to the Corinthians*, II, 269).

agrees that it does not make tongues identical to prophecy.[1] It is concluded, therefore, that Paul did not see interpreted tongues identical to Corinthian prophecy, but only occasionally and indirectly edifying to the whole church if interpreted.

4.6 The Cessation or Continuation of Congregational Prophecy (1 Cor 13:8-10)

Having defined the nature, function, and possible content of Corinthian congregational prophecy above, it is most important to ask the question of its cessation or continuation in the post-apostolic church and today. It was stated in Chapters 1 and 2 that canonical prophecy ceased with the completion of the NT Scripture. The main query here has been to decide whether this was also the case for congregational prophecy. Does Paul ever indicate in 13:8-10 a particular time of the cessation of Corinthian congregational prophecy (and other gifts) before the coming of the τέλειον (*teleion*, "complete, perfect, mature" in 1 Cor 13:10)? This text has been greatly debated among scholars, being used by both the cessationists and the continuationists to support their respective views. The key word here is τέλειον (*teleion,* "perfect") which is a *crux interpretum* in determining the time of the cessation or continuation of congregational prophecy. In other words, what Paul meant by τέλειον (*teleion,* "perfect") and what it referred to.

A good number of views exist in regard to the meaning of τελειον (*teleion,* "perfect"). Three main views are considered here.[2] It has been traditionally held by some cessationists that τέλειον (*teleion,* "perfect") in 13:10 refers to the completion of the NT canon since once the full revelation had been given in the NT the partial forms of revelation (i.e. prophecy and tongues) disappeared.[3] Gromacki argues that the τέλειον

[1] Carson, *Showing the Spirit,* 105.

[2] For other views, see Farnell, "When Will the Gift," 191 n. 66.

[3] Cf. Gentry, *Gift of Prophecy,* 54; Gromacki, *Modern Tongues Movement*, 125-26; John F. Walvoord, *The Holy Spirit*, 168-88; Unger, *The Baptism and Gifts*, 141-42; Ferguson, *Holy Spirit,* 227; Robert L. Thomas, "Tongues ... Will

(*teleion,* "perfect") refers to something that is "partially here now, is presently developing, and one day will become complete. This word fits the concept of the progressive revelation of the New Testament."[1] He agrees that τέλειον (*teleion,* "perfect") in the NT usually refers to the perfection or maturity of the believers (the church) but he argues that such maturity was achieved when the NT canon was completed.[2] This view has become increasingly less popular among modern exegetes and is considered hermeneutically questionable even by some cessationists.[3] Garland points out that this view "is driven more by the intent to limit the validity of tongues to the apostolic age than by any credible historical analysis."[4] The main arguments against this view are as follows[5] –

1) Paul had no idea of the formation of a canon after the death of the apostles. In fact, he seems to expect the *parousia* to happen in his lifetime (1 Thess 4:15-16; 1 Cor 15:51). Fee declares that "it is an impossible view … since Paul himself could not have articulated it."[6]
2) Similarly, it is unlikely that Paul expected the Corinthian church to understand τέλειον (*teleion,* "perfect") as referring to the completed canon of Scripture. The idea of a canon of Scripture would have been alien to the Corinthians.
3) The expression "face to face" in v. 12b does not fit with this view since no one sees God "face to face" (cf. Num 12:8) or knows him perfectly. The knowledge of him and

---

Cease," *JETS* 17 (1974): 81-89. Douglas Judisch, *An Evaluation of Claims to the Charismatic Gifts* (Grand Rapids: Baker Press, 1978).

[1] Gromacki, *Modern Tongues Movement*, 125-26.

[2] Gromacki, *Modern Tongues Movement*, 125-26.

[3] Cf. Gaffin, *Perspectives,* 109; Farnell, "When Will the Gift," 191 n. 66; Hodge, *I & II Corinthians,* 271-73; Calvin, *Corinthians,* 425-29.

[4] Garland, *1 Corinthians,* 622.

[5] See Turner, *Holy Spirit,* 286, for further critique.

[6] Fee, *First Epistle to the Corinthians,* 645 n. 23.

heavenly things is still imperfect and incomplete even with the Scripture available (v. 9).

4) This view incorrectly assumes that prophecy was essential for writing the NT Scripture, and so ceased when the NT was completed. Chapters 1 and 3 demonstrated that the gift of prophecy was not always needed for the writing of Scripture. In fact, not all prophecy was recorded in Scripture.

The second widely-held interpretation regards τέλειον (*teleion,* "perfect") as a process that leads to the maturation of the Church.[1] M. Miguens has argued that the three contrasts: partial/complete, infancy/adulthood, now/then, refer to the gradual development of the Christian life.[2] Therefore, Paul expected these gifts to pass away soon, since they hinder growing in love (maturity). Lexically this view is possible since τέλειον (*teleion,* "perfect") could literally mean "perfect" (with ethical reference)[3] and Paul's illustration of v. 11 (child vs. man) seems to support it. However, such perfection cannot be achieved before the *parousia* as proposed by this view. Forbes points out that even a clear passage about the maturation of the church, such as in Eph 4:13 (cf. Col 1:27-28), points to an eschatological situation, not a pre-*parousia* temporal maturity.[4] Turner clarifies that the point of the illustration in 13:11 is not to suggest that the apostolic church would transform believers into perfect people on earth where knowledge would no longer be ἐκ μέρους (*ek merous*, "in part or partial" [cf. v. 9-10]). On the contrary, it shows that the church's existence on earth is "characterised by partial knowledge," in comparison with the perfection to

[1] Cf. J. R. McRay, "To *Teleion* in 1 Corinthians 13:10," *RestQ* 14 (1971): 168-83; Thomas, *Understanding Spiritual Gifts*, 123, 202-203; Donald G. MacDougall, "Cessationism in 1 Corinthians 13:8-12," *TMSJ 14* (2003): 177-213; also Farnell, "When Will the Gift," 192-95, who tries to incorporate in this view the third view as well.

[2] M. Miguens, "1 Cor 13:8-13 Reconsidered," *CBQ* 37 (1975): 87 (cf. 76-97).

[3] See H. Hubner, "τέλειος," *EDNT* 3: 343.

[4] Forbes, *Prophecy,* 88-91 (cf. Turner, *Holy Spirit,* 287).

be possessed "when the kingdom is fully realised."[1] Garland explains that Paul's purpose through his discussion in chapter 13 was not "to persuade the Corinthians to abandon their prized spiritual gifts ... (but) to convince them to employ the gifts with love" since the gifts "are neither essential for, nor indicative of, Christian maturity in an individual," but are only "necessary for the functioning of the (church)."[2]

An increasingly popular view today is the eschatological interpretation of τέλειον (*teleion,* "perfect"), where it refers to either the *Parousia* or, more specifically, to "the state of affairs brought about by the arrival of the *parousia*."[3] Carson prefers to call it a state "*related to parousia* rather than *parousia* itself, because some have objected that the word *parousia* is feminine, whereas the word for *perfection* is masculine."[4] Hence, it is concluded that prophecy and tongues would continue until the *parousia* that will usher in the new heaven and new earth. Support for this view is found in the following – 1) The phrase "face to face" (v. 12b; cf. 1 John 3:2b) is best explained "as being with God in the new heavens and new earth since it is in glory that we will know as we are known (v. 12)";[5] 2) Not only the meaning of τέλειον (*teleion,* "perfect") as "perfect" best describes the period

---

[1] Turner, *Holy Spirit,* 287.

[2] Garland, *1 Corinthians,* 622.

[3] Carson, *Showing the Spirit,* 69 (also see Garland, *1 Corinthians,* 622; Grudem, *Prophecy,* 210-21; Jon Ruthven, *On the Cessation of the Charismata: The Protestant Polemic on Post-Biblical Miracles* (Sheffield: Sheffield Academic, 1993), 138-51; Forbes, *Prophecy,* 85-91; Grosheide, *First Epistle to the Corinthians,* 309-310; Robertson and Plummer, *I Corinthians,* 297 (cf. 299-300); Barrett, *First Epistle to the Corinthians,* 306; Fee, *First Epistle to the Corinthians,* 646; Conzelmann, *First Epistle to the Corinthians,* 226; Gaffin, *Perspectives*, 109; MacArthur, *Charismatic Chaos,* 230 n. 20; Clowney, *Church,* 249-50; W. W. Klein "Perfect, Mature," *DPHL*, 699-701; Stanley D. Toussaint, "First Corinthians Thirteen and the Tongues Questions," *BSac* 120 (1963): 311-16; Turner, *Holy Spirit,* 288; F. F. Bruce, *1 and 2 Corinthians*, NCB (London, 1971), 127-28; also almost similar are Calvin, *Corinthians*, 428 and Hodge, *I & II Corinthians,* 272-74.

[4] Carson, *Showing the Spirit,* 69-70.

[5] MacArthur, *Charismatic Chaos,* 230 n. 20 (also Clowney, *Church*, 250).

after Christ's return, but ἔλθῃ (*elthe,* "to come") carries the idea of the precise moment of Christ's second coming;[1] 3) Complete maturity of believers, in Paul's letters, is often connected to the end time (Col 1:5, 22, 27-28) and not as something to be fully realised prior to the *parousia*; 4) Paul and other NT writers use the related term τέλος (*telos,* "end") to refer to the second coming (Rom 8:18-30; 1 Cor 1:7-8; 15:24; Matt 24:6, 13-14). Wright's suggestion that the whole of chapter 13 "looks forward … to … resurrection, the new world"[2] also supports the view that τέλειον (*teleion,* "perfect") refers to the coming of the new heaven and new earth and not to anything else.

While the first two views specifically represent the cessationist view of prophecy from two different perspectives, the third view includes almost all continuationists and also a few cessationists.[3] This book agrees with the third view and proposes that Paul did not indicate the cessation of congregational prophecy in 1 Cor 13:8-12. On the contrary, the text appears to support the continuation of congregational prophecy until the second coming of Christ. The text below confirms this.

Paul's main purpose in chapter 13 is not to set a particular time for the cessation of spiritual gifts but to demonstrate the temporary nature of spiritual gifts (particularly the gifts of tongues, prophecy, and knowledge [vv. 8b-9] that were highly esteemed by the Corinthians), as opposed to the permanence of love.[4] Paul looks at the three gifts "from an eschatological perspective" and sees them limited to this side of the *eschaton*.[5] Fee suggests that the notion that gifts will pass away forms the heart of the entire

---

[1] See Godet, *First Epistle to the Corinthians,* II, 252, for further details.

[2] N. T. Wright, *The Resurrection of the Son of God* (Minneapolis: Fortress Press, 2003), 296.

[3] Cessationists like Gaffin do not base the cessation of prophecy (and tongues) on 1 Cor 13:8-12 (see Gaffin, *Perspectives,* 89-116).

[4] Cf. Garland, *1 Corinthians,* 621; Thiselton, *First Epistle to the Corinthians,* 1060; Ciampa and Rosner, *First Letter to the Corinthians,* 624; Farnell, "When Will the Gift," 191; Calvin, *Corinthians,* 418.

[5] Garland, *1 Corinthians,* 623 (also Hodge, *I & II Corinthians,* 271).

argument (vv. 8b-12).[1] Paul clearly affirms this in v. 8 as gifts are temporary and will pass away since they are given only for between the times, i.e., for the "church's present eschatological existence."[2] The verse presents a chiastic structure where the same verb (καταργέω [*katargeo,* "to abolish"]) is used to describe what will happen to prophecies and to knowledge but a different verb (παύσονται [*pausontai*, "to cease"]) for tongues.[3] The term καταργέω (*katargeo*, "pass away or cease," BDAG, 417) has an eschatological connotation and has been used by Paul in his letters to refer to that which does not "survive the transition from this age into the fullness of the age to come (1:28; 2:6; 6:13; 13:8, 10; 15:24, 26; 2 Thess 2:8)," similar to "the day of the LORD" (Isa 13:6-13; 65:17; 66:22; Joel 1:15-2:11; 3:14-16) in the OT and in Jewish apocalyptic.[4] In other words, it describes the temporal, transitory nature of spiritual gifts. Garland also insists that καταργέω (*katargeo,* "to abolish") indicates that the gifts "are not permanent and do not get perfected."[5] Therefore, the use of καταργηθησεται (*katargethesetai,* "will be abolished") in v. 10 supports the view that τέλειον (*teleion,* "perfect") has to do with eschatology, "not with maturity of some kind,"[6] or completion of the NT canon. Furthermore, the passive καταργηθήσονται (*katargethesontai,* "they will be abolished") and καταργηθήσεται (*katargethesetai,* "it will be abolished" in v. 8) do not mean that prophecies and knowledge will cease on their own at some point of time in the future. They are brought to an end by an external force, i.e., the *eschaton* (τέλειον [*teleion,* "perfect"]).[7]

The verb παύσονται (*pausontai,* "to cease") for tongues (middle voice) at first appears to suggest that tongues will "stop" of their own accord (BDAG, 638) or come to an end, rather than

---

[1] Fee, *First Epistle to the Corinthians,* 642.

[2] Fee, *First Epistle to the Corinthians,* 643.

[3] Ciampa and Rosner, *First Epistle to the Corinthians*, 653.

[4] Ciampa and Rosner, *First Epistle to the Corinthians,* 653-54.

[5] Garland, *1 Corinthians*, 621.

[6] Fee, *First Epistle to the Corinthians*, 643-44.

[7] Thiselton, *The First Epistle to the Corinthians*, 1061.

"be stilled" (BDAG) by an external force (τέλειον [*teleion*, "perfect"]).[1] For this reason, some suggest that the middle voice indicates that tongues would come to an end on their own before prophecies and knowledge cease.[2] Wallace argues that "if the voice of the verb here is significant, then Paul is saying … that tongues will … more likely, cease of their own accord, i.e., 'die out' without an intervening agent (indirect middle)."[3] He further points out that Paul uses the passive voice of καταργέω (*katargeo,* "to abolish") in regard to prophecy and knowledge, and also for μέρους ([*merous,* "partial"] v. 10) where it is used in relation to its passing away when the τέλειον (*teleion,* "perfect") comes. Since in vv. 9-10 only prophecy and knowledge (not tongues) are mentioned in relation to the passing away of μέρους (*merous,* "partial") at the coming of τέλειον (*teleion,* "perfect"), Wallace concludes, only "tongues were to have 'died out' of their own before the perfect comes."[4] However, he also recognises that the middle voice used for tongues in 13:8 still does not necessarily prove that tongues have already ceased since the verse does not "address when tongues would cease."[5] In other words, while prophecy and knowledge will be brought to an end only by the coming of the τέλειον (*teleion*, "perfect" i.e., the *parousia*), παυσονται (*pausontai,* "it will cease") indicates that tongues could cease on their own at any time since they do not need an agent (i.e. τέλειον [*teleion,* "perfect"]) to bring them to an end. The issue is whether tongues have already ceased at some point in history or will cease in future at some indefinite time before the coming of the τέλειον (*teleion,* "perfect"). This is not addressed in the text. In any case, even if Wallace's suggestion is followed in regard to tongues, the cessation of prophecy is not indicated in

---

[1] Wallace, *Greek Grammar*, 422-23.

[2] See Toussaint, "First Corinthians Thirteen," 311-16; MacArthur, *Charismatic Chaos,* 230 n. 20; also idem, *1 Corinthians* (Chicago: B M H C Press, 1984), 359.

[3] Wallace, *Greek Grammar*, 422. Suspension points mine.

[4] Wallace, *Greek Grammar*, 422-23.

[5] Wallace, *Greek Grammar*, 422-23.

the text before the coming of the τέλειον (*teleion,* "perfect"). In other words, even if tongues have already ceased, though there is no way to know that, prophecy ceases only at the *eschaton*.

On the other hand, some argue that this grammatical structure cannot be taken to support the notion that the cessation of tongues has taken place already. Ciampa and Rosner claim that the middle voice, παύσονται (*pausontai,* "it will cease"), does not necessarily indicate that tongues would cease or stop "at any point in time other than ... at the final consummation."[1] The support for this is sought in γάρ ([*gar*, "for"] v. 9), which not only applies to prophecy and knowledge but also to tongues since it indicates why the three gifts in v. 8 will come to an end. As such, γάρ (*gar,* "for") introduces vv. 9-10 as the basis for Paul's statement in v. 8 about the temporary nature of the gifts.[2] Another support for this is found in the fact that the three gifts are representative of all the spiritual gifts and are only used here as examples. What applies to the three gifts also applies to other gifts.[3] This means when the τελειον (*teleion,* "perfect") comes, not just the three, but all spiritual gifts will cease since they would no longer be needed. The reason for the different verbs and voices is only for stylistic (rhetorical) purposes to add and create "more chiasm" in the passage.[4]

While the latter argument seems to be more convincing, neither of the two suggests that Corinthian prophecy either has ceased or will cease in the future at some time before the coming of the τελειον (*teleion,* "perfect"). In fact, the debate regarding the cessation of tongues does not address the debate between cessationists and non-cessationists regarding the time of its cessation since Paul simply states that like prophecy and

---

[1] Ciampa and Rosner, *First Letter to the Corinthians,* 655 (Suspension points mine); also Carson, *Showing the Spirit*, 66-67.

[2] See Ciampa and Rosner, *First Letter to the Corinthians*, 655; Garland, *1 Corinthians,* 622; Fee, *First Epistle to the Corinthians*, 644.

[3] Ciampa and Rosner, *First Letter to the Corinthians*, 655-56 (cf. Fee, *First Epistle to the Corinthians*, 643 n. 17; Garland, *1 Corinthians,* 622 n. 13.

[4] Ciampa and Rosner, *First Letter to the Corinthians*, 655.

knowledge, tongues too will become redundant either sometime before or at the last day. What is evident is simply that prophecy ceases at the *eschaton*, not any time before that.

4.7 Conclusion

This chapter has endeavored to define the nature, function, and possible content of Corinthian prophecy along with the question of its continuation or cessation. It sought to prove from the biblical text that Corinthian congregational prophecy was a common gift of the Spirit exercised in the Corinthian church. Any Corinthian believer was eligible to prophesy; hence it was the congregational form of prophecy, not the canonical. This also makes the Corinthian congregational prophecy the dominant form of prophecy in all post-Pentecost churches.

It has been shown that Corinthian prophecy was deeply rooted in revelation but did not bring new doctrinal revelation for inscripturation like canonical prophecy. Due to its revelatory nature, it was also both spontaneous and essentially distinct from preaching and teaching though it may include a teaching and preaching aspect or outcome. It was also distinct from the Spirit's work of illumination.

Some of the possible content of the Corinthian prophecy has been indicated, namely that it was diverse, ranging from reiteration of doctrinal truths and their applications for general edification of the church to addressing specific issues and situations. It has been pointed out that though other speech gifts could also produce the same results as Corinthian prophecy and even have similar content, the revelatory nature of Corinthian prophecy makes it a unique activity of the Spirit. It has been observed that though Corinthian prophecy could include gospel-proclamation and convert unbelievers, it was primarily a church phenomenon, addressed to the church.

Corinthian prophecy was subject to evaluation and testing by the whole church. The standard for such evaluation was mainly the written OT Scripture and the apostolic traditions. Moreover, Corinthian prophecy was also subjected to the apostolic authority.

This confirms that it was unlike canonical prophecy since it was subjected to the OT. The apostles would not subject canonical prophecy to their apostolic authority.

This book rejects the view that interpreted tongues could be identified with congregational prophecy. The text shows that the two were completely different phenomena, addressed to different targets and with different types of content. Moreover, while there was a Godward form of prophecy in Acts, Corinthian prophecy was strictly humanward.

And lastly, but not least, it has been made evident that Paul does not indicate the cessation of Corinthian congregational prophecy in the text but rather sees it continuing until the *parousia.*

Conclusion

This book has endeavored to define the nature and function of prophecy as discussed in 1 Corinthians 12-14. It argued that due to the non-inscripturation of this prophecy and to its function, Corinthian prophecy was the "congregational form" of prophecy, and, as a gift of the Spirit, it was potentially available to every believer whether a prophet or not. In doing so, it proposed a redefined understanding of Corinthian prophecy that can build bridges between the three popular views on Corinthian prophecy without challenging the sufficiency and absolute authority of written Scripture.

To this end, Chapter 1 argued that there were two forms of prophetic revelation operating in the NT: canonical and non-canonical prophecy. The former was inscripturated and was ordinarily limited to those known as prophets and apostles. It often consisted of new doctrinal, redemptive revelation. This form of prophecy came to an end when the NT Scriptures were completed, at which point no new doctrinal revelation was needed. In addition to canonical, there was another form of prophecy in the post-Pentecost NT church that was not meant for inscripturation but provided specific guidance and edification to the church often based on previously revealed truths. This book labels this second form of prophecy as "congregational" or "non-canonical" prophecy. It was exercised in the Corinthian church and in other NT churches as the dominant form of prophecy, and it still continues today. Since, congregational prophecy was subjected to canonical prophecy (which comprised part of Scripture), there is a qualitative difference between the two forms of prophecy in regard to their authority and content.

The proposed view in this book also found support for congregational prophecy through a survey of relevant scholarship in Chapter 2. It was noted that several scholars who hold to the cessation of canonical prophecy, propose a non-canonical form of prophecy in the NT. Furthermore, it also noted that Corinthian prophecy is not identical to preaching and teaching.

Having discussed the theological debates among NT scholars on Corinthian prophecy, this book looked at the biblical data on prophecy in Chapter 3. This survey of biblical data has provided support to this book's assertions that OT prophecy was normally humanward and was largely confined to those designated as prophets. Its content consisted of both new and previous revelation that became inscripturated in the OT. On the other hand, there was also a Godward form of prophecy among the "sons of the prophets" and some individuals not known as prophets. It was rare and only found in the Pentateuch and in the historical books but absent in the latter prophets. Its content consisted of doxological praise to God and was not inscripturated. There is also a hint of non-canonical congregational type prophecy operating during the intertestamental period.

The NT found similarities and differences from the OT phenomena of prophecy. There are occasional occurrences in the NT of Godward prophesying in Luke-Acts similar to the OT phenomenon, although this is absent in the later books of the NT, including 1 Corinthians. Furthermore, there is the canonical type of prophecy (that brought new doctrinal, redemptive revelation and predictions to be inscripturated) in the NT similar to that found in the OT. This canonical NT prophecy was limited to a few individuals known as prophets and the apostles. On the contrary, most other references to prophecy in the NT epistles concern a form of prophecy that is not confined to prophets alone but was common among believers. This is the congregational prophecy that Paul discusses in 1 Corinthians, and elsewhere, as one of the gifts of the Spirit. The fact that none of the Corinthian prophecies was inscripturated in the NT supports there being a congregational form of prophecy. Indeed, a result of the Spirit's coming upon the Church on the day of Pentecost was the beginning of a new prophetic era under the new covenant as predicted by the prophet Joel. In the NT era, congregational prophecy became widely distributed and practised in NT churches.

Having established the distinction between canonical and congregational prophecy in the biblical data in Chapter 3, it attempted to define the main features, function, and possible content of congregational prophecy in the text of 1 Corinthians 12-14. The approach was to allow the text to control and define the nature of Corinthian prophecy, being supported and further explained by other non-Corinthian biblical texts. It identified the high priority texts in 1 Corinthians 12-14 as those that mention the phenomenon of prophecy. These texts were divided into six categories that defined the features, function or possible content of Corinthian congregational prophecy. They affirmed that Corinthian prophecy:

1) was a common gift of the Spirit exercised in the Corinthian church by believers;
2) was revelatory and distinct from preaching, teaching, illumination, though having some overlap with them in function;
3) was diverse and responsive in content covering reiteration of previously known doctrinal truths, rather than the prediction of future events, with applications to specific issues;
4) was subject to weighing and apostolic authority;
5) was distinct from the phenomenon of tongues;
6) was not to cease, in Paul's understanding, before the coming of the new state of affairs brought by the *parousia.*

It summarizes then, that Corinthian congregational prophecy consisted of spontaneous revelations given by the Spirit to any believer to be proclaimed in the church to provide specific guidance and edification for the whole body, having diverse content from general to specific nature. Such prophetic revelations did not add anything to written Scripture, rather they re-affirmed and applied scriptural truths to specific situations that were not directly addressed in Scripture.

There are a few pastoral and theological implications to this reconstruction of Corinthian prophecy. Since it has been established that congregational prophecy did not bring any new doctrinal or redemptive revelation to be inscripturated in the NT, the assertions that the continuation of prophecy denies the doctrine of the sufficiency of Scripture loses force. Joel's prophecy (2:28-29), fulfilled on the day of Pentecost, does not only cover the first century period but "the last days" (Acts 2:17) that are continuing until the second coming of Christ ("in those days I will pour out my Spirit, and they shall prophesy," [Acts 2:18]). It has been argued by some cessationists that in the absence of written Scripture in the first century Corinthian church, such prophetic revelations were needed to guide and edify the church. Such an argument does not provide a logical support to the cessation of congregational prophecy since there are difficult situations to which Scripture needs to be applied with direct specificity. It also incorrectly assumes that Scripture was and is the only way that God uses to speak to his people. The Scripture is undeniably sufficient and is the absolute authority for the church in matters of faith and life. It has been the God-given source to provide guidance and edification to the church throughout history. However, it does not mean that God has not spoken in the past or cannot speak today to people outside of written Scripture. The Holy Spirit, who was active in the Corinthian and the first century churches, has been active in the church throughout history. The Spirit still endows Christians with various gifts to serve the church. If congregational prophecy is a gift of the Spirit, there is no reason why it should not be available to believers today. Furthermore, it was seen that the gift of prophecy was not restricted to the office of a prophet. Prophecy as a gift was available to believers then and is still available to believers now. The gift can function without the office.

While written Scripture is sufficient for Christians today, and is the ultimate authority by which all prophecies must be weighed, there are pastoral circumstances of a specific nature that are not always addressed in Scripture directly. Accepting the Scripture's silence on many specific issues does not challenge its sufficiency or authority. Even the WCF (I. VI), while affirming the sufficiency of Scripture "concerning all things necessary for … man's salvation, faith and life," leaves room for the "new revelations of the Spirit" to come that are not "to be added" to Scripture but can provide specific guidance and edification to the church and individuals. The completion of Scripture does not stop the Spirit's work of guiding and edifying the Church "as he wills" (1 Cor 12:11). Congregational prophecy is one of such means.

Bibliography

Aune, D. E. *Prophecy in Early Christianity and the Ancient Mediterranean World*. Grand Rapids: Eerdmans. 1983.

Baker, D. L. "The Interpretation of 1 Corinthians 12-14." *Evangelical Quarterly* 46 (1974): 224-34.

Baker, J. P. "Prophecy, Prophets." Pages 972-74 in *New Bible Dictionary*. Edited by I. Howard Marshall, Millard, Packer, Wiseman. Leicester: IVP, 1996.

Barnett, Paul. W. *The Corinthian Question*. Nottingham: Apollos, 2011.

_______. *1 Corinthians*. Focus on the Bible. Ross-shire: Christian Focus, 2000.

_______. "The Jewish Sign Prophets – A.D. 40-70: Their Intentions and Origin." *New Testament Studies* 27/5 (1981): 679-97.

Barrett, C. K. *The First Epistle to the Corinthians*. Black's New Testament Commentaries; London: Adam & Charles Black, 1971.

Beale, G. K. *The Book of Revelation*. New International Greek Testament Commentary; Grand Rapids: Eerdmans, 1999.

Best, E. "Prophets and Preachers." *Scottish Journal of Theology* 12 (1959): 129-50.

Bittlinger, A. *Gifts and Graces: A Commentary on 1 Corinthians 12-14*. Translated by H. Klassen. London: Hodder and Stoughton, 1967.

Bloomberg, Craig. *1 Corinthians.* NIV Application Commentary; Grand Rapids: Eerdmans, 1994.

Boring, M. E. "What Are We Looking For? Toward a Definition of the Term 'Christian Prophet,'" *SBL Seminar Papers* (Missoula, MT: Society of Biblical Literature, 1973), 135-54.

_______. "Prophecy (Early Christian)." Pages 495-502 in vol. 5 of *Anchor Bible Dictionary*. Edited by D. N. Freedman. 6 vols. New York: Doubleday, 1992.

Bruce, F. F. *The Book of Acts.* New International Commentary of New Testament; Grand Rapids: Eerdmans, 1988.

_______. *1 and 2 Corinthians.* NCB; London, 1971.

Bultmann, R. *The Theology of the New Testament,* vol 1. Translated by K. Grobel. New York: Scribner, 1951.

Callan, T. "Prophecy and Ecstasy in Greco-Roman Religion and 1 Corinthians," *Novum Testamentum* 27 (1985): 125-40.

Calvin, Jean. *Commentary upon the Epistle of Saint Paul to the Romans.* Edinburgh: Calvin Translation Society, 1844.

_______. *Commentary on the Epistles of Paul the Apostle to the Corinthians,* vol. XX.1. Grand Rapids: Baker Press, 2009.

Carson, D. A. *Showing the Spirit: A Theological Exposition of 1 Corinthians 12-14.* Grand Rapids: Apollo, 2010.

_______., and Douglas J. Moo, *An Introduction to the New Testament.* Nottingham: Apollos, 2005.

_______., and John. D. Woodbridge, eds. *Hermeneutics, Authority and Canon.* Leicester: IVP, 1986.

Cartledge, Mark J. "Charismatic Prophecy: A Definition and Description," *Journal of Pentecostal Theology* 5 (1994): 79-120.

Chantry, Walter J. *Signs of the Apostles: Observations on Pentecostalism Old and New.* Carlisle, PA: Banner of Truth, 1976.

Ciampa, Roy E., and Brain S. Rosner. *The First Letter to the Corinthians.* Pillar New Testament Commentary; Grand Rapids: Eerdmans, 2010.

Clements, R. *Word and Spirit: The Bible and the Gift of Prophecy Today.* Leicester: UCCF, 1986.

Clowney, Edmund P. *The Church.* Illinois: IVP, 1995.

Collins, R. *First Corinthians,* Sacra Pagina 7. Collegeville, Minn.: Liturgical Press, 1999.

Conzelmann, Hans. *1 Corinthians.* Philadelphia: Fortress Press, 1975.

_______. *Die Apostelgeschichte.* Tübingen: Mohr, 1963.

Cousland, J. R. "Prophets and Prophecy." Pages 830-35 in *Dictionary of New Testament Background.* Edited by Craig A. Evans and Stanley E. Porter. Leicester: IVP, 2000.

Crone, T. M. *Early Christian Prophecy: A Study of its Origin and Function.* Baltimore: St. Mary's University Press, 1973.

Dautzenberg, G. *Urchristliche Prophetie.* Stuttgart: W. Ko1hlhammer, 1975.

_______. "Zum religionsgeschichtlichen Hintergrund der Διά κρισις πνευμάτων (1 Kor 12:10)." *Biblische Zeitschrift* 15 (1971): 93-104.

Davies, J. G. "Pentecost and Glossolalia." *Journal of Theological Studies* 3 (1952): 228-31.

Deere, Jack. *Surprised by the Power of the Spirit.* Grand Rapids: Zondervan, 1993.

Dunbar, David G. et al. "The Canon: How God Gave His Word to the Church: Viewpoints." *Christianity Today* 32, no. 2 (1988): 23-38.

Dunn, James. *Jesus and the Spirit.* London: SCM Press, 1975.

Edgar, Thomas R. *Miraculous Gifts: Are they for Today?* Neptune: Loizeaux, Brothers, 1983.

Ellis, E. Earle. *Prophecy and Hermeneutic in Early Christianity.* Grand Rapids: Eerdmans, 1978.

_______. "The Role of the Christian Prophet in Acts." *Apostolic History and the Gospel.* Edited by W. W. Gasque and Ralph Martin. Grand Rapids: Eerdmans, 1970.

Farnell, F. D. "The Current Debate about New Testament Prophecy." *Bibliotheca Sacra* 149 (1992): 277-303.

_______. "The Gift of Prophecy in the Old and New Testaments." *Bibliotheca Sacra* 149 (1992): 387-410.

_______. "Does the New Testament Teach Two Prophetic Gifts?" *Bibliotheca Sacra* 150 (1993): 62-88.

_______. "When Will the Gift of Prophecy Cease," *Bibliotheca Sacra* 150 (1993): 171-202.

_______. "Fallible New Testament Prophecy/Prophets? A Critique of Wayne Grudem's Hypothesis." *The Master's Perspective on Contemporary Issues*. Edited by R. Thomas. Grand Rapids: Kregel, 1998.

Fascher, E. *Prophetes: Eine sprach- und religionsgeschichtliche Untersuchung.* Geissen: Topelmann, 1927.

Fee, Gordon. *The First Epistle to the Corinthians*. NICNT; Grand Rapids: Eerdmans, 1987.

_______. *God's Empowering Presence: The Holy Spirit in the Letters of Paul.* Peabody: Hendrickson, 1994.

_______. *Paul, the Spirit, and the People of God.* Grand Rapids: Baker Press, 1996.

_______., and Douglas Stuart. *How to Read the Bible for all Its Worth*. Grand Rapids: Zondervan, 1982.

Ferguson, Sinclair B. *The Holy Spirit.* Downers Grove: IVP, 1996.

Findlay, G. G. *St Paul's First Epistle to the Corinthians*. EGT; Grand Rapids: Eerdmans, 1900 (1961).

Forbes, Christopher. *Prophecy and Inspired Speech in Early Christianity and its Hellenistic Environment.* Peabody: Hendrickson. 1997.

Gaffin, Richard B. *Perspectives on Pentecost.* Phillipsburg, NJ.: P&R, 1979.

Garland, David E. *1 Corinthians*. Baker Evangelical Commentary on the New Testament; Grand Rapids: Baker Press, 2003.

Gee, D. *Concerning Spiritual Gifts.* Springfield, MO: Gospel, 1980.

Geisler, Norman. *Signs and Wonders*. Wheaton: Tyndale, 1988.

Gentry, Kenneth L. *The Charismatic Gift of Prophecy: A Reformed Response to Wayne Grudem*. Memphis, TN: Footstool, 1989.

Giles, K. N. "Prophecy, Prophets, False Prophets." Pages 970-76 in *Dictionary of the Later New Testament and its Development.* Edited by Ralph P. Martin and Peter H. Davids. Downers Grove: IVP, 1997.

Gilliespie, Thomas W. *The First Theologians: A Study in Early Christian Prophecy*. Grand Rapids: Eerdmans, 1994.

_______. "A Pattern of Prophetic Speech in 1 Corinthians," *Journal of Biblical Literature* 97 (1978): 74-95.

Godet, F. *Commentary on St. Paul's First Epistle to the Corinthian,* vol. II. Translated by A. Cusin. Edinburgh: T & T Clark, 1887.

Grant, Robert M. *Paul in the Roman World: The Conflict at Corinth.* Louisville: Westminster John Knox Press, 2001.

Gray, R. *Prophetic Figures in Late Second Temple Palestine: The Evidence from Josephus.* New York: Oxford, 1993.

Green, Micheal. *I Believe in the Holy Spirit.* London: Hodder and Stoughton, 1975.

Greenbury, James. "1 Corinthians 14:34-35: Evaluation of Prophecy Revisited." *Journal of Evangelical Theological Society* 51 (2008): 721-31.

Greenspahn, F. E. "Why Prophecy Ceased." *Journal of Biblical Literature* 108 (1989): 37-49.

Gromacki, Robert G. *The Modern Tongues Movement.* Philadelphia: P&R, 1967.

Grosheide, F. W. *The First Epistle to the Corinthians.* NICNT; Grand Rapids: Eerdmans, 1953.

Grudem, Wayne. *The Gift of Prophecy in the New Testament and Today*. Wheaton: Crossway, 2000.

_______., ed. *Are Miraculous Gifts for Today? Four Views.* Grand Rapids: Zondervan, 1996.

_______. "Prophecy/Prophets." Pages 702-03 of *New Dictionary of Biblical Theology*. Edited by T. Desmond Alexander, Rosner, Carson, Goldsworthy. Wheaton: IVP, 2000.

_______. "A Response to Gerhard Dautzenberg on 1 Corinthians 12:10." *Biblische Zeitschrift* 22:2 (1978): 253-270.

Gundry, R. H. "'Ecstatic Utterances' (NEB)" *Journal of Theological Studies* 17 [1966]: 299-307.

Guy, H. A. *New Testament Prophecy: Its Origin and Significance*. London: Epworth, 1947.

Hawthorne, G. F. "Prophets, Prophecy." Pages 636-42 in *Dictionary of Jesus and the Gospels*. Edited by Joel B. Green, Scot McKnight, I. Howard Marshall. Downers Grove: IVP, 1992.

Hays, Richard B. *First Corinthians*. Louisville: Westminister John Knox Press, 1997.

Hering, J. *The First Epistle of St. Paul to the Corinthians*. Translated by A. W. Heathcote and P. J. Allcock. London: Epworth, 1962.

Hilber, John W. "Diversity of Old Testament Prophetic Phenomena and New Testament Prophecy." *Westminster Theological Journal* 56 (1994): 243-58.

Hill, David. *New Testament Prophecy*. London: Marshall Morgan & Scott, 1979.

Hodge, Charles. *I & II Corinthians*. Edinburgh: The Banner of Truth, 1857.

Hoekema, Anthony A. *What about Tongue-Speaking*? Grand Rapids: Eerdmans, 1966.

Horrell, David G., and Edward Adams, eds. *Christianity at Corinth: The Quest for the Pauline Church*. Louisville: Westminster John Knox Press, 2004.

Horsley, R. A. "Wisdom of Word and Words of Wisdom in Corinth." *Catholic Biblical Quarterly* 39 (1977): 224-39.

_______. "Pneumatikos vs. Psychikos: Distinctions of Spiritual Status among the Corinthians." *Harvard Theological Review* 69 (1976): 269-88.

Horton, Michael. *The Christian Faith: A Systematic Theology for Pilgrims on the Way*. Grand Rapids: Zondervan, 2011.

Houston, G. *Prophecy: A Gift for Today?* Downers Grove: IVP, 1989.

Judisch, Douglas. *An Evaluation of Claims to the Charismatic Gifts*. Grand Rapids: Baker Press, 1978.

Keener, Craig S. *Gifts and Giver: The Holy Spirit for Today*. Grand Rapids: Baker Press, 2001.

Kistemaker, Simon J. *I Corinthians*. New Testament Commentary; Grand Rapids: Baker Press, 1993.

Kittle, G., and G. Friedrich, eds. *Theological Dictionary of New Testament*. Translated by G. W. Bromiley. 10 vols. Grand Rapids: Eerdmans, 1964-1976.

Knight, George W. *The Pastoral Epistles*. NIGTC; Grand Rapids: Eerdmans, 1992.

Levison, J. R. "Did the Spirit Withdraw from Israel? An Evaluation of the Earliest Jewish Data." *New Testament Studies* 43 (1997): 35-57.

MacArthur, John F. *Charismatic Chaos*. Grand Rapids: Zondervan, 1992.

_______. *1 Corinthians*. Chicago: B M H C Press, 1984.

Macchia, F. D. "Groans Too Deep for Words: Toward a Theology of Glossolalia." *Asian Journal of Pentecostal Theology* 1 (1998): 149-73.

MacDougall, Donald G. "Cessationism in 1 Corinthians 13:8-12." *The Master's Seminary Journal* 14/2 (2003): 177-213.

Martin, D. B. *The Corinthian Body*. New Haven: Yale University Press, 1995.

_______. "Tongues of Angels and other Status Indicators." *Journal of the American Academy of Religion* 59 (1991): 547-89.

Martin, R. P. *The Spirit and the Congregation: Studies in 1 Corinthians 12-15*. Grand Rapids: Eerdmans, 1984.

Mathis, David. *Piper on Prophecy and Tongues* (Unpublished). Assessed on 10 Sep, 2013. Online: http://www.desiringgod.org/blog/posts/piper-on-prophecy-and-tongues.

Maudlin, Michael G. "Seers in the Heartland." *Christianity Today* 35 (January, 1991): 18-22.

McRay, J. R. "To *Teleion* in 1 Corinthians 13:10." *Restoration Quarterly* 14 (1971): 168-83.

Michaels, J. Ramsey. *Interpreting the Book of Revelation.* Grand Rapids: Baker Press, 1998.

Miguens, M. "1 Cor 13:8-13 Reconsidered." *Catholic Biblical Quarterly* 37 (1975): 76-97.

Mills, W. E. *Glossolalia: A Bibliography.* New York: Edwin Mellen Press, 1989.

Moffatt, J. *The First Epistle of Paul to the Corinthians.* The Moffat New Testament Commentary; London: Hodder & Stoughton, 1938.

Morris, Leon. *1 & 2 Thessalonians.* Tyndale New Testament Commentary; London: Tyndale, 1956.

_______. *1 Corinthians.* TNTC; London: Tyndale, 1958.

Mortyr, J. A. "Prophecy, Prophets." Pages 964-72 in *New Bible Dictionary.* Edited by I. Howard Marshall, Millard, Packer, Wiseman. Leicester: IVP, 1996.

Muller, U. B. *Prophetie und Predigt im Neuen Testament.* SNT 10; Gutersloh: Gerd Mohn, 1975.

O'Brien, Peter T. *The Letter to the Ephesians.* PNTC; Grand Rapids: Eerdmans, 1999.

Packer, J. I. *Keep in Step with the Spirit.* Leicester: IVP, 1984.

Palmer, Edwin H. *The Holy Spirit.* Philadelphia: P&R, 1974.

Panagopoulos, J. ed. *Prophetic Vocation and in the New Testament and Today.* Novum Testamentum Supplements 45. Leiden: E. J. Brill, 1977.

Pearson, B. A. *The Pneumatikos-Psychikos Terminology in 1 Corinthians: A Study in the Theology of the Corinthian*

Opponents of Paul and its Relation to Gnosticism. Society of Biblicaliterature Dissertation Series 12. Missoula: SBL, 1973.

Raymond, Robert L. *What about Continuing Revelations and Miracles in the Presbyterian Church Today: A Study of the Doctrine of the Sufficiency of Scripture.* St. Louis: P&R, 1977.

Reitzenstein, R. *Hellenistic Mystery Religions.* Translated by J. Steely. Pittsburgh: The Pickwick Press, 1978.

Robeck, C. M. "The Gift of Prophecy in Acts and Paul." *Studia Biblica et Theologica.* 5/1 (1975): 15-38; vol 5/2, 37-54.

_______. "Prophecy, Prophesying" Pages 755-62 of *Dictionary of Paul and His Letters.* Edited by Gerald F. Hawthorne, Ralph P. Martin, and Daniel G. Reid. Leicester: IVP, 1993.

Robertson, Archibald., and Alfred Plummer, *A Critical and Exegetical Commentary on the First Epistle of St Paul to the Corinthians.* ICC; Edinburgh: T & T Clark, 1911.

Robertson, O. Palmer. *The Final Word.* Edinburgh: Banner of Truth, 1993.

Ruthven, Jon. *On the Cessation of the Charismata: The Protestant Polemic on Post-Biblical Miracles.* Sheffield: Sheffield Academic, 1993.

Ryrie, C. C. *The Holy Spirit.* Chicago: Moody, 1965.

Sandmel, S. *Judaism and Christian Beginnings.* New York: Oxford, 1978.

Sandnes, K. O. *Paul – One of the Prophets? A Contribution to the Apostle's Self-Understanding.* Tubingen: J. C. B. Mohr (Paul Siebeck), 1991.

Schaff, P, ed. "The Homilies of St John Chrysostom on the Epistles of Paul to the Corinthians," *A Select Library of the Nicene and Post-Nicene Fathers.* Edinburgh: T & T Clark, 1889.

Schnider, F "προφητης" Pages 182-86 in vol. 3 of *Exegetical Dictionary of New Testament.* Edited by H. Balz and G. Schneider. 3 vols. Grand Rapids: Eerdmans, 1991.

Schrage, W. *Der erste Brief an die Korinther,* vol 3. Zurich: Benziger, 1991-2001.

Sommer, Benjamin D. "Did Prophecy Cease? Evaluating a Re-evaluation." *Journal of Biblical Literature* 115 (1996): 31-47.

Starling, David. "The Analogy of Faith in the Theology of Luther and Calvin." *Reformed Theological Review* 72 (2013): 5-19.

Stendahl, K. "Glossolalia and the Charismatic movement." *God's Christ and His People: Studies in Honor of Nils Alstrup Dahl.* Edited by J. Jervell and W.A. Meeks. Olso: Universitetsforlaget, 1977.

Storm, Samuel. "A Third Wave View," in *Are Miraculous Gifts for Today? Four Views.* Edited by Wayne Grudem. Grand Rapids: Zondervan, 1996.

Stott, John. *Baptism and Fullness: The Work of the Holy Spirit Today.* Leicester: IVP, 1964.

_______. *The Message of Thessalonians.* Bible Speaks Today; Nottingham: IVP, 1991.

Sumney, J. L. *Identifying Paul's Opponents: The Question of Method in 2 Corinthians.* Sheffield: JSOT Press, 1990.

Theissen, Gerd. *Pshychological Aspects of Pauline Theology.* Translated by J. P. Galvin. Edinburgh: T & T Clark, 1987.

Thomas, Robert L. *Understanding Spiritual Gifts.* Chicago: Moody, 1978.

_______. "Tongues ... Will Cease," *Journal of the Evangelical Theological Society* 17 (1974): 81-89.

Toussaint, Stanley D. "First Corinthians Thirteen and the Tongues Questions," *Bibliotheca Sacra* 120 (1963): 311-16.

Turner, Max. *The Holy Spirit and Spiritual Gifts: Then and Now.* Carlisle: Paternoster, 1996.

_______. "Spiritual Gifts: Then and Now." *Vox Evangelica* 15 (1985): 7-64.

Unger, Merril F. *The Baptism and Gifts of the Holy Spirit.* Chicago: Moody, 1974.

Wallace, Daniel B. *Greek Grammar beyond the Basics: An Exegetical Syntax of the New Testament.* Grand Rapids: Zondervan, 1996.

Waltke, Bruce K. *An Old Testament Theology: An Exegetical, Canonical, and Thematic Approach*. Grand Rapids: Zondervan, 2007.

Walvoord, John F. *The Holy Spirit at Work Today*. Wheaton: Van Kampen Press, 1954.

Ward, Rowland S. *Blessed by the Presence of the Spirit: The Authentic Charismatic Church* Melbourne: New Melbourne Press, 1997.

Warfield, B. B. *Counterfeit Miracles*. Carlisle, PA: Banner of Truth, 1918.

Wilkinson, T. L. "Tongues and Prophecy in Acts and 1 Corinthians," *Vox Reformata* 31 (1978): 1-20.

Wilson, R. R. "Prophecy and Ecstasy: A Reexamination," *Journal of Biblical Literature* 98 (1978): 321-337.

Wire, A. C. *The Corinthian Women Prophets: A Reconstruction through Paul's Rhetoric*. Minneapolis: Augsburg/Fortress, 1990.

Witherington, Ben. *Conflict and Community in Corinth: A Socio-Rhetorical Commentary on 1 and 2 Corinthians*. Grand Rapids: Eerdmans, 1995.

Wright, N. T. *The Resurrection of the Son of God*. Minneapolis: Fortress Press, 2003.

Yocum, B. *Prophecy: Exercising the Prophetic Gifts of the Spirit in the Church Today*. Ann Arbor: Word of Life, 1976.

Index of Authors

A

Aune, David 2, 9-11, 45-49, 53-54, 61, 67-68, 70, 72, 74, 114, 120

B

Baker, D. L 2, 6, 11
Baker, J. P 39, 52-54, 63
Barnett, Paul 11, 13, 49, 126
Barrett, C. K 68, 71, 78, 103, 114, 116, 120-121, 126, 134
Beale, G. K 63
Best, E 2
Bittlinger, A 117
Bloomberg, Craig 127
Boring, M. E 2, 74
Bruce, F. F 56, 134
Bultmann, R 126

C

Callan, T 2, 61
Calvin, John 76
Carson, Don 2, 6, 8-9, 12, 16, 21, 34, 42, 63, 69, 72, 76, 84, 93, 104-106, 108, 116-117, 120-123, 125, 127-129, 134, 138
Cartledge, Mark J 2, 21
Chantry, Walter J 16
Ciampa, Roy E 7, 12-13, 67, 69-70, 73, 77, 79, 82-84, 90, 94-96, 99-101, 103-106, 108-109, 111, 119, 122, 126, 129-130, 135-136, 138
Clements, R 2-3
Clowney, Edmund P 4, 17, 19, 123, 134
Collins, R 126
Conzelmann, Hans 67, 69-70, 76, 96, 114, 120, 124, 126, 134
Cousland, J. R 48, 49, 74
Crone, T. M 2, 10

D

Dautzenberg G 2, 11, 117, 126
Davies, J. G 126
Deere, Jack 21
Dunbar, David G 6, 34
Dunn, James 12, 24, 27, 57, 62, 74, 84, 88, 90, 96, 105, 114, 116, 126, 129

E

Edgar, Thomas R 74, 89, 93
Ellis, E. Earle 2, 27, 29, 35, 96-97, 123-124, 126

F

Farnell, F. D 2, 4, 6, 16-20, 34, 46, 63, 72, 74, 82, 84, 89-90, 92-93, 131-133, 135
Fascher, E 2, 10

Fee, Gordon 2, 8-9, 12, 21
Ferguson, Sinclair 4, 17, 19, 67, 70, 86-87, 123, 126, 131
Forbes, Christopher 3, 5-6, 8-10, 21, 25-27, 32, 45, 56-57, 61-62, 66-74, 105-106, 120, 126, 129, 133-134

G

Gaffin, Richard B 1, 4-5, 8-9, 13, 16-20, 35, 41, 44, 60, 66, 68, 70-71, 74, 79, 86, 88, 92-93, 99, 114-115, 117, 122, 132, 134-135
Garland, David 11, 28, 67, 69-70, 72-76, 78-79, 82-84, 90, 92, 95-97, 103, 105-106, 108-109, 117-122, 126-127, 129-130, 132, 134-136, 138
Gee, Donald 2, 21
Geisler, Norman 16
Gentry, Kenneth L 4, 16-18, 32, 131
Giles, K. N 55, 57, 63
Gillespie, Thomas 2, 28, 32, 72, 95-96, 98, 102, 104, 106, 114, 120
Godet, F 93, 130, 135
Grant, Robert M 10
Green, Michael 20, 24
Greenbury, James 55, 67, 72, 74, 79, 88-89, 99
Greenspahn, F, E 47
Gromacki, Robert G 16
Grosheide, F. W 120, 134
Grudem, Wayne 3-6, 20-25, 27, 38-39, 42, 44, 49-51, 54, 59, 61, 63, 67, 72, 74-76, 80-81, 84, 88-90, 93-100, 109-110, 115-123, 134
Gundry, R. H 126
Guy, H. A 2, 22

H

Hawthorne, G. F 74
Hays, Richard B 72
Hering, J 28
Hilber, John W 38, 44, 46, 50, 53
Hill, David 2, 10, 27, 30-33, 35, 44-45, 50, 67, 74, 97, 102, 104, 106, 114, 120
Hodge, Charles 17-18, 51, 71, 76-79, 99, 109-110, 112, 125-126, 132, 134-135
Hoekema, Anthony A 16
Horrell, David G 11
Horsley, R. A 10
Horton, Michael 28, 39, 66
Houston, G 2-3, 31

J

Judisch, Douglas 132

K

Keener, Craig S 6, 21, 34, 89, 99, 114
Kistemaker, Simon J 129
Knight, George W 59

L

Levison, J. R 48-49
Luther, Martin 32

M

MacArthur, John F 16-17, 19, 123, 134, 136
Macchia, F. D 127
MacDougall, Donald G 133
Martin, D.B 2, 126
Martin, R. P 2, 27, 124
Maudlin, Michael G 22
McRay, J. R 133
Michaels, J. Ramsey 63
Miguens, M 133
Mills, W. E 125
Moffatt, J 114
Morris, Leon 58, 68, 71, 110, 126
Motyer, J. A 38
Muller, U. B 2, 28, 104

O

O'Brain, Peter T 55, 59-60

P

Packer, J. I 21, 28-30, 35, 93
Palmer, Edwin H 16
Panagopoulos, J 2
Pearson, B. A 10
Plummer, Alfred 28, 73, 75-76, 95-96, 114, 117, 120, 134

R

Raymond, Robert L 16
Reitzenstein, R 10
Robeck, C. M 61, 67, 69, 71, 74-77, 80-81, 90, 105
Robertson, Archibald 28
Robertson, O. Palmer 4, 16
Rosner, Brain S 7, 12-13, 67, 69-70, 73, 77, 79, 82-84, 90, 94-96, 99-101, 103-106, 108-109, 111, 119, 122, 126, 129-130, 135-136, 138
Ruthven, Jon 134
Ryrie, C. C 16-17

S

Sandmel, S 47
Schaff, P 88, 99
Schnider, F 53-54
Sommer, Benjamin D 46-47
Starling, David 32-33
Stendahl, K 126
Storm, Samuel 21-23, 74-75, 88-89
Stott, John 16-18, 55, 58, 66
Sumney, J. L 11

T

Theissen, Gerd 127
Thiselton, Anthony C 3, 11, 28, 33, 69, 80, 84-86, 88, 90, 92-98, 102-104, 107, 109, 111, 125, 127, 129, 135-136
Thomas, Robert L 4, 16, 131
Toussaint, Stanley D 134, 137
Turner, Max 3-4, 6, 21, 24-27, 30, 32, 34, 39, 41-42, 44-45, 47, 49-50, 57, 62, 74, 82, 89, 92, 132-134

U

Unger, Merril F 16

W

Wallace, Daniel B 127, 137
Waltke, Bruce K 46
Walvoord, John F 16, 89, 131
Ward, Rowland 3
Warfield, B. B 16
Wilkinson, T. L 2
Wilson, R. R 2
Wire, A. C 2
Witherington, Ben 12, 126
Wright, N. T 135

Y

Yocum, B 2

Index of Subjects

A

Aaron 38-40
Advice 6, 23, 92, 119
Agabus 51, 107
Anna 52-53
Apocalyptic 11, 51, 62-63, 111, 126, 136
Apostle(s) 3-5, 17-19, 22-23, 31-33, 51, 59-61, 71, 87, 90, 114, 122-123, 132, 140-142
Apostolic 3-4, 6-8, 17, 21-23, 25, 27, 32, 34, 61, 66, 113, 116, 119, 122, 132-133, 139-140, 143
Applications 7, 34, 85-86, 99-100, 139, 143
Authoritative 3-4, 21-23, 31, 51, 70, 123
Authority 5-6, 8, 19, 23, 31, 42, 44, 49, 60-61, 66, 74, 113-123, 139-145

B

Bands 23, 41, 64

C

Caiaphas 54-55
Canonical prophecy 3-8, 13-14, 19, 22, 30, 34-35, 37, 50, 52, 58-60, 65-66, 74, 93, 109, 113, 119, 122-123, 131, 139, 142
Canonical prophets 50, 107, 123
Canonical revelation 5, 19, 34, 51, 80-81, 87, 92, 123
Canonisation 5, 19, 64-65
Ceased, cease 3-4, 8-9, 17, 19-20, 22-23, 32-34, 46-48, 50, 65, 87, 123, 127, 131, 133, 136-139, 143
Cessation 8, 15, 17, 19, 21, 47-48, 54, 61, 131-140, 142, 144
Cessationist 3, 9, 14-20, 22, 32, 34-35, 82, 88, 91, 99, 131-132, 135, 138, 144
Charismatic 1, 20, 24, 31, 48, 50
Community 31, 47-48, 50-51, 68, 70, 81, 105, 121-122, 129
Complete, completed 3, 8, 17, 19, 33, 47, 50, 65, 88, 117, 123, 129-133, 135, 140-141
Completion 17, 19-20, 34, 131, 136, 145
Congregational prophecy 4-9, 13-15, 20-22, 27, 29, 31, 33-34, 37-38, 46, 50, 52, 59-66, 68, 71, 73-75, 79, 81, 92-93, 95, 99, 102-103, 106-108, 110, 113, 120, 123, 129, 131-145
Consolation 7, 30, 60, 62, 96
Contemporary preaching 3, 15, 27-35
Contents 93, 95, 98, 100

Continuation 8, 15, 17, 21, 48, 91, 131-140, 144
Continuationist 3, 9, 14-15, 20-28, 34-35, 65, 88, 91, 131, 135
Control 11-12, 84, 111, 143
Controlled 12, 35, 60, 86
Corinthian Church 1, 7, 12, 37, 52, 66, 83, 132, 139, 141, 143-144
Corinthian prophecy 1, 3-5, 7, 9-15, 18, 20, 23-25, 27, 35, 58, 60-61, 65-144
Corinthian prophets 61, 66, 84, 87, 123

D

Deborah 40
Decline of prophecy 46
Didactic 26, 60, 93, 130
Difference 6, 8, 13-14, 22, 31, 44, 49, 51, 54, 61, 81, 86, 93, 99, 110, 125, 128, 142
Direct, directed 24, 28-29, 39-40, 42-44, 46, 56, 75, 89, 94, 98-99, 103, 106, 124, 130, 144
Discerning 114, 116-117, 120, 122
Distinct 3-4, 7, 13, 24-25, 27, 38, 46, 50, 59-60, 63, 74, 76, 85, 88-91, 93, 120, 129, 139, 143
Distinction 4-6, 18-19, 24-25, 27, 29, 35, 37, 56, 58, 61-62, 65, 69, 77-78, 82, 86-88, 90, 98, 100, 111-112, 116, 118, 123-131, 143
Distinguish 7, 18, 31, 49, 56, 61, 88, 90, 98
Distinguishing 26, 31, 35, 49, 58, 98, 117-118, 122
Diverse 7, 37, 45, 48, 91-93, 139, 143-144
Diversity 17, 27, 33, 127
Doctrinal 7-9, 19, 22, 26, 58, 60, 64, 92, 99-102, 109, 123, 139, 141-144
Doxological praise 38-40, 42, 52-53, 92, 124, 127, 142

E

Ecstatic 34, 49, 84, 126
Edification 3, 5, 7-9, 19, 24-25, 27, 29, 60, 64, 75, 78, 81-83, 86, 89, 93-96, 98-99, 101, 105, 107-108, 110, 122, 125, 128, 130, 139, 141, 144-145
Edify, edifying 24, 65, 86, 91, 93, 96, 106, 116, 119, 128-131, 144-145
Elders 39, 42, 59, 121
Encouragement, encourage 7, 25, 29, 46, 57, 60, 82, 91-94, 96-100
Eschatological 25-26, 44, 47, 51-54, 63, 80, 105, 109, 111-112, 133-136
Eschaton 127, 135-136, 138-139
Established 23, 40, 42-43, 51, 71, 79, 112, 143-144
Evaluate, evaluated 47, 116-122
Evaluation 8, 12-13, 15, 84, 113, 117-118, 121-122, 139
Evangelistic, evangelism 18, 102, 104, 128
Exegetical, exegesis 7-8, 11-14, 20, 26, 28, 31, 33-34, 46, 48, 50
Exercised, exercise 1, 5, 7, 12-13, 22, 37, 43, 50, 52, 58, 67-68, 71, 73, 83, 105, 109, 129, 139, 141, 143
Exhortation 30, 38, 40-42, 50, 58, 62-63, 68-69, 89-90, 93-94, 96-98, 104, 114, 123-124
Experience, experienced 25, 49, 52, 58, 61-62, 74, 85-86, 98, 128
Exposition 26, 50, 89
Ezra Nehemiah 46-47

F

Fallible 4, 22
False prophets 39-40, 45, 48-49, 54, 62, 113, 116, 118
Feature(s) 13, 31, 33-35, 37-38, 45, 51, 54-55, 58, 63-64, 66, 74, 92, 94, 103, 107, 113, 143

Forms 7, 19, 24, 26, 30, 37, 48, 53, 57, 60, 65, 76, 80-81, 88-89, 125, 131, 135, 141-142
Forth-telling 18, 28-29
Foundational 3, 17, 19, 22, 38, 60, 76
Frenzy, frenzied 34, 42, 84
Function 1, 3, 9-10, 13, 17, 19, 32, 46-48, 59-60, 66, 68, 70-71, 83, 91, 93-104, 115, 120, 128, 130-131, 139, 141, 143, 145

G

Gift of prophecy 1, 6, 17, 25, 28, 33, 47, 52, 58, 67-68, 73, 76, 79, 90, 109, 112, 114, 120, 133, 144
Gift(s) of the Spirit 51, 66-74, 86, 128, 139, 141, 143-144
Glossolalia 61, 130
Godward 8, 13, 24, 31, 37, 40, 42-43, 45, 51-53, 56-57, 61-62, 64-65, 93, 111, 124-125, 127, 129, 140, 142
Gospel proclamation 8, 26, 60, 93, 95-96, 102-108, 139
Guidance 5, 9, 19, 25, 27, 35, 41, 50, 57, 59, 64, 81, 92-93, 108, 122, 141, 144, 145

H

Human 4, 6, 22-24, 35, 44, 52, 71, 75, 80, 84-86, 90, 106, 108-111, 118-119, 124-127, 130
Humanward 8, 13, 31, 37, 40-45, 51, 53, 57, 60, 64-66, 125, 129, 140, 142

I

Identical 19, 23, 50, 56, 95, 97, 100, 102, 106, 124, 126, 130-131, 142
Illumination 80, 86-88, 119, 139, 143
Immediate 18, 26-27, 34, 41, 43-45, 51, 55, 79, 83, 89-90, 92, 99, 108
Indiscriminately 8, 60, 74
Individual(s) 3, 7-8, 13, 19, 31, 37-38, 40-45, 51-53, 57, 64, 66, 69-76, 82-83, 85, 87, 103, 106-108, 117, 119, 121, 125, 128-129, 134, 142, 145
Infallible 3, 21-22, 29, 59, 123
Inscripturated 3-5, 7, 18-19, 22, 27, 29, 33-34, 45, 51, 57-58, 63-64, 80-81, 141-144
Inspiration 18, 39, 62, 86
Inspired 18, 22, 24, 26, 30-31, 42, 48, 50-51, 81
Intelligible 8, 31, 34, 42, 81-82, 84, 96, 101-103, 106, 121, 125, 129-130
Interpretation 4, 11, 18-19, 22, 32, 50, 63, 69, 78-79, 95, 112, 120, 125, 127-130, 133-134
Intertestamental 3, 22, 46-50, 64, 142

J

Jesus 52-55, 60, 89, 122
John the Baptist 46, 51, 53, 55
Josephus 46, 48-49
Judgment, judge 25, 32, 38, 41, 53-54, 63, 104-105, 113-123

K

Knowledge 2, 18, 26, 33, 54, 76-79, 87, 91-92, 100-102, 106-113, 122, 127, 132-133, 135-139

L

Languages 125-129
Limited 8, 22, 25, 28, 30, 37, 45, 54, 70, 73-74, 114, 135, 141-142
Luke, Lukan 52-57, 61-62, 64-66, 83, 92-93, 96-97, 107, 124-126, 142

M

Maturity 95, 132-136
Miriam 39
Moses 38-40, 49, 69
Mysteries, mystery 10, 17, 25, 31, 48, 60, 78, 80, 108-113, 127, 129-130

N

Necessity, necessary 6, 15, 26, 33-35, 37, 58, 92, 110, 125, 134, 145
New Covenant 18, 30, 55, 74, 143
New revelation 30, 44-45, 53-54, 145
Non-canonical 1, 5, 19-20, 29-30, 33, 35, 65, 81, 142
NT prophecy 1, 3-5, 14-35, 37-38, 50-51, 61-62, 64, 68, 82, 92, 102, 118, 142
NT prophets 5, 17-19, 21-22, 26, 29, 32, 51, 53, 59, 92, 97, 102

O

Occasional 6, 9, 12, 18, 27, 31, 33-34, 37-38, 40, 52, 64, 68, 92, 142
Occasionally 5, 22, 30-31, 37, 41-43, 45, 50-53, 57, 61, 65-67, 69, 73, 85, 131
Office 17, 39, 68, 70-71, 144-145
Oracles 32, 48
Oracular speech 24, 42
Ordinary 21-23, 84, 101
Origin, originates 6, 44, 74-83, 85, 88, 91, 95
OT prophecies 52-54
OT prophets 23, 29, 31, 48-49, 51-54, 59, 61, 63, 118
Other prophets 19, 72, 120
Overlap, overlapping 76, 95-96, 100, 102, 112, 116, 143

P

Parousia 8, 54, 61, 132-135, 137, 140, 143
Pastoral 14, 26, 30, 32-33, 85-86, 97, 104, 107, 144-145
Pauline 5-6, 12-13, 27, 58-63, 67, 79-80, 113
Pentateuch 38-40, 43-44, 64, 142
Pentecost 1, 8, 20, 24, 55-57, 66, 74, 92, 124, 139, 141, 143-144
Perfect, perfection 8, 54, 131-138
Phenomenon 3, 7, 12, 27, 34, 37-38, 48, 52, 55, 57-60, 62, 82-88, 91-93, 103, 105, 125, 127-128, 139, 142-143
Philo 48-49
Post-apostolic 3, 9, 15, 21
Post-Pentecost 55, 57, 139, 141
Potentially, potential 7, 22, 25, 29-30, 35, 52, 67, 70, 86, 120, 141
Preaching 3, 7, 15, 18, 24-30, 32-33, 35, 53, 65, 74, 82, 85-86, 88-91, 95, 97-98, 102, 104, 106, 128, 139, 142-143
Prediction 18, 25, 27, 29-30, 34, 38, 41, 45, 49-50, 53-55, 57, 61-62, 69, 82, 92-93, 142-143
Previous, previously 7-8, 15, 18, 27, 30, 33-34, 40, 43, 45, 50, 53, 55, 60, 64, 69, 73, 77-78, 87-88, 91-92, 104, 107-108, 110, 141-143
Prophetic Formula 38, 40-41, 44, 51, 75

Q

Qualitative, qualitatively 6, 8, 81, 95, 113, 119, 123, 142

R

Redemptive 7, 9, 17-20, 22, 27, 63, 109-110, 141-142, 144
Reflection 14, 32, 55, 75, 85-86, 88, 90-91
Reiteration 8, 18, 27, 50, 53, 55, 99, 108, 110, 139, 143
Revelatory 7, 17-19, 24-25, 27, 30-31, 34-35, 50, 53, 57, 60, 62-63, 75-76, 81-82, 85, 88-89, 91, 98, 106, 115, 139, 143
Rooted 22, 27, 34-35, 45, 74-82, 88, 91, 139

S

Second Coming 135, 144
Second Temple 46-49

Sermon 23, 25, 28, 32, 88, 119
Situation(s) 7, 24-27, 33, 62, 75, 85-86, 89, 92-93, 97-98, 103, 107-109, 120, 133, 139, 144
Speech 7, 24, 26, 29, 32, 42, 50, 56, 60-61, 75, 81, 84, 88-91, 94, 96-98, 100, 126, 130, 139
Spiritual gifts 1, 12-13, 21, 81, 90, 94, 105, 107, 109, 134-136, 138
Spontaneous, spontaneity 7, 18, 22, 24-25, 27, 33, 35, 38-40, 52-53, 60, 82-92, 124, 139, 143
Standard 40, 62, 113, 115, 139
Synonymous 56, 96

T

Teaching 3, 6-8, 18, 24-29, 33-35, 46, 58, 65, 74, 76-79, 81-82, 85, 88-91, 95, 97-102, 122, 139, 142-143
Temporal 6, 92, 133, 136
Testing 39-40, 62, 114-117, 119, 122, 139
The book of Revelation 51, 62, 64, 92
Tongues, tongue 1, 8, 12, 19, 32, 55-57, 61-62, 65, 79, 83, 94, 101, 106, 110-111, 120, 123-132, 134-140, 143
Tradition(s) 10, 18, 25-26, 34, 63, 88-89, 91, 99, 116, 119, 122, 131, 139
Truth 7, 18, 28-30, 33-34, 44, 77, 85-86, 92, 96, 99, 103-104, 110, 112, 139, 141, 143-144

U

Unbeliever(s) 8, 60-61, 95, 102-108, 128-129, 139
Unintelligible 8, 42, 101, 126, 129
Utterance(s) 32, 38, 40-41, 43-44, 52, 78, 81, 84-85, 88, 96, 98, 106, 108

W

Weighing, weigh 8, 73, 93, 113, 115-120, 122-123, 143
Women 43, 45, 57, 60, 68, 70
Worship 24, 42, 68-69, 75, 82-83, 85, 95, 105, 108, 118, 121, 129